# MORAL DEVELOPMENT
## Current Theory and Research

## CHILD PSYCHOLOGY

A series of volumes edited by **David S. Palermo**

# MORAL DEVELOPMENT
## Current Theory and Research

Edited by

DAVID J. DePALMA
JEANNE M. FOLEY

*Loyola University of Chicago*

 LAWRENCE ERLBAUM ASSOCIATES, PUBLISHERS
1975    Hillsdale, New Jersey

DISTRIBUTED BY THE HALSTED PRESS DIVISION OF

JOHN WILEY & SONS
New York    Toronto    London    Sydney

Lawrence Erlbaum Associates, Inc., Publishers
62 Maria Drive
Hillsdale, New Jersey 07642


Distributed solely by Halsted Press Division
John Wiley & Sons, Inc., New York



**Library of Congress Cataloging in Publication Data**

Moral development.

   Includes indexes.
   1. Ethics.   I. DePalma, David J.   II. Foley,
Jeanne M.
BJ1012.M63   170      75-14211
ISBN 0-470-20950-X

Printed in the United States of America

# Contents

# Preface

The purpose of this volume is to present a collection of contemporary theory and research in moral development. The coverage, as further discussed in the Introduction, is selective rather than comprehensive with the emphasis on current contributions that focus on various provocative issues pertinent to both moral judgment and moral behavior. The fact that there is no existing collection of papers and critical evaluation of this type makes this book a unique resource for workers and students in the area of moral development.

Although the subject matter of the book is suited primarily for use on the graduate level, the material is also appropriate for special readings or seminars with advanced undergraduate students. We believe that the book can be used most effectively in conjunction with other readings, such as Derek Wright's (1971) *The psychology of moral behaviour*, Martin Hoffman's (1970) chapter in *Carmichael's manual of child psychology* (Vol. 2), and, for an introduction to cognitive-developmental theory, Lawrence Kohlberg's (1964) chapter in Hoffman and Hoffman's *Review of child development research* (Vol. 1). More recent articles and publications might then be used as supplementary material or for coverage of specific topics.

We are deeply indebted to the administration of Loyola University of Chicago and the staff of the Department of Psychology. The symposium on which this volume is based would not have been possible without their financial and clerical assistance.

Finally, we wish to acknowledge and thank Lawrence Erlbaum and his staff for their vital part in publishing this book and for their helpfulness and editorial support in guiding all of its authors, and especially the editors, from initial copy to final product.

DAVID J. DEPALMA
JEANNE M. FOLEY

# Introduction

Jeanne M. Foley
*Loyola University*

The material in the following chapters was first presented at the Symposium on Moral Development at Loyola University of Chicago in December, 1973. The editors' interest in planning this symposium was founded primarily in the belief that work in this area was in a period of rapid growth and that an opportunity to have various investigators share their thinking and research would be worthwhile. As the area of moral development is broad and has many ramifications, it was apparent that a certain amount of sampling would be necessary if reasonable limits of time and funding were not to be exceeded. The guiding principles in selecting the participants included their current contributions and continuing focus on moral development in terms of research and theory. It also seemed desirable to have a certain amount of diversity, with the participants representing different orientations to add breadth and to avoid a soporific atmosphere of amiable head nodding and agreement. In brief, we wanted a group whose emphasis would be prospective and provocative and who might be anticipated to be in the forefront in setting the direction for future work and thought in moral development. Although we have resisted the urge to add another to the "current issues" or "recent trends" series, such a title would have reflected our intent.

To the extent that the participants were encouraged to present recent and ongoing research (or simply ideas for research that were still a gleam in the investigator's eye), our approach was something of a gamble. We hoped, however, that by eschewing the relatively well established, the presentation of new ideas and the possibility of creating a certain amount of disequilibrium would contribute to restructuring and lead to new levels of integration. Or, for those of a different persuasion, we hoped that some of the ideas would be sufficiently reinforcing to provide for continued research and gains in knowledge of a quantitative nature.

As a reader who is somewhat prone to skipping introductions, I recognize that one may plunge into Chapter 1 without grave feelings of guilt or disadvantage. As the writer of this introduction, I hope, of course, that it will be read, but I also believe that it serves a real purpose in providing an overview of the topics discussed and in supplying a degree of cohesiveness that might otherwise be lacking. This orientation seems especially important because the participants in the symposium had not been assigned particular topics that would then fit together as logical parts of the whole. However, although there is considerable diversity, the fact that there are recurring concerns and emphases gives some sense that the participants have been, after all, considering the same elephant and, further, that there is considerable agreement about specific aspects of moral development that merit our attention.

In recognition of the major contributions of Lawrence Kohlberg to work on moral judgment and to the cognitive–developmental tradition in general, the first four participants explored certain ramifications or possible extensions of thought and methodology in this area. Attention was focused on the previously rather neglected relationships between several aspects of cognitive development (the attainment of concrete and formal operations and social perspective taking) and the attainment of higher stages of moral judgment, the exploration of a structure different from moral judgment (as exemplified by the thinking inherent in the development of social rules), and an attempt to develop an objective measure of moral judgment.

Specifically, Elliot Turiel argues that Kohlberg's formulation of the development of moral judgment is not applicable to the development of thinking about social rules or conventions, that is, that the two involve different structures. Instead of Kohlberg's moral dilemmas, such as stealing an expensive drug to save a life, Turiel deals with what appear to be the homely, everyday type of dilemmas—the shoulds and should nots of eating with one's hands, of dressing too casually to suit a professional partner, and of children calling teachers by their first names. Turiel's presentation provides the basis for this formulation as well as some initial qualitative findings about children's thinking about social rules. Although the levels of thought that he describes suggest stages, he is careful to note that his data, as yet, are not adequate for establishing this possibility.

In the next two chapters, Charles Blake Keasey and Robert Selman focus on cognitive variables that they hypothesized are associated with the development of moral judgment or thought. Although their interests and conclusions are similar, their approaches differ in several respects. Keasey considers cognitive development, especially as it is represented by the attainment of concrete and formal operations, to be a prerequisite for attaining higher stages of moral judgment as measured by subjects' responses to Kohlberg's dilemmas. On the basis of investigations conducted by him and his colleagues, he argues for a "specific–dependent" model in which the attainment of concrete operations is a necessary but not sufficient condition for the progression to Stage 2 moral judgment, with a similar relationship holding for formal operations and Stage 5. As these cognitive operations do not appear to be associated with the attainment of Stages 3, 4, and 6 of moral judgment, Keasey suggests that social factors or other noncognitive variables may be crucial in these transitions. In further considering variables that may affect moral judgments, Keasey provides evidence that the evaluation of issues involved in the moral dilemmas is a function of both the respondent's agreement or disagreement with the opinion expressed and the stage of the supportive reasoning relative to the respondent's own level.

The implication of social factors in moral development as noted by Keasey, and particularly those associated with social perspective taking (or role taking) provides the basis for the chapter by Selman and Damon. However, instead of dealing with Kohlberg's moral dilemmas and stages, their presentation spotlights the social perspective–taking skill of younger respondents (4–10 years of age) and the relationship of these skills to their ideas about justice. As in Turiel's argument that the development of thought about social conventions involves structures distinct from moral judgment, Selman and Damon argue that social perspective taking is structurally different from moral reasoning and that given levels of perspective taking (or the structures implied by these levels) are a necessary but not sufficient basis for attaining the concommitant stage of justice reasoning. Their formulation, which is based on four levels of perspective taking and three levels of reasoning about justice is, as they note, largely deductive and is not yet supported by extensive hypothesis testing and quantitative data.

In the final chapter in this section, James Rest reviews recent research by himself and his colleagues on his objective test of moral judgment, the Defining Issues Test (DIT). In taking this test, the respondent is asked to read hypothetical moral dilemmas of the Kohlberg type and then to select for each dilemma the most important issues as they are represented in 12 statements. These issue statements represent the thinking characteristic of Kohlberg's stages. The assumption underlying the DIT, therefore, is that it provides a measure of moral judgment based on the respondent's selection of issues. On the basis of Rest's systematic investigations relevant to the reliability and validity of the DIT, it appears that he has made considerable progress toward his goal of an objectively scored measure of moral judgment, particularly for somewhat older subjects, such as adolescents and young adults.

In the second half of this book, the interest in variables associated with, or prerequisite to, moral development remains high but the emphasis switches from stages, structures, and judgment to moral behavior in the life situation. In a further division of focus, the chapters by James Bryan and Ervin Staub provide extensive reports of experimental research on situational variables and their relationship to altruistic behavior, whereas the chapters by Martin Hoffman and Robert Hogan are mainly theoretical.

With respect to children's actions in the life situation (or at least life as represented by bowling games in a trailer), Bryan reviews much of the research by him and his colleagues on the effects of models on children's donation behavior. Their findings are based on comparisons of the effects of models' words (preaching greed or generosity) and their actions (generous or selfish) and especially the effects of hypocrisy (as preaching generosity but practicing greed). Although the models' actions appear to speak louder than words in facilitating donation behavior, children's, and even adults', apparent insensitivity to hypocrisy is intriguing, particularly when the implications of these findings are considered not only for child rearing but for reactions to some of our leaders in business and government.

In Staub's report, the interest is on what one, as teacher or parent, can teach a child to facilitate prosocial behavior. In this research, teaching is considered broadly and includes techniques ranging from direct instruction (how the other feels) to techniques for practice (as teaching others). As with Bryan's research, the findings suggest that the variables affecting prosocial behavior are indeed complex and preclude a simple formulation of rules to promote helping behavior. That is, the variables hypothesized by Staub to facilitate such behavior in their child subjects receive some support from the data, but the effects of unanticipated variables, such as sex of child, the experimenter doing the training, and even the child's assignment to a particular classroom, are also significant. Such complications are discouraging, and the research approaches exemplified by the work of both Bryan and Staub suggest that researchers in this area must have the virtue of persistence to a high degree in order to pursue elusive relationships through a whole series of systematic studies. They also must be constantly alert to the challenge of unanticipated findings and show readiness and ingenuity in incorporating them into their thinking.

The final chapters, by Martin Hoffman and Robert Hogan, with their emphasis on theory, appear especially appropriate in representing quite different but relatively broad and cogent conceptions of moral development. Hoffman focuses on both affective and cognitive components in the development of altruistic motives in children. His thesis is that empathic responses to another's distress (and the subsequent development of sympathetic empathy) in interaction with cognitive development as represented by role-taking skills (the observer's "sense of the other") provides the basis for altruistic motives and actions. Hoffman's concern with role taking and its development is, of course, similar to that of Selman. However, his focus on empathy both as an affective element and a motive for action suggests an additional variable that is involved in prosocial behavior. The emphasis on empathy also reflects concern with a variable that enters into Hogan's formulation. It may also be noted that Hoffman's treatment of empathy (as responses to distress and sympathetic empathy) and role taking provides a distinction between the two that is frequently not observed, that is, when conceptions of role taking appear to include the child's ability to recognize or understand the feelings of another as distinct from his own.

Finally, Hogan's plea in the final chapter that: "Theory and research in the area of moral development must be related to a broader conceptualization of social action if it is not to become merely a special topic in social psychology" sounds a warning that merits our attention. Hogan, in taking his own advice, has indeed set moral development in the context of a developmental theory of personality. He emphasizes the ontogenesis of role and character structures and devotes attention to variations in the latter that are posited to account for individual differences in moral thought and behavior. Although it seems likely that most of us have learned at some point during our education that a theory of development or personality should be able to account for both the commonalities and uniquenesses of behavior, Hogan's presentation reminds us of this important requirement.

To those of you who have read this far, we may now say, "Onward to the chapters." In reading them and the subsequent comments by the two discussants, Shirley L. Jessor and David J. DePalma, we can only wish that you will experience the immediacy, the challenge, and the stimulation of sharing ideas and findings that were felt by those who braved the ice and snow to hear it "live."

# 1

# The Development of Social Concepts: Mores, Customs, and Conventions[1]

Elliot Turiel

*Harvard University*

The research and related theory discussed in this chapter concerns the thinking of children and adolescents about social mores, customs, and conventions, as well as their more general conceptions of society as a system. Most previous work on the development of social concepts has focused on moral judgments (Kohlberg, 1969, 1971; Kohlberg & Turiel, 1971; Piaget, 1932). However, findings from studies on mechanisms of developmental change in the moral judgments of adolescents (Turiel, 1973a, 1974) have indicated that the form of moral judgment is distinguishable from other social concepts. In particular, it has been found necessary to differentiate moral thinking from thinking about the customary and conventional. This implies that although moral judgments are social in nature, not all social judgments are moral judgments.

The research on the development of "social–conventional" thinking stems from analyses of stage changes in moral judgment during late adolescence. Working with the six-stage scheme formulated by Kohlberg (1969), data were obtained (Turiel, 1973a, 1974) relevant to the movement from Stage 4, the authority and social order maintaining orientation to Stage 5, the contractual–legalistic orientation. These studies have shown that the transition from Stage 4 to Stage 5 involves a phase of conflict or disequilibrium (see

[1]Expanded version of a paper presented for a symposium on "Contemporary Issues on Moral Development," Loyola University, Chicago, Illinois, December 13, 1973. The work reported in this paper was supported by a grant from the Russell Sage Foundation and a fellowship from the John Simon Guggenheim Memorial Foundation.

Turiel, 1973b, 1974, for a discussion of the role of disequilibrium in develop-ment) in which responses are not classifiable at any given stage. Judgments made during this phase are characterized by a great deal of inconsistency, conflict, and internal contradiction. The central inconsistency expressed by transitional adolescents is between (a) a relativism, in which there is an apparent rejection of moral judgments or moral terminology, and (b) a moralism, in which moral judgments are made and moral terminology used. The simultaneous rejection of morality and presence of moral assertions reflects the transitional process, which entails both a reevaluation of the existing mode of thinking and the construction of a more adequate mode. Our analyses have indicated that the apparent rejection of morality by the transitional adolescents is not a blanket rejection; it is instead a partial rejection of Stage 4 conceptions, which they are beginning to consider inadequate.

Characterizing the judgments made during the transition from Stage 4 to Stage 5 is a distinction between society and the individual as moral agents and a recogni-tion of the diversity of value systems. This calls into question the definition of morality as a code of fixed rules derived from and dictated by society. External standards (e.g., law, authority, God) are no longer seen as adequate criteria for verifying the validity and objectivity of moral values. Of particular relevance to the discussion in this chapter is that a concern with adequate verification of the validity of moral values also includes a concern with the basis for distinguish-ing between moral issues and conventional issues. Within the moral domain are considered such issues as the value of life, trust, deception, honesty, responsi-bility, and individual rights. Examples of conventional issues include sexual mores, dress codes, forms of address, traditional sex roles, and national and religious rituals or customs. Those adolescents attempting to draw distinctions between these two realms are moving toward a conceptualization of two types of values: (a) values or principles considered to be objectively valid and universalizable, and (b) values, such as customs or conventions, considered specific to a given individual or society.

These analyses of stage change clearly pointed to further study. From the observation that during late adolescence universal moral principles were dif-ferentiated from relativistic social conventions, it was plausible, from a de-velopmental perspective, to hypothesize that social–conventional thinking would have an earlier genesis. That is, such conceptualization in adolescence should have originated from prior forms of thinking and have had its own onto-genetic history.

It is being proposed, therefore, that moral judgment constitutes only one aspect of social conceptions and that there exist other dimensions of social development that should be analyzed separately. The theoretical basis for hypothesizing that the form and development of thinking about social conventions is different from that of moral thinking is discussed in the following section.

## PARTIAL SYSTEMS IN THE STRUCTURE OF THOUGHT

The theoretical perspective taken in the research on change is one that views the individual's development as progressing through a series of organized structures of thought. As the concept of structure is used here, it is not meant to imply that all of the individual's thinking forms a unitary organization or system. In fact, valid structural distinctions have been made between physical and social concepts (Kohlberg, 1969; Piaget, 1970). It is proposed here that distinctions need to be made within the category of social thinking—that the development of social-conventional thinking takes a different form from other social concepts. In proposing that there may be different and distinct realms of social thinking I am not hypothesizing that there exist a number of isolated or unrelated concepts that are to be analyzed independently. Instead, the hypothesis is that there exist different realms of thought, within which development proceeds through a sequence of structures of interaction with the environment. This approach is consistent with the following definition of structure:

> We shall define structure in the broadest possible sense as a system which presents the laws or properties of a totality seen as a system. These laws of totality are different from the laws of properties of the elements which comprise the system. I must emphasize the fact that these systems are merely partial systems with respect to the whole organism or mind. The concept of structure does not imply just any kind of totality and does not mean that everything is attached to everything else [Piaget, 1967, p. 143].

The theoretical basis for making distinctions between conceptual domains (i.e., considering partial systems) rests on the developmental assumption that structures of thought stem from the individual's interaction with the environment (Turiel, 1974). The hypothesis is that thought is a construction, the source of which is the child's actions on objects and events. Knowledge is generated from the way the individual orders and transforms objects and events. If the child encounters fundamentally (structurally) different objects, then the construction of different forms of thought can be expected.

As a relatively unambiguous example, consider the distinction just mentioned between physical and social concepts. Studies of children's thinking about the physical world have led to descriptions of the form of physical concepts in development (e.g., Inhelder & Piaget, 1958, 1964; Piaget, 1952; Werner, 1957). As discussed in the previous section, studies of children's thinking about the social world have led to descriptions of forms of moral judgments (e.g., Kohlberg, 1969). Descriptions of the structures of physical concepts differ from descriptions of the structures of moral judgments. This is not to say that the two forms of thought are entirely independent of each other. Although they may inform and influence each other, one is not reducible to the other.

The formulation of different developmental stages for physical and social concepts is consistent with the idea that thought stems from action. The child's experiences with the physical world are of a different kind from his experiences with the social world. First, the structure of physical and social objects or events differ, which implies differences in the way the child can manipulate and experiment with them. Furthermore, the child's methods of verifying his knowledge about each domain should differ. From this perspective, therefore, knowledge of the physical world is considered to define a different realm from moral knowledge.

The hypothesis of "partial systems" can be clarified by considering the alternative possibility, that the individual's thinking forms one unitary structure, and its implications for an explanation of the interactive and developmental processes. If it is proposed (a) that thought forms a unitary structure, and that is combined with (b) the view that structure stems out of interaction with the environment, then the implication is (c) that the environment is structurally uniform and all knowledge is of one kind. Assuming that thought is constructed out of actions on objects and that structure defines the way the individual interacts with his environment, the development of a unitary stage sequence would mean that all interactions or experiences are basically the same. Returning to the example of physical and moral concepts, the existence of one structure means: (a) that physical and social objects are not structurally distinct, (b) that physical and social concepts are not structurally different, and therefore (c) that the two realms are not epistemologically distinct from each other.

It may be maintained, however, that the environment is not structurally uniform, that there exist different realms of knowledge, and yet, that mental structure is unitary. Such a view alters the meaning of "structure" as interactional and the conception of development as construction. If it is assumed that there are basically different objects and events and only one global structure, then the individual must use the same way of thinking in relation to different environmental structures. Therefore, hypothesizing a unitary mental structure without also hypothesizing a unitary environmental structure implies that mental structure is independent of the environment and that thought represents, not an interaction with the environment, but an application of mental activity to differing events. This would be akin to defining mental activity as the use of a skill or series of skills in solving a variety of problems (e.g., physical, social). Such a view contradicts the notion that thought is a construction out of organism–environment interaction. For, if development is construction, there is a synthesis between thought, actions, and the structure of the environment.

It is claimed here, therefore, that viewing development of thought as the formation of a unitary, global structure does not allow for conceiving knowledge as constructions that take more than one form. The idea of a unitary structure implies either (a) that the environment is structurally uniform and all knowledge is of one kind, or (b) that the environment is not structurally uniform, but the individual applies his thought to different aspects of the environment. My own view, that structure should be defined in terms of partial systems, is based on the hypothesis that thought is constructed out of the individual's interactions with the environment. Additionally, it is hypothesized that the environment is not uniform and that there exist different realms of knowledge. These assumptions imply that thought does not form a unitary structure but that there exist distinguishable domains of thinking.

This approach raises a variety of theoretical and empirical problems. In particular, it may lead into a morass filled with so many partial structures that each no longer has the property of wholeness. However, it is only through the delineation of such boundaries that the development of thought and knowledge can be explained as involving the organization of experience. It becomes necessary, therefore, (a) to determine how and where to draw the lines between different realms or systems of thought and (b) to verify that the proposed distinctions are valid. To demonstrate that thinking about a given realm represents a developmental dimension, distinct from other realms, it is necessary to fulfill the following three criteria:

1. The observed sequential forms of reasoning are qualitatively distinct from other domains.
2. The actions and interactions that are the genesis of these forms of reasoning are qualitatively distinct. On the environmental side, this implies different structural properties of objects and events.
3. At the most advanced developmental level (or end point) the domain is differentiated by the subject from other realms of thought.

## DISTINCTIONS BETWEEN FORMS OF SOCIAL CONCEPTS

The differences between stages of cognitive development and stages of moral development has been mentioned as one example in which the research findings support the plausibility of distinguishing domains of thought. Implicit in this discussion of the developmental basis for "partial structures" is the view that it may be necessary to make further distinctions within the cognitive and social realms. In fact, this has been the case in studies of cognitive development. For example, Piaget and Inhelder have studied the distinctions and interrelations between seriation and classification (Inhelder & Piaget, 1964), as well as conservation (Piaget, 1952) and relativity (Piaget, 1927). Such distinctions, however, have not been pursued within the social domain.

I have hypothesized that social–conventional thinking represents a developmental dimension. That is, it is a form of social thinking that is distinguishable from other forms, such as moral judgments. This hypothesis stems from two sources. First, my research has shown that in adolescence social conventions are differentiated from moral principles, which leads to the hypothesis that development within the two domains may take different forms. The plausibility of this hypothesis is also strengthened, in my view, by existing research on social development. Studies from various theoretical perspectives and approaches, including anthropology, social–learning theories, and structural–developmental theories, have actually included both the conventional and the moral domain. However, there has been a failure to make clear distinctions between the two that has, in my opinion, resulted in ambiguities for students of the development of social judgments. Some of these ambiguities may be clarified by a better understanding of the development of social–conventional thinking.

The most explicit analyses of customs and conventions have been provided by anthropologists. Certain anthropologists have viewed custom as playing an important role in societies, as well as in the individual's development and behavior (Benedict, 1934; Le Vine, 1969; Mead, 1928; Whiting & Child, 1953). It is generally assumed that customs and norms serve social and evolutionary functions, of which the individual members of the society are not necessarily aware. From this perspective, a variety of values and actions, which are placed under the category of custom, form integrated cultural patterns. This is expressed by Benedict (1934):

> It is a corollary of this that standards, no matter in what aspect of behavior range in different cultures from the positive to the negative pole. We might suppose that in the matter of taking life all peoples would agree in condemnation. On the contrary, in a matter of homicide, it may be held that one is blameless if diplomatic relations have been severed between neighbouring countries, or that one kills by custom his first two children, or that a husband has right of life and death over his wife, or that it is the duty of the child to kill his parents before they are old . . . .
>
> The diversity of custom in the world is not, however, a matter which we can only helplessly chronicle. Self torture here, head-hunting there, pre-nuptial chastity in one tribe and adolescent license in another, are not a list of unrelated facts, each of them to be greeted with surprise wherever it is found or wherever it is absent. The tabus on killing oneself or another, similarly, though they relate to no absolute standard, are not therefore fortuitous. The significance of cultural behaviour is not exhausted when we have clearly understood that it is local and man-made and hugely variable. It tends also to be integrated. A culture, like an individual, is a more or less consistent pattern of thought and action [pp. 45–46].

As can be seen, the term "custom" is used to cover a wide variety of values, ranging from attitudes toward killing to attitudes toward sexuality. The thesis is that these customs or standards are culturally determined and their meaning and import can be understood in relation to their role in a particular cultural pattern. "Patterns" of culture may vary from one place to another, and, therefore, customs are relative to their specific society. In this formulation no conception can be seen of universal moral values or principles. Consequently, no distinction is made between moral values and nonmoral (conventional) values. The value of life, prenuptial chastity, adolescent license, etc., are all regarded as part of the same class of values: that is, values that contribute to the formation of cultural patterns.

In sum, a series of assumptions are made regarding the relation between the individual and his social environment. Starting from the premise that the source of values and standards is the culture, it is assumed that (a) values are organized at the societal level to serve collective functions and that (b) individual social development is equivalent to the learning of, and conformity to, cultural values: "The life history of the individual is first and foremost an accommodation to the patterns and standards traditionally handed down in his community [Benedict, 1934, pp. 2–3]." It follows, therefore, that (c) the individual makes no cognitive distinctions between different cultural values and (d) the individual's conformity to society's values allows him to adapt to the social environment (Le Vine, 1969).

This perspective does not deal with the possibility that distinctions may exist between the ways in which different types of values are acquired or reasoned. A major difficulty in evaluating the validity of this approach stems from the fact that claims regarding the individual's development and behavior are based, not on ontogenetic study, but on study of social organizations. Theory based on analysis at the societal level is used to generate hypotheses regarding the individual. However, verification of these hypotheses requires study of individual development. Indeed, alternative hypotheses regarding the development of individual social judgments underlie my approach to customs and conventions. First, as already mentioned, the research on moral judgments suggests that certain values and concepts are not learned but represent the transformation of structures of interaction with social experiences. Second, it may be that individuals do not merely adapt to social custom and convention but instead act on the socially given; i.e., they actively structure and transform that which is socially conventional and customary. In such a case, criteria used in making judgments about customs and conventions may be different from those used in other types of social thinking.

Existing research on the development of social concepts and actions does not clarify the question of how individuals think about social conventions. In most cases, this domain of social thought has not been dealt with explicitly. For example, social-learning theorists have assumed that the process of learning all social values and behavior is the same. Consequently, distinctions are not made between different types of social concepts, as the following statement shows:

> . . . the present paper makes no sharp distinction between social and moral rules. Rather, it assumes that an evaluative tendency is an integral part of social conduct, and that morality has a social job to do; that is, the function of morality is to regulate and moderate human affairs [Hogan, 1973, p. 219].

The assumption that no distinctions exist between social and moral rules is made prior to a study of individual judgments about social conventions. Therefore, research based on this proposition is unlikely to determine whether or not such distinctions ought to be made.

In contrast, studies have been conducted by both Piaget (1932) and Kohlberg (1969, 1971) in which there has been an attempt to define the distinctive characteristics of the moral realm. Starting with the idea that moral judgments are qualitatively distinct from other types of judgments, Piaget has formulated a two-stage scheme, which has later been modified and extended by Kohlberg into a six-stage scheme. One of the strengths of Kohlberg's analysis lies in the attempt to isolate the distinctive features of morality (morality defined as "justice"; see Kohlberg, 1971). This has allowed for studies of the universal characteristics of basic moral values (Kohlberg & Turiel, 1971; Turiel, Kohlberg, & Edwards, 1973). However, one of the weaknesses in Kohlberg's analysis is that the stages of moral judgment are extended to encompass areas of social conception other than morality. Other domains of social conception have not been examined directly but have been viewed through the lens of the moral judgment sequence.[2]

In my view, the moral stages have been defined too globally, so that other areas of social thought are treated as subcategories of moral judgment. In this way, the stages have been applied to judgments in such domains as politics (Kohlberg & Lockwood, 1970; Lockwood, 1970) and sexuality, (Gilligan, Kohlberg, Lerner, & Belenky, 1970). Exemplifying this approach is a study of adolescent thinking about sexuality (Gilligan et al., 1970). The procedures Gilligan et al. have used to study "sexual development" are simple and straightforward. Hypothetical stories dealing with sexual activities (e.g., a high school age couple engaging in sexual intercourse) were constructed and subjects were asked to judge those activities. Subjects were also administered a standard moral judgment interview. Responses to both interviews were scored for stage of moral judgment according to the six-stage sequence. That is, sexuality is regarded as another area to which moral judgments can be applied.

Although it is likely that moral judgments are applied in certain sexual situations, it appears to us that in thoughts and feelings about sex other factors not reducible to moral judgment, such as intimacy and conventionality, are more primary. In the Gilligan et al. study reasoning about sexuality and moral reasoning have been treated interchangeably; that is, a system for scoring stage of moral judgement is used to assess stage of reasoning about sexuality. There is no independent analysis of the subject's reasoning about sexuality.

The results of the Gilligan et al. study do, indeed, suggest that reasoning about sexuality may not be reducible to the stages of moral judgments. It was

---

[2]In Piaget's (1932) early work on the child's moral judgment and behavior can be seen an example of how the failure to distinguish domains of social thought may have resulted in ambiguities. To study the development of morality, Piaget first observed children's attitudes and behavior in regard to rules for playing marbles. From that research he concludes that moral development proceeds from: (a) a stage of heteronomous morality, in which rules are viewed by the child as sacred and unalterable; to (b) a stage of autonomous morality, in which the child understands rules to be alterable, based on mutual agreement and for the purpose of cooperation. In his analysis, however, Piaget has not determined the nature of the child's sense of cooperation independently of his conception of rules. In using rules of marble playing as the object of study, Piaget is dealing with a category of events in which, in the child's mind, the force of rule may be minimal as compared to rules and laws of government or commandments of religion, for instance. In the realm of games, therefore, it is more likely to appear that, by a fairly early age, the child conceives of rules to be in the service of cooperation. It is plausible, however, to suppose that a sense of cooperation stemming from interpersonal activities may not be interchangeable with conceptions of broader social rules, which may entail a different set of interactions for the child.

found that responses on the sexual stories are (*a*) more variable and (*b*) scored at lower stages than responses on the standard moral judgment interview stories. Of particular interest is the finding that the sex stories are scored Stage 2 (instrumental–egoistic orientation) with greater frequency than the standard stories, whereas there is a greater frequency of Stage 4 scores (authority and social order maintaining orientation) on the standard stories than on the sex stories.

Two hypotheses are suggested by this observed discrepancy between stage scores on the sexual and standard stories. First, it may be that moral reasoning regarding sexual relations is systematically lower (as a function of cultural attitudes toward sex, for instance) in the population studied. This hypothesis implies that the moral judgment analysis of sexuality is accurate. However, if thinking about sexual situations is not reducible to moral judgments, then it is likely that the responses scored Stage 2 reflect something other than an instrumental and egoistic stance. That is, nonmoral responses to the sexual situations can closely resemble, in content, responses characteristic of Stage 2 in moral judgment scheme. The second hypothesis, therefore, is that the discrepancy indicates moral reasoning and reasoning about sexuality to be distinct domains. This hypothesis is supported by the results of a longitudinal follow-up (Stein, 1973) of subjects in the Gilligan *et al*. study. Stein has found that over a 2-year interval moral stage changes are sequential on the standard stories, but not on the sexual stories. This suggests that the moral development sequence is not applicable to ontogenetic changes in thinking about sexual situations.[3]

It should be clear from this discussion that a tendency exists in anthropological and psychological research to group different social values into the same category. It should also be clear that there is no agreement regarding the appropriate category into which these values ought to be placed. We have seen that some treat all these values as conventions or customs and others regard them to be in the moral realm. In each case the same epistemological status is attributed to a variety of values.

One exception to this can be found in the sociological analyses of Max Weber (1947). In describing social organization, Weber identified three categories of social action: custom, convention and ethics. Unlike Benedict (1934), who viewed the study of *custom* as central to an understanding of societies, Weber reserves the use of this term for actions which are performed with some uniformity but do not serve a function in social organization. Customs are not regulated by external sanctions: "Today it is customary every

---

[3]In actuality, Gilligan *et al*. (1970) stated, at times, that they were studying the development of moral reasoning about sexual situations; at other times, however, they stated that they were studying sexual development. Even with the former intent, it is necessary to base such a study on an understanding of sexual development; the proper aim of the research must then be the study of interrelationships between moral reasoning and judgments made about sexual situations. Furthermore, for such a study to be developmental, it becomes necessary to include subjects of different ages; whereas the Gilligan *et al*. subjects are all high school juniors.

morning to eat a breakfast which, within limits, conforms to a certain pattern. But there is no obligation to do so [Weber, 1947, p. 122]." In contrast, conventions are a significant aspect of the "legitimate order" of social organization and are regulated by sanctions:

> The term convention will be employed to designate that part of the custom followed within a given social group which is recognized as 'binding' and protected against violation by sanctions of disapproval. . . . Conformity with convention in such matters as the usual forms of greeting, the mode of dress recognized as appropriate or respectable, and various of the rules governing the restrictions on social intercourse, both in form and in content, is very definitely expected of the individual and regarded as binding on him [pp. 127–128].

In turn, the conventional is distinct from the ethical:

> Every system of ethics which has in a sociological sense become validly established is likely to be upheld to a large extent by the probability that disapproval will result from its violation, that is, by convention. On the other hand, it is by no means necessary that all conventionally or legally guaranteed forms of order should claim the authority of ethical norms [p. 130].

Our own orientation is to the way convention, as a category of social organization, is an aspect of the individual's social judgment. While Weber's criteria for distinguishing convention from other social values and actions are useful, they do not bear directly on the development of the conceptualization of convention. The research described in the following section has been designed to examine social–conventional thinking and to explore the hypothesis that it represents a distinct developmental dimension.

## THE DEVELOPMENT OF SOCIAL–CONVENTIONAL REASONING

The research discussed in this section has been guided by the idea that members of society (a) formulate their own conceptions regarding customs and conventions, which (b) are not reducible to their moral conceptions and (c) undergo changes with age. As has been seen, these assumptions are in contrast with the view, held by some anthropologists, that the nature and functions of conventions are generally unknown to individuals. On the one hand, it is thought that individuals adhere to conventions, whereas on the other hand, it is thought that individuals are largely unaware of the basis for their behavior. My assumptions are also in contrast with the view that the individual does not distinguish between different types of values.

To determine how individuals related to customs and conventions, it was necessary to examine directly the thinking of children, adolescents, and adults. In addition, to determine whether social–conventional thinking represented a distinct developmental dimension, it was necessary to analyze this domain independently of other forms of social thinking. Through items used in a "clinical interview" (see Piaget, 1928), the social–conventional domain was empirically defined. This interview contained a series of hypothetical stories and questions revolving around specific social conventions (such as forms of address or modes of formal and informal dress), sex roles, sources of social status and prestige, and customs. For example, one story used in the interview concerns a boy brought up to call people by their first names who is expected to address the teachers in his new school by their formal titles. He comes into conflict with the teachers and principal, who insist on conformity to the rules. Other stories are alluded to in the context of the analyses of subjects' responses.

In the research so far completed the "social–conventional" interview, as well as a moral judgment interview, has been administered to approximately 175 males and females between the ages of 9 and 30 years. Subjects are currently being reinterviewed in longitudinal followups at 2- or 3-year intervals. The analyses are still underway and the results discussed here are tentative. Consequently, I cannot yet fulfill the criteria, mentioned earlier, which would verify that social–conventional thinking defines a distinct developmental dimension.

Some examples of reasoning about social–conventional issues in late childhood and adolescence that illustrate the developmental trends emerging from this study are presented below. It should be stressed that the sequence discussed represents preliminary age-related observations. For the sake of convenience these are referred to as "levels"; they should not be construed as stage descriptions. Age-related observations do not, in themselves, constitute developmental stages. A stage system requires: (a) structural, rather than descriptive, analyses; (b) analyses of the structure of processes of change; and (c) experimental verification of the validity of the invariance of the sequence.

Although one long-term goal of the research is to determine whether development in this domain has stagelike properties, it is desirable to avoid a premature and misleading labeling of the observed differences as forming a developmental stage sequence. Therefore, two developmentally related observations are presented. First, three levels of social–conventional judgment can be characterized that are roughly associated with ages 9–11, 12–13, and 14–16. Second, the transitional periods between these levels are characterized.

## Levels of Development

*Level 1.* The first level observed in the sample (appoximately ages 9–11 years) is one in which the child displays no clear conception of social systems. Individual behavior is not related to organized forms of group or social activity, nor are social phenomena seen as serving social functions. In addition, at this level children do make some clear distinctions between the issues covered in our social–conventional interview and those represented in the moral judgment interview. That is, their evaluation of social–conventional acts changes according to whether or not such acts are covered by rules. In contrast, the class of acts included in the moral judgment interview, such as killing, stealing, or cheating, are regarded by these children as intrinsically good or bad: in this case, the child's evaluation does not depend on the existence of rules or laws. Instead, rules are viewed as an intrinsic part of the nature of the act itself.

First, consider examples of children's reactions to the stories regarding the use of titles or first names in addressing teachers. The following responses are characteristic:

Bruce (11 years, 5 months)[4]:

DO YOU THINK PETER WAS RIGHT OR WRONG TO CONTINUE CALLING HIS TEACHERS BY THEIR FIRST NAMES?

Wrong, because the principal told him not to. Because it was a rule. It was one of the rules of the school.

AND WHY DOES THAT MAKE IT WRONG TO CALL A TEACHER BY HIS FIRST NAME?

Because you should follow the rules.

DO YOU THINK IF THERE WEREN'T A RULE, THAT IT WOULD BE WRONG—OR WOULD IT BE RIGHT TO CALL TEACHERS BY THEIR FIRST NAMES?

Right. Because if there wasn't a rule, it wouldn't matter.

WHAT DO YOU MEAN, IT WOULDN'T MATTER?

It wouldn't matter what they called her if there wasn't a rule.

WHAT ABOUT THE RULE MAKES IT WRONG?

They made the rule because if there wasn't any rules, everybody would just be doing things they wanted to do. If they didn't have any rules everybody would, like, be running in the corridor and knocking over people.

Robert (11 years, 0 months):

I think he was wrong because those were the rules of the school and they were different rules than at his house.

DO YOU THINK THAT RULE WAS FAIR?

Yes, because it was just another rule that they have to call the teachers by Mr. or Mrs.

DO YOU THINK IT MATTERS WHAT PEOPLE ARE CALLED? WHETHER THEY ARE CALLED BY THEIR TITLES OR THEIR FIRST NAMES?

No, because as long as someone is understanding you and they know what you are talking about, I don't think it is wrong.

THEN WHY DO YOU THINK PETER SHOULD FOLLOW THAT RULE IF HE DOES NOT THINK IT IS WRONG EITHER?

---

[4]Throughout this chapter, in the initial reference to each subject the age will be included. Thereafter only the name will be used.

Well, that is the rule in the school.

WHY IS IT IMPORTANT TO FOLLOW THE RULES?

Because they make the rules for safety and stuff like that and some of the rules like you have to do your math homework and stuff like that.

These children also responded in a similar way regarding situations outside the school context. Here is a response to the question of whether or not Ken, a lawyer, was right to dress informally in the law office despite objections from his partner.

Mark (10 years, 9 months):

DO YOU THINK KEN WAS RIGHT OR WRONG IN HIS DECISION TO CON-TINUE WEARING SPORTS CLOTHES TO THE OFFICE?

I think that you can wear whatever you want as long as you get the work done.

HOW COME?

It doesn't matter what you look like, it's how the work is and what it's like, not how you dress, because no one's going to care, I don't think.

WHY SHOULDN'T THEY CARE? OR DO YOU THINK THEY SHOULD CARE?

I think they shouldn't because it really doesn't matter what you look like, it's just for looks.

WHAT IF THERE WAS A RULE IN THE OFFICE—DO YOU THINK HE WOULD BE RIGHT OR WRONG IN BREAKING THAT RULE?

I think he would be wrong, because you shouldn't break any rule, really.

WHY NOT?

Because if he made a rule, that means you should stick to it or else you don't even have to make the rule. There's no sense in making a rule if no one's going to pay any attention to it.

WHY SHOULD YOU FOLLOW IT THOUGH IF YOU DON'T BELIEVE IN IT?

Rules are rules, and you have to stick to the rules.

WHY IS THAT?

If nobody else stuck to any other rules, like I was saying about the corridor, everybody would be hitting each other.

All of these examples demonstrate that for children at this level the evaluation of social–conventional acts depends on whether or not there are rules pertaining to the situation. In the reasoning of these children, a rule has an independent existence with a purpose of its own; the children do not relate its purpose with the nature of the particular act covered by the rule. The reasoning observed at the first level, therefore, takes the following form:

1. The act does not lead to disorder.
2. The rule prohibits the act.
3. Adherence to the rule prevents the act from occurring and therefore no disorder.
4. Violation of rule (i.e., performance of the act) leads to disorder.

In contrast, a chain of reasoning in which the action is coordinated with the rule may be characterized as follows:

1. The act leads to disorder.
2. Therefore a rule is needed to prevent the act from occurring.
3. Adherence to the rule prevents the act from occurring and therefore no disorder.
4. Violation of the rule (i.e., performance of the act) leads to disorder.

In both of these sequences the conclusions are the same: violation of the rule leads to disorder. The difference between the two is that in the former sequence (1) is disjointed from (2)–(4). That is, the rule is treated as obligatory and invariable even though it pertains to an act that is treated as arbitrary and variable from place to place and time to time. If a rule prohibiting the act does exist, then the rule must be followed and the action is judged to be wrong. For these children the rule subordinates the act.

Therefore, in these children's thinking the existence of a rule gives the rule reason and reason lies in its existence. Their conception of a social rule is circular: the existence of a rule implies regularity and, in turn, regularity implies the rule. They thus confuse the prescriptive nature of a rule for a description of empirical regularity. In a sense, they define a social rule in the way an adult may define a natural law. A violation of the rule, therefore, is incompatible with the existence of the rule.

We have said that children at the first level view social–conventional acts as arbitrary but that they judge such acts as obligatory when covered by a rule. However, these same children do not reason in this way about all social acts. Their thinking about life, trust and property rights takes another form. In response to questions concerning such acts as killing, stealing, and cheating, it could be seen that life and property rights are not regarded as variable and that evaluations of such issues do not depend on the existence of rules or laws.

Responses to two types of interview questions are relevant here. Drawing from one of the stories used in the moral judgment interview, subjects were questioned about a boy who has cheated an old man of 500 dollars. We asked whether or not cheating would be wrong if there were no rule prohibiting such cheating and everyone agreed it was all right to do so. Subjects were also asked whether or not stealing would be wrong in the absence of rules prohibiting theft.

Here are examples of responses to these questions:

Mark:

SUPPOSE THAT EVERYBODY FELT IT DIDN'T MATTER IF YOU CHEATED AN OLD MAN OUT OF MONEY. THEY CONSIDERED IT ACCEPTABLE IF THE PERSON WAS STUPID ENOUGH TO GET SWINDLED IN THE FIRST PLACE.

I still think that would be wrong.

WHY?

Because you're still cheating the old man. It doesn't matter whether he's stupid enough or not, and it's not really fair to take the money.

WHAT DO YOU MEAN, IT'S NOT FAIR TO STEAL?

It's not nice to do it, because maybe he needs it too.

WHAT IF THE RULE WERE CHANGED ABOUT CALLING PEOPLE BY THEIR FIRST NAMES SO THAT EVERYBODY COULD CALL THEIR TEACHERS BY THEIR FIRST NAMES? DO YOU THINK IT WOULD BE RIGHT OR WRONG IN THAT CASE TO DO IT?

I think it would be all right then, because the rule is changed. Right? And everybody else would probably be doing it too.

HOW COME THE TWO THINGS ARE DIFFERENT? YOU'RE SAYING IN CHEATING, IF YOU CHANGED THE RULE IT WOULD STILL BE WRONG, BUT IF YOU CHANGED THE RULE ABOUT CALLING PEOPLE BY THEIR FIRST NAMES, THEN YOU COULD DO IT.

Because it's sort of a different story. Cheating an old man, you should never do that, even if everybody says you can. You should still never cheat off an old man.

WHY?

Because he's sort of helpless. He can't try to get it back if he has to and you could easily steal it off him too, because he can't defend himself.

Philip (10 years, 8 months):

WHAT IF THERE WAS NO RULE ABOUT STEALING? WOULD IT BE RIGHT OR WRONG TO DO THAT?

Wrong.

WHY?

Well, because the guy who say went in and robbed a jewelry store, the guy who owned the jewelry store had bought all that stuff for money and then the robber who stole the stuff just had to go in and take it instead of work for it.

WHY WOULD THAT BE WRONG?

Well, because if just one person worked for everything in the world, and everybody would just be able to go in and steal something, it wouldn't be right.

These responses show that children do not reason about all rules in the same way. In regard to stealing, cheating, or killing, the judgment of the act is based on the child's view of the intrinsic nature of the act itself and not the rules or sanctions that apply to the act. Stealing is viewed as wrong because it violates the right to one's property or possessions. Killing is also seen as intrinsically wrong because everyone wants to live and death is irreversible. It is assumed that both types of acts are against the law and should be against the law. For these children there is a natural and necessary correspondence between such rights and laws that prohibit the violation of these rights. The existence of laws does not determine the wrongness of the act. Instead, it is assumed that laws correspond to wrong actions. This type of reasoning, because of the close correspondence between the acts and the laws, sometimes appears circular:

Bruce:

WHAT'S THE DIFFERENCE BETWEEN BREAKING A CUSTOM, LIKE GOING INTO A JOB THAT USUALLY ONLY WOMEN GO INTO, AND BREAKING A RULE THAT SAYS YOU SHOULDN'T STEAL? WHAT'S THE DIFFERENCE BETWEEN THE TWO?

There's no law against doing something that ladies usually do, but it's like against the law to steal something.

HOW COME THERE'S NO LAW AGAINST GOING INTO SOMETHING THAT LADIES USUALLY DO BUT THERE IS A LAW AGAINST STEALING? WHAT MAKES THE TWO THINGS DIFFERENT?

Because when you steal, that's doing something wrong, but there's nothing wrong with doing what Joe did [becoming an infant nurse].

WHAT DO YOU MEAN, THERE'S NOTHING WRONG WITH IT?

Well, it's not against the law or anything.

*Level 2.* The second level (approximately 12–13 years of age) of social–conventional thinking emerges with the child's changing conceptions of social rules. At the second level rules are no longer defined as descriptive of social regularity. Instead, rules are conceived to be prescriptions for behavior set down by individuals (e.g., parents, teachers) or institutions (e.g., schools).

With this change in the conception of rules, evaluation of a given rule is coordinated with evaluation of the act involved. Bill's (12 years, 11 months) responses to two stories are typical of this second level:

DO YOU THINK PETER WAS RIGHT OR WRONG TO CONTINUE CALLING HIS TEACHERS BY THEIR FIRST NAMES?

I think it is up to him what he calls them because a name is just like a symbol or something and it doesn't really matter, just as long as the teacher knows or everybody else knows who you are talking about.

WHAT ABOUT THE RULE, DO YOU THINK IT WOULD BE WRONG TO DISOBEY IT IN THE SCHOOL?

No.

IN SOME SCHOOLS IT IS GENERALLY ACCEPTED TO ADDRESS TEACHERS BY THEIR FIRST NAMES. DO YOU CONSIDER IT WRONG TO CALL A TEACHER BY HIS FIRST NAME EVEN IN A SCHOOL WHERE IT IS ALLOWED?

No.

IS THERE A DIFFERENCE IN DOING IT IN A SCHOOL WHERE IT IS ALLOWED AND IN A SCHOOL WHERE IT IS NOT ALLOWED?

I don't think so.

HOW COME?

I don't really think it makes that much difference. I think that kids should call teachers by their first names, so I don't see any difference in it.

WHY DO YOU THINK KIDS SHOULD CALL TEACHERS BY THEIR FIRST NAMES?

They call everybody else by their first names, and it seems more friendly too.

SOME PEOPLE MIGHT ARGUE THAT IT SHOWS A LACK OF CONSIDERA-TION AND RESPECT TO CALL A TEACHER BY THEIR FIRST NAME. WHAT WOULD YOU SAY TO THAT?

I think that is stupid. There is nothing wrong with a name no matter which you say. It doesn't really matter.

DO YOU THINK KEN WAS RIGHT OR WRONG IN HIS DECISION TO CON-TINUE WEARING SPORTS CLOTHES TO THE OFFICE?

I don't see any difference about wearing clothes, like it does not change how he works or anything like that. It isn't very important.

DO YOU THINK IT WOULD MAKE ANY DIFFERENCE IF IT WAS THE BOSS
THAT TOLD HIM IT WAS THE OFFICE POLICY TO GET DRESSED UP TO GO
TO THE OFFICE?

It's up to him, what he wants to wear. Unless he signed a contract or
something saying that he would always wear a shirt and tie, then he should
have to, but it's really up to him what he wants to wear.

HOW COME?

It is something, that it does not affect anybody else, what he wears, it is
up to him, what he prefers.

The distinguishing features of thinking at the second level are: (*a*)
social–conventional acts are regarded as arbitrary and unnecessary, (*b*) rules
are evaluated on the basis of the acts involved, and (*c*) those rules pertaining to
social–conventional acts are seen as unduly constraining. As has been seen in
Bill's responses, use of titles or mode of dress are regarded as arbitrary. It is
the ability to communicate with others that these children regard as important.
Names are seen as ways of identifying people and it is thought that communication can be achieved via the use of first names or titles. Similarly, modes of
dress have little meaning to these children. In both cases, they believe that
these kinds of decisions are up to individual choice. The preferences of
children and adults or employer and employee are considered equally valid.
Therefore, each individual has the right to make his own choice of how to
address teachers, how to dress at work, etc.

Responses at the second level support the interpretation of judgments at the
first level. It may be argued that children at the first level do have a conception
of social systems and that they subordinate individual acts to the need for
adherence to rules so as to provide order in the system. Responses at the first
level have been interpreted here to mean that those children do not have a
conception of society as a system and that rules are defined as descriptive of
social regularity. Consequently, it is only when rules exist pertaining to
social–conventional acts that they are regarded as obligatory. Children at the
second level do not define rules as descriptive and, therefore, they evaluate
social convention and custom in terms of individual choice. The following
responses are additional examples reflecting this type of thinking.

John (13 years, 0 months):

DO YOU THINK KEN WAS RIGHT OR WRONG IN HIS DECISION TO CON-
TINUE WEARING SPORTS CLOTHES TO THE OFFICE?

I think well, I don't think that really what he wears should make any
difference, I don't see why anyone should have to wear a coat and tie or
anything like that, because you know, they just may not be as comfortable
or something like that to the person who does not want to wear them, and

therefore, I don't think that anybody should have to. I think he was probably, I don't know, I think he may have been right in still wearing them because he was sort of telling them that he really thinks they don't have to wear a coat and tie and he was standing up for what he thought was right.

HOW COME IT DOES NOT MATTER WHAT PEOPLE WEAR, AND PEOPLE CAN WEAR WHAT THEY WANT? THAT PEOPLE SHOULD BE ABLE TO WEAR WHAT THEY WANT TO?

Well, clothing is just like names. Certain people, like it doesn't signify anything, except maybe someone when they are rich and have nicer clothes or something like that. But then you can't tell someone's personality by what they wear the same as you can't tell someone's personality by their name, it just really does not make any difference. Like one day I wore shorts to school, a couple of days ago, and I don't see anything wrong with that, it was a hot day and I knew it.

Robert (12 years, 11 months):

DO YOU THINK PETER WAS RIGHT OR WRONG TO CONTINUE CALLING HIS TEACHERS BY THEIR FIRST NAMES?

Well, all the teachers were strict right, and felt that he should call them sir, or mister. Well if I were a teacher, I don't think it should bother a teacher that he be called by his first name and if I had anything to say about it, I would call a teacher by his first name, but the way it is now, you really can't. But Peter actually should not have done it, because he could get himself into trouble, but I guess he could because that was the way he had been brought up and that was the way he thought it should be done.

WHY DO YOU THINK HE SHOULD NOT BREAK THE RULE?

He shouldn't break the rule. Because he could get into trouble for it and if you have to go to school you might as well not make it harder for yourself.

WHAT IF PETER REALLY BELIEVED THAT THE RULE WAS WRONG? DO YOU THINK THEN IT WOULD BE RIGHT OR WRONG FOR HIM TO BREAK A RULE?

Well, still, it is actually not wrong, because it is not going to make any difference because like I said before, maybe it is right for him to do it, but he would be getting himself into trouble if he did it.

These children judge rules in relation to the relevant act. Therefore, both rules and adult expectations regarding these acts are treated as instances of constraint. Insofar as sanctions are associated with violation of the rule, then the combination of (*a*) the relative unimportance of these issues and (*b*) punishment for their performance leads these children to highlight the sanctions. Furthermore, the necessity of a given rule and its adherence is evaluated pragmatically. In like fashion, the validity of demands of one individual on another is judged on pragmatic grounds rather than on ones of social conformity or accommodation.

Robert:

DO YOU THINK KEN WAS RIGHT OR WRONG IN HIS DECISION TO CON-TINUE WEARING SPORTS CLOTHES TO THE OFFICE?

Well, there are sometimes we need to get dressed and sometimes we don't need to, like if you are sitting there all day signing papers and not going out or talking to clients and stuff, it really does not matter, but if you are going to be going to meetings and stuff, people may not think much of you if you come in sports clothes, although I don't think it really matters, although some people would.

SO WHY SHOULD YOU FOLLOW THE RULE OF WEARING A SUIT AND TIE?

Well, just sometimes something that you wear, one reason is that everyone else is doing it, and another reason is because this is what everybody does and it is a dress-up occasion.

WHAT IF YOU DO NOT BELIEVE IN IT. DO YOU THINK IT WOULD BE RIGHT OR WRONG NOT TO DO IT?

Well, if he didn't believe in it, it would depend on what you were doing to the business or what you were doing for the business.

Bill:

SAY WHEN KEN BREAKS THE CUSTOM OF DRESSING FORMALLY AND WEARS CASUAL CLOTHES, BUT MOST OF HIS CLIENTS OBJECT—DO YOU THINK IT WOULD BE WORSE THEN TO DO IT?

Well, he shouldn't really have to wear anything special, but if it is going to take business away, he should, but it is really up to him, but it would probably be better for the business if the clients did not like it, but if they didn't really mind, then he should have kept on wearing what he wanted to.

IF MOST OF HIS CLIENTS MINDED, DO YOU THINK THEN HIS GOING AGAINST THE CUSTOM AND WEARING SPORTS CLOTHES WAS BAD?

Well, not really. No matter what he wears, he is still going to do what he has to do and I wouldn't see any reason why the clients would object to it.

In these responses it can be seen that, unlike children at the previous level, these children are aware of general social expectations regarding an individual's behavior. However, they do not attribute importance to social expectations. Decisions are made on practical grounds and social expectations are subordinated to their judgment of the intrinsic worth of the acts themselves. This is evident in the ways the children discuss the expectations of teachers, business clients, or employers. The social aspects of relationships and interactions are not salient in their decisions. One of our subjects, John, makes this explicit when he is asked to compare the violation of customs of formal dress with dishonest actions.

That is not the same as doing something dishonest. It is doing something people really don't take to, like eating with your hands at the dinner table. It's not wrong—like other people might not like it that much.

In this case, John spontaneously raises the issue of table manners. Other children have responded similarly to a story in the interview about a boy who wants to eat with his hands in public. Ken's answer also reflects a lack of concern with social expectation as a guide to behavior.

DO YOU THINK HE WAS RIGHT OR WRONG IN CONTINUING TO USE HIS HANDS TO EAT?

It's up to him if he wants to. If it created anything bad I think he ought to change it. If there was something actually wrong with it, not socially but healthwise. I think he should keep on doing this if this is what he wants, if there's no health hazard.

DO YOU THINK IT IS RIGHT FOR PEOPLE TO EXPECT OTHERS TO EAT IN CERTAIN WAYS?

Well, I think most people do, but I think it doesn't really. . . they expect everyone to but I don't think it really matters. Everyone does so they expect him to, but if someone else came along and did it differently and it didn't harm anyone or anything I think it doesn't matter.

Finally, it should be noted that children who are at the second level of social–conventional thinking generally do not respond relativistically to questions regarding life and individual rights. A typical example can be seen in the following responses made by Bill:

SUPPOSE THAT IN PETER'S FAMILY THEY DON'T CARE ABOUT CHEATING FROM AN OLD MAN. THEY CONSIDER IT ACCEPTABLE TO CHEAT SOMEONE OUT OF MONEY IF THE PERSON WAS STUPID ENOUGH TO ALLOW HIMSELF TO GET SWINDLED. WOULD IT BE RIGHT OR WRONG IN THAT CASE TO CHEAT SOMEONE OUT OF $500?

Wrong.

WHY IS THAT?

They are still taking something away and they said they would help someone, so it doesn't really matter what they think, it is what they do. And what they say.

WHAT DO YOU MEAN?

Well, what difference does it matter that they think it was right or they think it is wrong, because it is still not right, it is still the same thing, what they think.

WHAT IF THE RULE WAS CHANGED FOR EVERYONE AND THERE WAS NO LAW AGAINST CHEATING OR BAD FEELING ABOUT CHEATING. EVERYONE THOUGHT IF THEY WERE STUPID ENOUGH TO GET CHEATED, IT WAS WORTH IT. DO YOU THINK IT WOULD STILL BE WRONG TO DO IT?

Yes.

WHY?

No matter what the law is or the rule, it doesn't change it being right or wrong.

*Level 3.* It has been seen that up to the second level of social–conventional thinking the child does not view his actions as an aspect of group, institutional, or societal functioning. Except in situations where the child can see the intrinsic worth or harmfulness of specific acts, social rules and expectations are regarded as arbitrary constraints. At the next level, which emerges during adolescence (14–16 years), a clear shift in reasoning about the issues in the social–conventional interview can be seen. Now these issues are regarded as meaningful and necessary.

One of the primary changes observed at this level (accounting for the shift in attitude toward such acts as the use of titles) is the formulation of ideas regarding the functions and form of the social environment. These adolescents consider social demands and expectations legitimate in the context of the social system from which they emanate..They take a collectivistic perspective such that group and institutional codes or mores are treated as the means of defining correct behavior.

Michael (15 years, 6 months):

I think it was wrong.

WHY?

His parents said it was all right for him to do it, and I think that was fine in his house, but I don't think that he should—what he's able to do at

home, I don't think he should be able to think what he's able to do there
he can do anywhere else. He should follow the rules of where he is and
act accordingly.

WHY SHOULD HE FOLLOW THE RULES OF WHERE HE IS?

I don't know, I guess if nobody ever followed the rules of what they were
supposed to do, we'd have chaos. Nobody would do anything that
anybody else would want to do, everybody would do everything that they
wanted to do. You'd just have chaos.

DO YOU THINK IT MATTERS WHAT YOU CALL PEOPLE, WHETHER YOU
CALL THEM BY THEIR TITLE OR BY THEIR FIRST NAME?

I guess this is a little thing, but it sort of hits on what you're able to do,
and it's kind of important because it's kind of a little thing but it concerns
what a person has a right to do. Whether he should—has to follow rules or
not.

James (15 years, 11 months):

I think he's wrong, because in his family he can call his mother and father
by their first names in his family, but when he's in public he's got to
respect the rules of the school.

WHY DOES HE HAVE TO RESPECT THE RULES OF THE SCHOOL?

How can you be one individual? If everyone else—he's one individual
and his family is brought up with first names. In school, it's a rule to call
people by their last names, and if it's a rule he can't be the only one who's
not going to do it. He's just going to have to live with it. Even if his
family taught him like that, he doesn't have to tell them . . . he cannot do
it. It's just the principle of the thing. Because it's different if a lot of
families did it, but I think he probably is just one exception. And he
should obey the rules of the school.

Social–conventional thinking forms part of a conception of society as an
entity. That is, social acts are now judged in relation to a group or social
system in which the individual is subordinate. This shift in thinking stems from
a transformation in the conception of society. Society is now viewed as a
system providing a context for rules, policies, and social expectations. Therefore, society is treated as an entity that guides social behavior. At this level
general consensus is reflected in the rules by which society functions. Uniformity is required in order to maintain and regulate the system. The following
examples are typical of the way subjects at this level discuss society:

Ben (16 years, 0 months):

DO YOU THINK IT WAS RIGHT OR WRONG TO CONTINUE USING HIS HANDS
TO EAT?

Uh . . . he was wrong because well, every place he goes, nobody else likes it, and he should have respect for other peoples' feelings. Just because he did it from when he was a child doesn't make it right.

WHAT MAKES IT WRONG?

Society says it's wrong. It's just not something you're supposed to do. It's impolite; society says it's impolite. You're not supposed to well, I've been brought up by society and I say it looks disgusting.

Marty (14 years, 7 months):

DO YOU THINK IT IS RIGHT OR WRONG FOR THE MEN TO LIVE APART FROM THEIR FAMILES?

Again, the thing that decides what's right or wrong is society, and what society has decided. I think it's right, and if that's what they decided and that's what they've worked out, then that's what they should do.

Jim (14 years, 6 months):

DO YOU THINK IT IS RIGHT OR WRONG FOR THE MEN TO LIVE APART FROM THEIR FAMILIES?

Well, I think that it is whatever is right or wrong in that society. I think if that society dictates that it is okay for the men to live here and the women to live there, it should be okay. But in our society, the people live together as a family, unless they die or get divorced or something, or separate.

It is through their conception of society that these subjects' understanding of, and commitment to, social–conventional acts can be explained. Of particular relevance to the types of issues studied is the subjects' definition of society as hierarchically organized. Here are some examples. The first comes from one of the younger subjects, who is beginning to make status distinctions, whereas the second example comes from an older subject.

David (13 years, 6 months):

SAY YOU FELT THAT CALLING PEOPLE BY THEIR FIRST NAMES WAS A MUCH MORE INFORMAL WAY OF TALKING TO PEOPLE AND YOU PRE-FERRED THAT?

Yeah, well, me, myself, I don't think that that's very respectful.

WHY IS THAT?

Because you call kids by their first names. Like you have a maid or something you call them by their first names. But that's sort of different because it's like one of the kids almost, you know? It depends how the person acts. Like John—do you know who that is? Well, I think he acts like a kid, so I just call him John. But Coach Jones, I don't call him "hey, Bob"—I say Coach because I respect him.

George (16 years, 0 months):

WAS PETER RIGHT OR WRONG TO CONTINUE CALLING HIS TEACHERS BY THEIR FIRST NAMES?

Wrong.

WHY?

A teacher can be called what he wants. If a teacher wants to be called Mr. or Mrs., then it's his right, it is his name and everybody if he wants to be called Mr. or Mrs. should be.

DO YOU THINK IT MATTERS IF PEOPLE ARE CALLED BY THEIR TITLES, MR., MRS., DR.?

Well, it makes some difference. At least to the person. If he worked through college for his title, he would probably like people to use it.

DO YOU THINK IT MAKES ANY DIFFERENCE?

Yeah, it makes you aware of what the person is. If he is above you, older, smarter.

IS THAT IMPORTANT TO KNOW?

Yeah, you've got to respect that.

WHY DO YOU HAVE TO RESPECT THAT?

They have had a lot more experience and they know a lot more than you do.

WHY IS CALLING A TEACHER BY HIS TITLE A SIGN OF RESPECT OR ACKNOWLEDGMENT OF THAT FACT?

Well, he is smarter than you if he is teaching and you should be somewhat thankful and call him what he wants to be called by.

BUT THE FACT THAT YOU CALL HIM A DOCTOR, WHY IS THAT A SIGN OF RESPECT? OR MR.?

Just Mr. or Dr. you recognize that he is a doctor and got his doctorate in something.

At this level, hierarchical distinctions are made between people of differing roles and status. Status distinctions are based on the social system's classifications of activities and accomplishments—classifications presumably determined by usefulness to the system. Conventions are seen to be necessary because they serve to distinguish the relative worth of individuals and to acknowledge merit and accomplishment. Social forms serve to guide interactions between people of lower and high status.[5]

## Transitional Periods

Three levels of social–conventional thinking have been analyzed so far. However, these levels of development do not explain the means by which change from one level to the next occurs. As has been discussed elsewhere (Turiel, 1974), transitional processes have characteristics that are different from those of stable forms of thinking. In this section, some hypotheses regarding the transitions from Level 1 to Level 2 and from Level 2 to Level 3 are discussed.

*Transition 1.* The first level of social–conventional thinking is one in which social rules are not coordinated with the acts to which the rules apply. At the second level, rules are no longer defined as descriptive of social regularity and the existence of a rule does not, in itself, imply that the act it pertains to is obligatory. The transitional process between these two levels entails a change in the conception of social rules, as well as an attempt to simultaneously consider social–conventional acts in relation to rules. In the transition from the first to the second level there is an attempt to consider the bases for both an individual's action and for the rule. In the following responses, a beginning awareness of the social source of rules, as well as a concern with the means by which they are established, can be seen.

Jonathan (10 years, 4 months):

Well, Ken was right about the whole thing. Bob shouldn't make him change the clothes. But Bob can ask and if Ken doesn't want to, Ken doesn't do it . . . Ken has the right to wear what he wants to wear.

WHAT GIVES HIM THE RIGHT?

Because it's his clothes and he has half the office, whatever he wants to do with it.

WELL, WHAT'S THE DIFFERENCE BETWEEN SOMETHING LIKE THIS AND CALLING SOMEONE BY THEIR FIRST NAME?

[5]At the third level we also see interconnections between the social-conventional and the moral. Although our hypothesis was that the two are distinct realms, it is possible that they may at times become confused with each other. We have seen that the social–conventional is differentiated from the moral at the first two levels. It is at the third level that these are sometimes treated interchangeably: the conventional can be moralized and the moral can be conventionalized. By the conventional being moralized we are referring to the transformation of social conventions or customs into moral issues. In the case of the moral being conventionalized, we are referring to judgments in which moral issues are regarded as convention.

Well, in the school thing you don't own anything. But in the lawyer business you own half the office. You bought half the office and it's yours to do with what you want to do.

BUT SAY YOU DON'T OWN THE OFFICE?

If you don't own the office, and there was a rule about that, you should. If there's a rule about something you should try to follow it.

Although Jonathan states that rules should be followed, he is aware that rules are not always obeyed. When he is asked to compare the act of cheating a man out of his money with the violation of school rules, he replies:

Cheating, it isn't right to do. But breaking a rule, if he was brought up that way, if he breaks it once or twice, it's not that bad. Everybody must break a rule sometime.

In the judgments of a number of subjects we observed a good deal of doubtfulness and uncertainty, which might have been reflective of transition. In particular, there was a failure to coordinate the conception of rules with the conception of the validity of individual choices:

Stuart (11 years, 6 months):

DO YOU THINK PETER WAS RIGHT OR WRONG TO CONTINUE CALLING THE TEACHERS BY THEIR FIRST NAMES?

I don't think he is right. He may be able to do things—say his parents let him smoke at home, but he should not be allowed to smoke in school or something. Maybe he can do it at home, but there is a law in school that he can't.

WHAT DO YOU MEAN THERE IS A LAW IN SCHOOL?

Like a rule, you know. Like you have rules you cannot stay after if you are just staying after to fool around, things like that, unless you have a reason.

WHY DO YOU THINK THEY MADE THAT RULE ABOUT USING TITLES?

Because it is more proper than just calling teachers by their first names. I really don't know.

DO YOU THINK IF SOMEONE BELIEVES THE RULE IS WRONG, THAT THEY WOULD BE WRONG IN CALLING TEACHERS BY THEIR FIRST NAMES?

It is kind of what the person thought. You would have to hear his opinion about it. I know we are not supposed to, but you would have to get his opinions about what he has to think about it.

WHAT IF HE THINKS THAT TITLES DON'T NECESSARILY MEAN RESPECT TO HIM AND HE IS USED TO CALLING PEOPLE BY THEIR FIRST NAMES AND HE DOES NOT BELIEVE THAT THAT RULE MAKES SENSE. DO YOU THINK HE WOULD BE RIGHT THEN?

I am not really sure, like maybe a lot of people think that a lot of the rules made by the police are not worthy, but they still have to abide by them, and I think they should. You just can't go and break a rule, you can try, but I don't think you are going to get anywhere. If it's a rule it is a rule and if you break it you are wrong.

WHY?

Well, you can break it when you want, but you can't change it, I don't think you will be able to change it, because it is a rule and the teachers want it that way, they should be able to have it that way. Because they work there and they teach the kids and they should have some rights, some laws to themselves, like people don't like you going up to them and calling them by their last names, I know our teachers don't, but I have done it before, and they say, "Mr. so and so to you." I don't know, it is just the way they like it.

Two aspects of Stuart's responses are of interest. First, he vacillates between a concern with an individual's reasons for an act and the view that rules must be followed. Unlike children at the first level, Stuart is aware that individuals may not necessarily approve of a given rule and, therefore, they may violate it. Second, Stuart is, at the same time, still uncertain as to whether or not a rule can be violated. He begins by stating that rules must be followed. When asked to justify that, he becomes less certain and says that rules can be violated but not changed. The uncertainty and vacillation may be reflective of changing conceptions of rules. In fact, in some of his responses Stuart reverts to judgments similar to those made by children at the first level.

*Transition 2.* The second level is a way of thinking that is minimally social in nature. Those children do not conceive of their actions in relation to groups or society. In general, the child's own role in social groupings is not a relevant consideration. It is expected that the mode of thinking characteristic of the second level has the potential for producing a state of conflict or disequilibrium for the adolescent that may lead to major developmental changes in social–conventional thinking. The disequilibrium hypothesized has its basis in a combination of two factors: (*a*) the child's thinking is in disparity with his social environment, and (*b*) the child still does not understand the form of that environment.

Consider the ways in which social–conventional thinking at the second level is disparate with the social environment. It has been seen that these children do not view conventions as important and do not see social acceptability as a basis for behavior. However, the adolescent functions in a social context that communicates a contrary viewpoint. Social roles, conventions, and status distinctions are presented as important from society's perspective.

During this age period attempts at socialization are made by conveying to the child that society should be respected: its symbols, conventions, and general will. Adherence to social expectations is treated as an expression of respect for authorities and the collectivity. Although these demands and expectations regarding how an individual ought to behave may be communicated explicitly, they are also implicit in the adolescent's environment. Implicit expectations of appropriate behavior and roles are embedded in the rewards, status, and achievements that can be observed.

Moreover, the individual's relation with his social environment is continually changing during this period. With increasing age he becomes more involved in social relations and groupings. Because of his greater participation in the social order, societal definitions of rules and conventions become more salient in the adolescent's experiences. As a consequence, the discrepancy between his own ideas and the nature of the social environment is likely to become apparent to him. Disequilibrium may be generated by the discrepancy between the adolescent's own ideas regarding social phenomena and the perceived social reality. Such a state primarily entails a tension between (*a*) the individual's own conception of the arbitrariness of aspects of social reality and (*b*) a social reality that presents itself in those aspects as nonarbitrary and meaningful.

The child also does not yet understand his social environment. The type of disequilibrium we are postulating, therefore, is not solely stimulated by external demands. Nor does it involve a process of adapting to an environment that forces the individual to do what he does not want to do. Instead, the conflict has its basis in the inadequacy of his concept of society and its components. He may view parents, teachers, institutions, etc., as having knowledge and understanding unavailable to him. During this phase he is in a position of conceptual dependence, from which he assumes there is an understanding of social phenomena still to be discovered. Subsequent changes, therefore, are likely to entail construction of concepts regarding the functions and form of the social environment. Indeed, it is just such a shift that occurs at the third level of social–conventional thinking.

## CONCLUSION

The developmental trends observed in this research substantiate the validity of its basic hypothesis: that the social–conventional domain forms a developmental dimension. By studying how individuals think about conventions and customs it has been determined that they do structure and transform the socially given and that changes in the ways they structure the social environment are age related. These findings indicate that individuals do not merely adapt their behavior to the customs and conventions of their culture without any awareness of the function and meaning of those customs and conventions. Instead, conceptions about the social–conventional form part of an understanding of social organization. As has been seen, individuals undergo systematic changes in the development of their understanding of social organization.

It should be reiterated, however, that the descriptions of social–conventional thinking presented here represent the product of a preliminary analysis and apply to a fairly narrow age range—from 9 or 10 years to 16 or 17 years. Additional analyses of the thinking of older subjects are currently underway. These are expected to show that further changes in social–conventional thinking do occur. In particular, changes in the individual's conceptions about, and understanding of, society should result in different ideas about the role and functions of social conventions.

In any event, the developmental trends discussed also support the hypothesis that social–conventional thinking represents a domain distinct from other dimensions of social conception. This research has focused on the distinction between social–conventional thinking and moral judgments because previous explanations of social development have either treated social and moral concepts alike or have subordinated all social concepts to moral reasoning. Neither approach is supported by this research: these findings show that moral judgments and social–conventional thinking are not reducible to each other. Therefore, the work reported here points to the hypothesis of partial systems in development. Verification of this domain as representing a partial system would require analyses of the distinctive features of the child's actions and interactions that produce social–conventional development. So far this domain has been distinguished only in terms of empirically defined content areas.

The hypothesis that all thought does not form a unitary whole is based on the principles of structure and interaction. This does not imply that different partial systems are necessarily unrelated to each other. Indeed, one of the aims of this research is to examine possible interrelations between social–conventional thinking and moral reasoning. However, I do not hold the view that all partial systems are necessarily integrated. For example, Werner's (1957) orthogenetic principle—that development is directed toward increased differentiation and integration—may be taken to mean that development progresses toward a state in which all systems are integrated into a total mental organization. In contrast, I propose the hypothesis that certain aspects of development may be directed toward integration, but others may be directed toward the segregation of systems. That is, some systems of thought inform each other and therefore become integrated, whereas some systems are not logically related and are therefore segregated.

## REFERENCES

Benedict, R. *Patterns of culture*. Boston: Houghton-Mifflin, 1934.

Gilligan, C., Kohlberg, L., Lerner, J., & Belenky, M. Moral reasoning about sexual dilemmas: the development of an interview and scoring system. Unpublished paper, Harvard University, 1970.

Hogan, .R. Moral conduct and moral character: a psychological perspective. *Psychological Bulletin*, 1973, **79**, 217–232.
Inhelder, B., & Piaget, J. *The growth of logical thinking from childhood to adolescence.* New York: Basic Books, 1958.
Inhelder B., & Piaget, J. *The early growth of logic in the child: (Classification and seriation).* New York: Harper, 1964.
Kohlberg, L. Stage and sequence: the cognitive-developmental approach to socialization. In D. Goslin (Ed.), *Handbook of socialization theory and research.* Chicago: Rand McNally, 1969.
Kohlberg, L. From is to ought: How to commit the naturalistic fallacy and get away with it in the study of moral development. In T. Mischel (Ed.), *Cognitive psychology and epistemology.* New York: Academic Press, 1971.
Kohlberg, L., & Lockwood, A. Cognitive-developmental psychology and political education: Progress in the sixties. Paper presented at the Social Science Consortium Convention, Boulder, Colorado, June 2, 1970.
Kohlberg, L., & Turiel, E. Moral development and moral education. In G. Lesser (Ed.), *Psychology and educational practice.* Chicago: Scott Foresman, 1971.
Le Vine, R. A. Culture, personality and socialization: an evolutionary view. In D. Goslin (Ed.), *Handbook of socialization theory and research.* Chicago: Rand McNally, 1969.
Lockwood, A. L. Stages of moral reasoning in students' analysis of public value controversy. Unpublished doctoral dissertation, Harvard University, 1970.
Mead, M. *Coming of age in Samoa.* New York: William Morrow, 1928.
Piaget, J. *The child's conception of time*, 1927. London: Routledge & Kegan Paul, 1969.
Piaget, J. *The child's conception of the world*, 1928. Patterson, New Jersey: Littlefield, Adams, 1960.
Piaget, J. *The moral judgment of the child*, 1932. Glencoe, Illinois: Free Press, 1948.
Piaget, J. *The child's conception of number.* New York: Norton, 1952.
Piaget, J. *Six psychological studies.* New York: Random House, 1967.
Piaget, J. Piaget's theory. In P. H. Mussen (Ed.), *Carmichael's manual of child psychology.* New York: Wiley, 1970.
Stein, J. L. Adolescents' reasoning about moral and sexual dilemmas: a longitudinal study. Unpublished doctoral dissertation, Harvard University, 1973.
Turiel, E. Adolescent conflict in the development of moral principles. In R. Solso (Ed.), *Loyola symposium: Contemporary issues in cognitive psychology.* Washington, D.C.: V. H. Winston & Sons, 1973. (a)
Turiel, E. Stage transition in moral development. In R.M. W. Travers (Ed.), *Second handbook of research on teaching.* Chicago: Rand McNally, 1973. (b)
Turiel, E. Conflict and transition in adolescent moral development. *Child Development*, 1974, **45**, 14–29.
Turiel, E., Kohlberg, L., & Edwards, C. Cross-cultural studies of moral development. Unpublished paper, Harvard University, 1973.
Weber, M. *The theory of economic and social organization,* 1947. Glencoe, Illinois: Free Press, 1964.
Werner, H. *Comparative psychology of mental development.* New York: International Universities Press, 1957.
Whiting, J. M. W., & Child, I. L. *Child training and personality: A cross-cultural study.* New Haven: Yale University Press, 1953.

# 2
# Implicators of Cognitive Development for Moral Reasoning

Charles Blake Keasey

*University of Nebraska, Lincoln*

At many points in the history of mankind various civilizations have undergone what may be termed grave moral crises. America is certainly no exception. Most recently we have been faced with atrocities committed by our own combat troops in Viet Nam, by the eruption of violence in our own country between police and students and between blacks and whites, and flagrant violations of the law by several of our highest public officials. With none of these instances has there been true consensus among our population as to who was in the right and who was in the wrong. Certainly sharp differences of opinion may be expected among those individuals directly involved in any of these instances (e.g., Ohio National Guardsmen, students at Kent State University, a U.S. Army private in Charlie Company entering the hamlet of My Lai in Viet Nam). However, sharp differences between people exist even among those agreeing about the rightness or wrongness of an act. Although they may reach agreement, they do so for very different reasons. Interestingly, they seem to come from a fairly systematic and consistent manner of thinking about moral issues.

One of the earliest attempts to systematically examine different modes of thinking about morality was carried out by Piaget (1932). From his extensive interviews and observations of children he concluded that their conception of morality shifted at about 7 years of age from a rather primitive view dominated by obedience and unilateral respect for adults to a more mature one characterized by cooperation and mutual respect. Working within the same cognitive-developmental framework, Kohlberg (1958) concluded that moral reasoning was more complex and long term in development than Piaget considered. Kohlberg delineated six qualitatively different modes of thinking about morality that extend beyond childhood, through adolescence, and well into adulthood.

Both Piaget and Kohlberg view their stages as forming an invariant sequence, with each stage representing a qualitatively different mode of thought. Consequently, an individual must pass through each preceding stage in the sequence in order to progress to the next stage. It is this issue of sequential invariance that has stimulated the most empirical attention. Research to, date strongly supports Piaget's two-stage sequence (see Hoffman, 1970, for a summary of relevant studies). Although much less research has been directed at Kohlberg's system, what has been done has generally been supportive.

With the issue of sequential invariance fairly well resolved, attention has been focused on factors responsible for movement from one stage to the next. Both Piaget (1932) and Kohlberg (1958) view moral development as an outgrowth of the interaction of cognitive development and social experience. Piaget's (1947). concept of structural parallelism implies that the structural transformations reflected in cognitive development cause children to redefine some of their social and moral perspectives. Given the above theoretical views, it comes as somewhat of a surprise that the hypothesized relationship between cognitive and moral development has been virtually untouched empirically (Kuhn, Langer, Kohlberg, & Haan, 1971; Lee, 1971).

In this chapter I will first review research to date on the relationship between cognitive and moral development and then present some new findings. The first section will be concluded with a discussion of the various theoretical models of the nature of the relationship between cognitive and moral development. In the second section attention will be shifted from the factors influencing how an individual reasons about moral issues to those involved in his or her evaluation of the moral reasoning of others. This process of evaluation appears to involve a complex interplay of thinking capacities in both moral and cognitive areas.

## STAGES OF COGNITIVE AND MORAL DEVELOPMENT

This section begins with consideration of the implications of studies relating IQ to moral development and continues with the few studies that have examined the relationship between cognitive and moral development. A substantial number of studies have found performance on standardized IQ tests to be positively related to several of the aspects of moral reasoning delineated by. Piaget (see Hoffman, 1970, for a summary of these studies). There are also a few studies (Keasey, 1971; Kohlberg, 1958; Kuhn et al., 1971) showing a moderate positive correlation (low .30's) between IQ and Kohlberg's stages of moral reasoning. It must be recognized that these findings do not really demonstrate a relationship between cognitive and moral development. First of all, the mental operations underlying Piaget's stages of cognitive development are only being assessed indirectly, at best, by standardized IQ tests. Support for this claim is indicated by the failure of Kuhn *et al.* (1971) to find any significant correlation between IQ and four Piagetian mental operations in a sample of 10-, 11-, and 12-year-olds. The two significant correlations (.31 and .50) they obtained in a sample of subjects in age ranging from 10 to 50 years are difficult to interpret and probably inflated because the influence of age was not partialled out. Even considering the highest correlations obtained, however, IQ only accounts for 25% of the variance in cognitive development. Clearly, if it is desired to assess the degree to which moral development is related to cognitive development, cognitive development, and not IQ, must be directly measured.

In addition to the above problem, which is strictly empirical in nature, there exists a potentially greater problem at the theoretical level. This problem grows out of the differing conceptions of intelligence held by Piaget and by mental testers (Elkind, 1970). The central issue is whether intellectual development is conceived as qualitative or quantitative in nature. If it is viewed as quantitative, as commonly done by mental testers, then it becomes extremely difficult to argue that different amounts of intelligence can lead to qualitatively different modes of reasoning about morality. In fact, none of the studies reviewed by Hoffman (1970) asserts that a certain amount of intelligence is predictive of one rather than the other of Piaget's stages of moral reasoning. It cannot even be argued that the positive correlations obtained indicate parallel development between IQ and moral reasoning. At best it can be claimed that children with higher IQ's move through either Piaget's or Kohlberg's stages of moral reasoning at a faster rate than children with average or below average IQ's. What is further implied by such a relationship is that IQ affects the rate of moral development and not the underlying structures that give rise to qualitatively different modes of moral reasoning.

A general model that does focus on these underlying structures has been advanced by Turiel (1967). He suggests that disequilibrium in the structures underlying moral reasoning can be induced by exposure to conflicting moral arguments. If these arguments contain some higher stage reasoning, then the individual undergoing the conflict can often use it to resolve his disequilibrium. If he does, then his or her newly evolved structures have incorporated some higher stage reasoning. Support for Turiel's model has come from three laboratory studies (Keasey, 1973; Tracy & Cross, 1973; Turiel, 1966) in which preadolescents have been exposed to conflicting moral arguments. In these studies, the subjects display an increased amount of higher stage reasoning following their exposure to conflicting moral arguments containing higher stage reasoning.

Although the form of Turiel's model closely parallels Piaget's notions of increasing equilibration of cognitive structures, it focuses on specific types of social interaction. Consequently, Turiel's model clarifies what types of social experience are likely to facilitate moral development but tells little about what cognitive factors are likely to be important. Also as a general model, it applies equally well to the transitions between all pairs of adjacent stages and therefore does not point out what specific factors are important to particular transitions.

From all that has been said above, it would seem appropriate to examine the issue of the dependency of moral development on cognitive development by first determining whether there is even an empirical relationship between the two. However, should this be done by examining the relationship between Piaget's theory of cognitive development and his theory of moral development, or between Piaget's cognition theory and Kohlberg's theory of moral development? Actually, the choice is a fairly simple one, because of the limited scope of Piaget's theory of moral development; for although the transition to Piaget's higher stage of moral reasoning occurs at around age 7, substantial changes in cognitive development continue well into adulthood. Consequently, research is limited to establishing the existence of a relationship between cognitive and moral development between the years 2 and 8. With Kohlberg's theory of moral development, however, it becomes possible to examine the nature of the relationship between the two processes over a much greater age range.

The inherent limitations in relating Piaget's theory of moral development to his theory of cognitive development were clearly recognized by Lee (1971). Instead of using Piaget's model of moral development, Lee devised her own five-stage system. Although it appeared somewhat like Kohlberg's six-stage system, it incorporated none of Kohlberg's techniques. Lee found substantial correlations (ranging from .26 to .70, with an average of .49) between six Piagetian measures of cognitive development and her stages of moral development. Because these correlations were based on her total sample of subjects, who ranged in age from 5 to 17 years, Lee recalculated the correlations with age partialled out. Although their magnitude decreased, the correlations were still substantial (ranging from .10 to .57, with an average of .33). Lee admitted that even with age partialled out, it could easily be contended that the main variable functioning in her study was still chronological age and its many correlates. Consequently, the interpretation of the correlation between cognitive and moral development became a difficult issue because of the possible influence of a larger number of factors that also varied with age. Possibly one of them would account for more of the variance in moral development than did cognitive development. Lee suggested that future studies could avoid some of these difficult interpretational problems by relating different levels of cognitive functioning within one age group to their level of moral reasoning. In spite of these interpretational problems, Lee concluded that her findings demonstrated that cognitive and moral modes of thought develop concomitantly.

These same interpretational problems, arising from a wide range in subjects' ages, are present in an unpublished study by Kuhn et al. (1971). They have obtained moderate positive correlations (ranging from .04 to .28, with an average of .20) between performance on Kohlberg's moral dilemmas and several Piagetian tasks designed to assess formal operational thought. Because Kuhn *et al.* have arranged their subjects in age groups (e.g., 10–15, 16–20, 20–30) for purposes of analysis, their obtained correlations are confounded with age. In spite of this, when their data are examined in 2×2 contingency tables (presence/absence of formal operations and principled moral reasoning) the resulting distributions strongly suggest that formal operations serve as a prerequisite for principled moral reasoning.

Although the confounding influence of age and its many correlates complicates the interpretation of the findings by Lee (1971) and Kuhn *et al.* (1971), it appears that some relationship does exist between cognitive and moral development. However, the two investigators do not agree as to the nature of that relationship. Kuhn *et al.* go well beyond Lee's conclusion that cognitive and moral modes of thought develop concomitantly. They clearly argue that some formal operational thought is a necessary condition for the emergence of principled moral reasoning. Their view of the relationship between the two processes adds specificity to the assertion by both Piaget (1932) and Kohlberg (1969) that moral development depends on cognitive development.

The confounding influence of age was avoided in a study conducted (Tomlinson-Keasey & Keasey, 1974) by examining the relationship between cognitive and moral development within two specific age groups—12 and 19 year olds. These two ages were selected because according to Piaget (Inhelder & Piaget, 1958) formal operations would be emerging in the younger group and would presumably be fairly well established in the older group. In addition to investigation of whether or not cognitive and moral development are related, several issues raised by the introduction of greater specificity in the relationship between cognitive and moral development were pursued. In particular, we wanted to determine whether formal operations were indeed a necessary but not sufficient condition for the emergence of principled moral reasoning. Last, it was desired to document the existence of the time lag implied between the emergence of formal operations and principled moral reasoning.

The question of whether or not the two processes were related was examined by correlating performance on three Piagetian measures of formal operations with moral reasoning given in response to six of Kohlberg's moral dilemmas. Substantial correlations were obtained for both the younger girls (+.60) and the women college students (+.58). These findings clearly indicate that a substantial relationship does exist between cognitive and moral development that is independent of age and its many correlates.

If formal operations are a prerequisite for becoming a principled moral thinker, then it can be expected that all principled moral thinkers evidence some capacity for formal operational thought. This is exactly the pattern found among the college women (see Table 1). In no instance is there a principled moral thinker who does not evidence a substantial amount of formal operational

## TABLE 1
### Cognitive and Moral Reasoning Levels
### of Girls and College Women[a]

| | Girls | | | | College women | | | |
|---|---|---|---|---|---|---|---|---|
| | Conventional | | Preconventional | | Principled | | Conventional | |
| | N | % | N | % | N | % | N | % |
| Integrated formal[b] | 1 | 100 | 0 | 0 | 3 | 38 | 5 | 62 |
| Early formal[c] | 3 | 43 | 4 | 57 | 1 | 11 | 8 | 89 |
| Transitional[d] | 0 | 0 | 12 | 100 | 1 | 20 | 4 | 80 |
| Concrete[e] | 0 | 0 | 10 | 100 | 0 | 0 | 2 | 100 |

[a] Source: Tomlinson-Keasey and Keasey. Reprinted by permission of the Society for Research in Child Development, Inc. (1974).

[b] Subject evidenced formal operational thought on all three tasks.

[c] Subject evidenced formal operational thought on two of three tasks.

[d] Subject evidenced formal operational thought on only one task.

[e] Subject failed to evidence formal operational thought on any task.

thought. It therefore appears that formal operations are necessary for the emergence of principled moral reasoning.

Turning to the 12 year olds, it can be seen from Table 1 that eight (27%) evidence substantial amounts of formal operational thought and another 12 (40%) evidence at least some facility with formal operations. Why, then, are there no principled moral thinkers within this age group? First of all, this finding is neither unusual nor unexpected, as normative data (Kuhn *et al.* 1971) indicate that the achievement of principled moral reasoning is rare at any age, especially as young as age 12. Second, this finding is still consistent with the notion that formal operations are necessary for the emergence of principled moral reasoning but not sufficient. However, to conclude that formal operational thought has no effect on moral reasoning among the younger subjects would be very misleading. For, in fact, at this age it appears that formal operations facilitate movement from preconventional (Stages 1 and 2) to conventional (Stages 3 and 4) moral reasoning (see Table 1).

To further substantiate the notion that formal operations were not sufficient for the emergence of principled moral reasoning, the levels of moral reasoning were compared for groups of young girls and college women who had achieved comparable mastery of formal operations. The underlying rationale for such comparisons was as follows: if formal operations were a sufficient condition for the emergence of principled moral reasoning, then groups evidencing similar mastery of formal operations should have attained similar levels of moral reasoning. When the appropriate comparisons were made, it was found that the moral reasoning of the college woman was significantly ($p<.001$) higher than that of the girls. Further support for the insufficiency of formal operations is indicated by the sizable proportion of both girls and college women (see Table 1) evidencing formal operational thinking who have not attained principled moral reasoning.

The conclusion that formal operations are a necessary but not sufficient condition for the emergence of principled moral reasoning implies the existence of a lag between the two. Although longitudinal data are needed to clearly document this lag, the distribution of subjects in Table 1 is quite consistent with the notion of a lag.

Because this study avoided the confounding influence of age and the resulting interpretational problems, it provided much needed support for the interpretations of both Kuhn *et al.* (1971) and Lee (1971) that their findings indicated the existence of a relationship between cognitive and moral development. It also provides substantiation for the contention of Kuhn *et al.* that formal operations are a necessary condition for the emergence of principled moral reasoning. To this picture, the above study adds evidence that formal operations are not sufficient for the emergence of principled moral reasoning, which seems to lag behind the emergence of formal operations.

In attempting to understand the findings from this study, speculations were made as to the nature of the relationship between cognitive and moral development. The concomitant development interpretation provided by Lee (1971) seemed to imply that development in the two areas was parallel but relatively independent. In contrast, both Piaget (1932) and Kohlberg (1969) claimed that the rate of moral development depended on cognitive development. Therefore, moral development might be either retarded or accelerated by one's rate of cognitive development. Not only did Piaget view moral development as dependent on cognitive development, among other things, but also his concept of structural parallelism implied that specific cognitive transformations led to specific moral transformations. Consequently, Piaget's view of the relationship between cognitive and moral development was one of specific dependency rather than general dependency. The documentation of the relationship between formal operations and principled moral reasoning (Kuhn *et al.*, 1971; Tomlinson-Keasey & Keasey, 1974) provided empirical support for specificity in the relationship between cognitive and moral development.

It is unlikely that a moral transformation will occur concurrently or immediately after a cognitive transformation. A time lag is expected because a cognitive transformation must consolidate before it transforms reasoning in the moral realm. If the above reasoning is correct, then what can be expected empirically? First of all, it can be expected that moral development will evidence a moderate positive correlation with both cognitive development and social experience throughout a rather wide age range. Second, the magnitude of the correlation between moral and cognitive development should be heightened during the emergence of a moral transformation. Finally, once the impact of the cognitive transformation has been fully reflected by a redefinition of moral reasoning, then the magnitude of the correlation between cognitive and moral development should return to its previous level.

A similar relationship presumably exists between moral development and social experience. The various types of social experience that are likely to play an important role in moral development have been discussed by Kohlberg (1969), Piaget (1932), and Turiel (1967). Findings by Keasey (1971) and Selman (1971) indicate that various types of social experience do relate systematically to moral development. Various dimensions of personality also appear to influence moral development, especially beyond Kohlberg's stages of conventional morality (Sullivan & Quarter, 1972).

In order to test some of the implications of the specific-dependent model, a study (Keasey & Weston, 1973) was conducted in which the relationship between concrete operations and Kohlberg's second stage of moral reasoning was examined. Kuhn *et al.* (1971) suggested that several characteristics of concrete operational thought gave rise to the naive instrumental hedonism embodied in Kohlberg's second stage of moral reasoning. An especially important cognitive advance was the child's ability to differentiate the objective, physical properties of an object from his own psychological actions relating to that object. Following this differentiation, the child came to view the moral value of an object or action strictly in terms of its relation to some psychological desire, motivation, or value on his part. The child was now also able to differentiate unobservable psychological states from observable physical appearances or behaviors of other people. This enabled him to redefine moral action as that which was instrumental to the actor's needs and desires.

A major issue under investigation was whether or not the magnitude of the relationship between cognitive and moral development shifted in the pattern implied by the specific-dependent model. If it did, then the relationship between cognitive and moral development should have been greater among 7-year-olds, who should have been entering concrete operations, than among 9-year-olds, who should have been well established in concrete operational thought. Although it was expected that the magnitude of the relationship between cognitive and moral development would differ between 7- and 9-year-olds, it was still anticipated that the presence of concrete operations in both age groups would serve as a necessary but not sufficient condition for the emergence of Kohlberg's Stage 2 moral reasoning. Finally, it was expected that there would be a lag between the emergence of concrete operations and Stage 2 moral reasoning.

The relationship between cognitive and moral development was examined by presenting all subjects (20 7- and 9-year-olds, half boys and half girls) with five Kohlberg dilemmas and Piagetian measures of the concrete operations of conservation and classification. For the 7-year-olds, moral judgment correlated significantly with all four indices of concrete operations (classification, .43; conservation of mass, .69; weight, .40, and volume, .48). A very different pattern of correlations emerged for the 9 year olds. Moral judgment failed to correlate significantly with any index of concrete operations (classification, .32; conservation of weight, $-.03$, and volume, $-.02$). Because all 20 9-year-olds conserved mass, it could not be correlated with moral judgment. The possibility that the very different magnitudes of the correlations for 7- and 9-year-olds were caused by corresponding differences in the ranges of the variables being correlated was examined and ruled out. It could therefore be concluded that the relationship between cognitive and moral development did shift in a pattern consistent with expectations derived from the specific-dependent model.

If concrete operational thinking is necessary for Stage 2 moral reasoning, then all Stage 2 subjects can be expected to evidence substantial amounts of concrete operational thought. Exactly this pattern has been found among both 7- and 9-year-olds. Table 2 indicates that all 15 children who are solidly at Stage 2 in their moral reasoning also evidence substantial amounts of concrete operational thought—none are still preoperational. These findings provide considerable support for the contention that concrete operational thought is necessary for the development of Stage 2 moral reasoning.

The findings summarized in Table 2 are also relevant to the contention that concrete operations are not sufficient to bring about Stage 2 moral reasoning.

TABLE 2
Cognitive and Moral Reasoning Stages
of 7- and 9-Year-Olds

|  | Integrated concrete[a] | Early concrete[b] | Preoperational[c] |
|---|---|---|---|
| 7-year-olds |  |  |  |
| Stage 1 | 2 | 0 | 7 |
| Moral reasoning[d] |  |  |  |
| Transitional[e] | 1 | 5 | 2 |
| Stage 2 | 1 | 2 | 0 |
| Moral reasoning[f] |  |  |  |
|  |  |  |  |
| 9-year-olds |  |  |  |
| Stage 1 | 1 | 1 | 0 |
| Moral reasoning[d] |  |  |  |
| Transitional[e] | 3 | 3 | 0 |
| Stage 2 | 5 | 7 | 0 |
| Moral reasoning[f] |  |  |  |

[a] Subject both classified and conserved.
[b] Subject either classified or conserved.
[c] Subject could neither classify nor conserve.
[d] At least 60% of subject's reasoning at Stage 1.
[e] Less than 60% of subject's reasoning at either Stage 1 or at Stage 2 or above.
[f] At least 60% of subject's reasoning at Stage 2 or above.

There are three subjects (two 7- and one 9-year-old) who both conserve and classify but are still at Stage 1 in their moral reasoning. Four more subjects (one 7- and three 9-year-olds), who both conserve and classify are still in transition between Stages 1 and 2. Clearly, functioning at the concrete operational level does not insure that moral reasoning has progressed to Stage 2.

The seven subjects discussed in the preceding paragraph indicate the existence of a lag between concrete operations and Stage 2 moral reasoning. It would be of interest to follow these seven children and observe the length of time required before their moral reasoning progresses to Stage 2.

In conclusion, this study strongly suggests that concrete operational thinking is necessary but not sufficient for the emergence of Stage 2 moral reasoning. It also provides support for the shifting magnitude of the relationship between cognitive and moral development that is implied by the specific-dependent model.

In reviewing these two studies, it is worth noting that substantial correlations have been found between cognitive and moral development at three ages (7, 12, and 19 years) but not at a fourth age (9 years). The adequacy of the different models of the relationship between cognitive and moral development (concomitant and specific-dependent) vary greatly in the extent to which they can account for these data. The obtained pattern of correlations makes it difficult to argue that the two processes develop concomitantly. It is possible to maintain such a conception of the relationship only if one of three assumptions holds. First, it may be that the 9-year-olds are unusual in some important ways. This is unlikely, as the 9-year-olds are from the same school, neighborhood, and occasionally the same families as the 7-year-olds. Second, it may be that there is a substantial amount of error in the measurement procedures. However, because the same individual applied the same measurement procedures to both age groups, this assumption seems unjustified. Some kind of an experimenter effect is also ruled out, for the experimenter was unaware of the expected difference between the 7- and 9-year-olds.

The inadequacy of the concomitant model is further demonstrated by the specificity of the relationship between cognitive and moral development. Clearly, two different cognitive transformations (concrete and formal operations) seem to be prerequisites for the emergence of two stages of moral reasoning (Stages 2 and 5). The prerequisite status of these two cognitive transformations is further suggested by what appears to be a time lag between their emergence and that of the corresponding stages of moral reasoning.

Even the specific-dependent model appears unable to handle the entire pattern of our findings. It leads to the expectation of substantial correlations between cognitive and moral development within the 7- and 12-year olds, for they have already experienced the beginnings of major cognitive transformations (concrete and formal operations). The minimal correlations between the two processes evidenced by the 9-year-olds are consistent with the model as this age group lies between major cognitive transformations. However, the model fails to explain the substantial correlation among the 19-year-olds.

Some of the interpretational difficulties that are encountered with the 19-year-olds may arise from some rather unique characteristics of the stage of formal operations. Relative to Piaget's other stages of cognitive development, formal operations appear to require more time to develop and are not initially mastered as completely nor applied as broadly (Tomlinson-Keasey, 1972). Perhaps, then, the 19-year-olds are still undergoing a major cognitive transformation. Such an interpretation is consistent with the finding that only eight (33%) of the 24 college women are at integrated formal operations, whereas 14 others (58%) are still in transition. In contrast, 55% of the 9-year-olds are firmly established at concrete operations. What must really be examined in terms of the model is the relationship between cognitive and moral development within a group of individuals evidencing integrated formal operations. For it is among these individuals that the major cognitive transformation (formal operations) should be largely completed and the influence of various noncognitive factors should stand a better chance of producing further individual differences in moral reasoning. Under such conditions it can be expected that the correlation between cognitive and moral development is less than that found among the 19-year-olds.

Assuming for the time being that concrete and formal operations are actually prerequisites for Stages 2 and 5, respectively, then what are the prerequisites for Stages 3, 4, and 6? It is not readily apparent what major cognitive transformations occur within the period of concrete operations that can give rise to Stages 3 and 4. Findings from two studies (Kuhn et al., 1971; Tomlinson-Keasey & Keasey, 1974) suggest that formal operations may serve to consolidate moral reasoning at Stage 4. The shift from Stage 2 to Stage 3 seems to be very much a function of increasing role-taking skills (Selman, 1971). Although cognitive abilities underlie skills at role taking, a number of noncognitive factors also seem to be involved. Factors accounting for movement from Stage 5 to Stage 6 are as yet unexamined, although a number of suggestions have been offered (Kuhn et al., 1971).

In conclusion, it appears that several of the transitions in Kohlberg's six-stage model of moral development can be accounted for in terms of either specific cognitive transformations or social experiences. Clearly, both cognitive and social factors play important roles in the development of moral reasoning. In the next section attention is turned from the relationship between cognitive and moral development to their interplay in the evaluation of moral judgments.

## THE EVALUATION OF MORAL JUDGMENTS

Today one is continually exposed to opinions presented by others and the mass media that carry moral overtones. Often these opinions are supported by reasoning. Presumably, an individual's evaluative reaction to these opinions and reasoning is influenced both by whether or not they agree with his or her own opinions and by the quality of their supportive reasoning.

The idea that individuals evaluate opinions agreeing with their own more highly than those disagreeing is consistent with a number of social psychological theories (Heider's balance theory, 1958; Osgood & Tannenbaum's congruity theory, 1955). Furthermore, it has been demonstrated (Hovland, Harvey, & Sherif, 1957) that an individual's evaluation of an opinion decreases systematically as the discrepancy between it and his own increases. Although it seems reasonable that the evaluation of an opinion should vary directly with the quality of the supportive reasoning, the issue has received little empirical attention. Because the opinion and its supportive reasoning typically occur together, it is important to know how these two components interact. Research in the area of prejudice suggests that the opinion component may indeed exert the greater influence. A consistent finding (Prentice, 1957; Schuman & Harding, 1964) is that prejudiced individuals tend to evaluate one of two logical arguments as better or more logically valid according to whether or not it agrees with their own prejudice and not according to its actual validity.

The extent to which the above trends generalize to the evaluation of moral judgments has been only partially investigated. Generally, individuals show a preference for moral judgments containing reasoning above rather than at or below their own developmental stage (Rest, Turiel, & Kohlberg, 1969; Rest, 1973). Whether an individual's evaluation of a moral judgment is influenced by its agreement or disagreement with his own opinion has not been examined. Consequently, nothing is known about the extent and nature of the interaction between these two components of a moral judgment (opinion agreement/ disagreement and stage of supportive reasoning).

The extent to which these two components influenced the evaluation of moral judgments and how they might interact were examined in a recent study (Keasey, 1974). Assuming that the findings from the areas of opinion research and prejudice would generalize to the evaluation of moral judgments, two trends were expected. First, it was expected that moral judgments in which the opinion agreed with that held by the evaluator would be rated higher than those disagreeing. Second, it was expected that the evaluation of moral judgments would be influenced more by opinion agreement/disagreement than by stage of reasoning. In considering the different cognitive capacities of the subjects (11- and 20-year-olds) it was expected that opinion agreement/disagreement would have a greater impact on the younger subjects. Because adolescents lack the cognitive capacities to deal effectively with abstract verbal statements (Inhelder & Piaget, 1958) they would be likely to have centered more attention on the more concrete opinion component. This greater attention should have increased the impact of the agreement/disagreement manipulation and lead to greater differentiation in the ratings made by the preadolescents.

Four weeks after a pretest consisting of six Kohlberg dilemmas, each subject rated four moral judgments. Each judgment consisted of an opinion that either agreed or disagreed with the subject's and supportive reasoning that was either at the subject's own developmental stage or one stage higher. Because individuals often give reasoning at different stages for different dilemmas (Tomlinson-Keasey & Keasey, 1972) each of the four moral judgments to be rated referred to one of the pretest dilemmas. In this way it was insured that the stage of reasoning contained in the moral judgment either matched the actual stage given by the subject to the same moral dilemma on the pretest or was one stage higher $(+1)$ than what she had given to the same dilemma on the pretest.

The extent to which the findings from the areas of opinion research and prejudice generalized to the evaluation of moral judgments was substantial. Moral judgments in which the opinion agreed with the subject's own were rated significantly higher $(F = 126.56, p < .005)$ than those in which the opinion disagreed. Because stage of reasoning had no effect on the evaluation of the moral judgments, it is obvious that the opinion-agreement component exerted the greater influence. The failure of stage of reasoning to produce any effect whatsoever came as a complete surprise. In fact, a second study was conducted to investigate the possibility that the lack of influence evidenced by stage of reasoning was an artifact of the two stages employed in this first experiment. Before that study is discussed, however, two other results of this first study need mentioning. The greater impact of the opinion-agreement component on the evaluations made by the younger subjects failed to appear. There was a consistent trend (see Table 3) for both girls and college women to assign slightly higher ratings to same-stage reasoning than to +1 reasoning.

The second study employed a different pair of contrasting stages of moral reasoning. It consisted of reasoning one stage above (+1) the subject's dominant stage and reasoning one stage below (−1). Except for this feature the procedures of the two studies were identical.

It seems that this effort was well rewarded, for in the second study, stage of reasoning ($F = 42.50$, $p < .005$) as well as opinion agreement ($F = 72.59$, $p < .005$) significantly influenced the evaluation of moral judgments. As in the first study, opinion agreement still exerted more influence than stage of reasoning. Opinion agreement also had a greater impact on the girls than on the college women. It was also found that both age groups rated same-stage reasoning significantly ($p < .005$) higher than −1 reasoning.

It can be concluded from these two studies that the evaluation of moral judgments is influenced by both opinion agreement and stage of supportive reasoning. It also appears that these two components do not interact. The

### TABLE 3
#### Mean Ratings of Moral Judgments[a]

|  | Opinion agreement | | Opinion disagreement | |
|---|---|---|---|---|
|  | Same-stage reasoning | +1 reasoning | Same-stage reasoning | +1 reasoning |
| Study 1 | | | | |
| Sixth graders | 6.50 | 5.92 | 4.50 | 4.42 |
| College students | 5.29 | 5.12 | 3.12 | 2.96 |
|  | −1 reasoning | +1 reasoning | −1 reasoning | +1 reasoning |
| Study 2 | | | | |
| Sixth graders | 4.92 | 5.83 | 2.50 | 3.83 |
| College students | 3.83 | 4.92 | 3.08 | 3.50 |

[a]Source: Keasey, *Journal of Personality and Social Psychology* (1974). Reprinted by permission of the American Psychological Association.

greater relative influence of opinion agreement in both studies probably reflects an inequality in the power of the experimental manipulations of the two components. Resolution of the question of relative influence requires that the power of their experimental manipulations be equal. Because such a demonstration is virtually impossible, a number of investigators (Byrne & Erwin, 1969; Dienstbier, 1972) are convinced that the question of relative strength cannot be meaningfully answered on logical grounds.

It is very tempting to account for the different impact of stage of supportive reasoning in the two studies in terms of the power of its experimental manipulations. However, such an account does not actually explain why the contrast of $-1/+1$ reasoning is more powerful than that of same-stage/ $+1$ reasoning. From a quantitative point of view, power may be equated with the degree of discrepancy between a pair of contrasting stages. Therefore, the contrast of same stage/ $+1$ represents a one-stage discrepancy, whereas the contrast of $-1/+1$ represents a two-stage discrepancy. Such an explanation seems reasonable until it is recalled that another one-stage discrepancy, $-1/$same stage, leads to differential evaluations.

Perhaps some of this confusion can be reduced by recognizing certain developmental considerations. Even though the contrasts of $-1/$same stage and same stage/ $-1$ are equal in a quantitative sense—both are one-stage discrepancies—from a developmental point of view they are unequal in a qualitative sense. This inequality comes about because individuals seem able to grasp the general orientation of $-1$ reasoning and explicitly reject it. Because of the newsness of $+1$ reasoning, however, an individual as yet lacks a good understanding of its general orientation and is therefore not well able to differentiate it from his or her own developmental stage (Rest et al., 1969). Consequently, it is much easier to differentiate between $-1$ and same-stage reasoning than it is between same-stage and $+1$ reasoning. If two stages of reasoning, such as same stage and $+1$ cannot be consistently differentiated, then it is quite unlikely that they can be differentially evaluated. This factor of ease of differentiation seems to be a major element underlying the power of the experimental manipulation of stage of reasoning.

Many of the above findings are directly relevant to the concept of a preference hierarchy for Kohlberg's stages of moral reasoning (Rest et al., 1969; Rest, 1973). The preference for $+1$ reasoning over $-1$ reasoning reported by Rest (1973) has been found in the present study. In addition, it has been found that same-stage reasoning is preferred over $-1$ reasoning. However, a preference for $+1$ reasoning over same-stage reasoning fails to emerge; if anything there is a consistent trend in the opposite direction. Actually, this same basic preference pattern has been found in a reanalysis of Rest's (1973) data.[1] Same-stage and $+1$ reasoning are preferred over $-1$ reasoning by his subjects ($t = 3.12, p<.01$, and $t = 4.02, p <.01$, respectively). Again, there is no clearcut preference between same-stage and $+1$ reasoning, although $+1$

[1]Jim Rest graciously made his data available for the reanalysis.

reasoning tends to be rated slightly higher ($t = 1.68$, $p < .20$). Even though the preference trends for same-stage and +1 reasoning in the present study and Rest's (1973) are in opposite directions, they are not significant and probably reflect little more than methodological differences. From these three studies (Keasey, 1974; Rest, 1973; Rest et al., 1969) it can be concluded that among stages comprehended, individuals prefer their own dominant stage of reasoning and the next higher one (+1) over lower stage reasoning (−1). However, there does not appear to be a clearcut preference between reasoning at one's own dominant stage and the next higher one.

A somewhat different pattern emerges, however, when preferences for all stages of reasoning are considered whether or not they are comprehended (Rest, 1973). Of the 38 subjects out of 47 for whom ranking data are complete, 19, or half, prefer Stage 6 reasoning (i.e., rank Stage 6 reasoning above all other stages on at least three of the five ranking trials). Because five of these 19 subjects are at Stage 6 and another three are at Stage 5, only 11 subjects out of 38 evidence a preference for a stage higher than +1. Because two of these 11 subjects evidence comprehension of Stage 6, only nine subjects are left who prefer Stage 6 reasoning but apparently cannot comprehend it. Rest (1973) suggests that the ambiguity of this finding can be resolved if either of two things can be demonstrated. First, it is possible that these nine subjects have been basing their preferences on the greater complexity and abstractness of Stage 6 reasoning. Second, it may be that they really understood Stage 6 reasoning but only intuitively or faintly and thus failed to express evidence of their understanding on Rest's comprehension test. Until this last set of findings is replicated and the ambiguity of its meaning resolved, it seems premature to try and integrate it with the previously obtained pattern of preferences.

My last point concerns the greater differentiation between opinion agreement and opinion disagreement evidenced by the girls in the second study. This finding suggests that preadolescents focus their attention more on the concrete and less abstract issue of whether the opinion in the moral judgment being evaluated agrees or disagrees with their own. Because nothing comparable was evidenced by the older college women, it is tempting to account for these age differences in terms of differing cognitive capacities.


## SUMMARY AND CONCLUSIONS

From the pattern of findings of the studies reviewed in the first section of this paper (Keasey & Weston, 1973; Kuhn et al., 1971; Lee, 1971; Tomlinson-Keasey & Keasey, 1974) it can be concluded that cognitive and moral development are definitely related. More specifically it appears that cognitive development facilitates moral development. This facilitation effect seems due primarily to the impact that major cognitive transformations (e.g., concrete and formal operations) have upon moral reasoning. The attainment of concrete operational thought seems to facilitate the emergence of Kohlberg's second stage of moral reasoning and formal operations seem to play a similar role for Kohlberg's Stage 5 moral reasoning.

It is quite likely that these two major cognitive transformations have similar facilitating effects upon other aspects of social development in addition to moral reasoning. Presently, I am conducting a longitudinal study that focuses on the relationship between cognitive development and several aspects of social development (e.g., communication skills, role taking).

The implication of Piaget's concept of structural parallelism, that the extent of the relationship between cognitive and moral development will vary in a predictable fashion, has received some initial support. It seems fruitful at this time to conduct a longitudinal study to further investigate the varying magnitude of the relationship between cognitive and moral development. Ideally, such a study can also obtain data on various types of social experience. With the collection of data on all three variables it will be possible to deal with the issue of the relative variance in moral development that is accounted for by either cognitive development or social experience at various ages.

To the extent that the relationship between cognitive development and other aspects of social development varies in magnitude at different ages, then, future studies need to employ a cross-sectional design that examines the relationship at several different ages. Ultimately, longitudinal studies of the relationship between cognitive development and various aspects of social development will be needed.

The studies presented in the second section clearly indicate that the evaluation of moral judgments is influenced both by the stage of their supportive reasoning and by whether or not the moral opinion advocated agrees or disagrees with that of the evaluator. The later component seems to exert the greater influence.

In addition to its role in the development of moral reasoning, cognitive development also appears to influence the evaluation of moral reasoning. The younger and therefore less cognitively sophisticated subjects are more influenced by the opinion-agreement/disagreement component than the older, more cognitively advanced subjects.

These findings strongly suggest that the preference hierarchy for Kohlberg's stages of moral development is not well differentiated. It does not seem that individuals have a clearcut preference for each stage over the preceding one. Instead, they seem to prefer their own stage and higher stages of reasoning over lower stages.

## REFERENCES

Byrne D., & Erwin, C. R. Attraction toward a Negro stranger as a function of prejudice, attitude similarity, and the stranger's evaluation of the subject. *Human Relations*, 1969, **22**, 397–404.

Dienstbier, R. A. A modified belief theory of prejudice emphasizing the mutual causality of racial prejudice and anticipated belief differences. *Psychological Review*, 1972, **79**, 146–160.

Elkind, D. *Children and adolescents: Interpretative essays on Jean Piaget*. London and New York: Oxford University Press, 1970.

Heider, F. *The Psychology of interpersonal relations*. New York: Wiley, 1958.

Hoffman, M. L. Moral development. In P. H. Mussen (Ed.), *Carmichael's manual of child psychology*. Vol. 2. New York: Wiley, 1970.

Hovland, C. I., Harvey, O. J., & Sherif, M. Assimilation and contrast effects in communication and attitude change. *Journal of Abnormal & Social Psychology*, 1957, **55**, 242–252.

Inhelder, B., & Piaget, J. *The growth of logical thinking from childhood to adolescence*. New York: Basic Books, 1958.

Keasey, C. B. Social participation as a factor in the moral development of preadolescents. *Developmental Psychology*, 1971, **5**, 216–220.

Keasey, C. B. Experimentally induced changes in moral opinions and reasoning. *Journal of Personality & Social Psychology*, 1973, **25**, 30–38.

Keasey, C. B. The influence of opinion-agreement and quality of supportive reasoning in the evaluation of moral judgments. *Journal of Personality & Social Psychology*, 1974, **30**, 477–482.

Keasey, C. B., & Weston, D. The impact of concrete operations upon moral reasoning. Unpublished manuscript, University of Nebraska-Lincoln, 1973.

Kohlberg, L. The development of modes of moral thinking in the years ten to sixteen. Unpublished doctoral dissertation, University of Chicago, 1958.

Kohlberg, L. Stage and sequence: The cognitive-developmental approach to socialization. In D. Goslin (Ed.), *Handbook of socialization theory and research*. Chicago: Rand McNally, 1969.

Kuhn, D., Langer, J., Kohlberg, L., & Haan, N. S. The development of formal operations in logical and moral judgment. Unpublished manuscript, Columbia University, 1971.

Lee, L. C. The concomitant development of cognitive and moral modes of thought: A test of selected deductions from Piaget's theory. *Genetic Psychology Monographs*, 1971, **83**, 93–146.

Osgood, C. E. & Tannenbaum, P. H. The principle of congruity in the prediction of attitude change. *Psychological Review*, 1955, **62**, 42–55.

Piaget, J. The moral judgment of the child (1932). Glencoe, Ill.: Free Press, 1948.

Piaget, J. *The psychology of intelligence*. London: Routledge & Kegan Paul, 1947.

Prentice, N. M. The influence of ethnic attitudes on reasoning about ethnic groups. *Journal of Abnormal & Social Psychology*, 1957, **55**, 270–272.

Rest, J. R. The hierarchical nature of moral judgment: A study of patterns of comprehension and preference of moral stages. *Journal of Personality*, 1973, **41**, 86–109.

Rest, J. R., Turiel, E., & Kohlberg, L. Level of moral development as a determinant of preference and comprehension of moral judgments made by others. *Journal of Personality*, 1969, **37**, 225–252.

Schuman, H., & Harding, J. Prejudice and the norm of rationality. *Sociometry*, 1964, **27**, 353–371.

Selman, R. The relation of role taking to the development of moral judgment in children. *Child Development*, 1971, **42**, 79–91.

Sullivan, E., & Quarter, J. Psychological correlates of certain postconventional moral types: A perspective on hybrid types. *Journal of Personality*, 1972, **40**, 149–161.

Tomlinson-Keasey, C. Formal operations in females from eleven to fifty-four years of age. *Developmental Psychology*, 1972, **6**, 364.

Tomlinson-Keasey, C., & Keasey, C. B. Long-term cultural change in cognitive development. *Perceptual & Motor Skills*, 1972, **35**, 135–139.

Tomlinson-Keasey, C., & Keasey, C. B. The mediating role of cognitive development in moral judgment. *Child Development*, 1974, **45**, 291–298.

Tracy, J. J., & Cross, H. J. Antecedents of shift in moral judgment. *Journal of Personality & Social Psychology*, 1973, **26**, 238–244.

Turiel, E. E. An experimental test of the sequentiality of developmental stages in the child's moral judgments. *Journal of Personality & Social Psychology*, 1966, **3**, 611–618.

Turiel, E. E. Cognitive conflict in the development of the child's moral judgments. National Science Foundation, January, 1967 (mimeo.).

# 3

# The Necessity (but Insufficiency) of Social Perspective Taking for Conceptions of Justice at Three Early Levels[1]

Robert Selman          William Damon

*Harvard University*    *Clark University*

In this chapter we shall present an analysis based on some of our related investigations into the cognitive aspect of early social development. More specifically, it is the "relatedness" of these investigations to each other that is of most interst to us, for which we shall make our case today.

For the past several years, Selman (1971a, 1974; Selman & Byrne, 1974) has studied the development of the child's ability to take perspectives in moral and interpersonal social contexts. A program of audiovisual and hypo-thetical–verbal techniques that tests this ability in children as young as 4 years old has been devised. Following the structural-developmental model proposed by Piaget (1970), an ordered sequence of social perspective-taking levels has been worked out, each of which describes a form of reasoning about the relation of the self's perspective on social events to that of others. A major interest has been the ontogenetic relation of perspective-taking ability to moral judgment and reasoning and for the past several years I have worked closely with Lawrence Kohlberg on this problem (Selman, 1971a, in press).

While this work has been progressing Damon has been investigating the development of young children's conceptions of justice (Damon, 1973, in press). Also working within a Piagetian framework, Damon has been interested in children younger than those considered by Kohlberg's moral judgment model. Consequently, he has designed a series of games and stories that test for justice

[1]Part of the research described here was presented at the Biennial Meeting of the Society for Research in Child Development, Philadelphia, Pa., April, 1973.

conceptions in children as young as 3 and 4 years old. A stage model has been proposed, labeled to match the existing Kohlberg system, that describes with greater specificity the development of the young child's ability to reason about problems of justice.

Now, because justice is a means of resolving conflicting claims between persons (Rawls, 1971), it is reasonable to suppose that one's mode of social perspective taking (which determines how one anticipates interpersonal claims) influences one's mode of conceptualizing justice. As we became aware of each other's work in the area of early social development, we decided to attempt a description of the logic of the relation of our two developmental systems. We shall attempt here to communicate to the reader what we believe that logic to be.

## SOCIAL PERSPECTIVE TAKING AND MORAL REASONING: DISTINCT ABILITIES OR TWO NAMES FOR THE SAME STRUCTURE?

In a dyadic or interpersonal exchange, the ability to consider another's point of view as both distinct from and yet related to and somehow contingent on one's own viewpoint is often seen as the crux of social intelligence (Mead, 1934). Referred to either as "social role taking" or "social perspective taking," this ability does not appear to function in infancy but does in various ways throughout childhood and adulthood. Psychologists, particularly those interested in the development of social cognition, investigate it as a means of clarifying the steps through which the child progresses in coming to know about the social world and social relations.

More exactly, a level of social perspective taking describes the way in which a child at that level understands the relations between the perspectives of self and other. Accordingly, such analysis emphasizes the form of the child's understanding of social perspectival relations rather than the content, and the ability to conceive of subjective perspectives rather than the accuracy of person perception. In Table 1, levels of social perspective taking are analyzed (*a*) in symbolic terms and (*b*) according to the development of the child's conception of self and other as subjects with subjective perspectives.

In the symbolic representations of Table 1, the term "S" is used to indicate the subject or the self; "O," the other or others; and "X," a social object or person considered as the object of social cognition by self or other. The symbol $\Theta$ represents a general judgment of social–psychological cognition (e.g., he is disappointed, angry), an inference about another's covert or psychological reality that does not necessarily invoke true social perspective taking. The symbol → indicates specific social perspective taking, putting one's self in another's place (e.g., "if I were he . . ."); and the symbol ↔ indicates mutual and simultaneous social perspective taking, i.e., the ability to step outside a dyadic relation and view each subject as each subject considers each other's point of view.

This model attempts to clarify how each social perspective-taking level incorporates the structure of the previous level into a newly organized social view.

**TABLE 1**
**Descriptive and Symbolic Representation**
**of Social Perspective-Taking Levels**

| Level | Symbolic | Descriptive |
|---|---|---|
| 0 | S ⊶ X = O ⊶ X | Egocentric perspective taking: Although the child can identify simple emotions in other people, he or she often confuses other's perspective with his or her own. He or she does not realize others may see things differently. |
| 1 | S → O ⊶ X | Subjective perspective taking: Child begins to understand that other people's thoughts and feelings may be the same or different from his or hers. He or she realizes that people feel differently or think differently because they are in different situations or have different information. |
| 2 | S → (O → S) or S → (S → O) | Self-reflective perspective taking: The child is able to reflect on his or her own thoughts and feelings. He or she can anticipate others' perspective on his or her own thoughts and feelings and realize that this influences his or her perspective on other. |
| 3 | S → (O ↔ S) | Mutual perspective taking: The child can assume a third-person point of view. He or she realizes that in a two-person interaction each can put her or himself in the other's place and view her or himself from that vantage point before deciding how to react. |

At each level a new organizing principle can be defined; at Level 0, that both self and other have a social perspective; at Level 1, that other's subjective social views are separate and distinct from the self's; at Level 2, that other can view the self as a subject just as self can view other as a subject; and at Level 3, that self and other can simultaneously consider each other as perspective-taking subjects.

Although of interest in its own right, social perspective-taking development has also concerned researchers because of its importance in the function of other social-cognitive abilities. Recent research indicates that a sequence of age-related levels of social perspective-taking ability similar to those defined in Table 1 can be applied to the analysis of such social behaviors as (a) communication skills (Flavell et al., 1968), (b) interpersonal relations (Feffer & Gourevitch, 1960), and (c) sociomoral judgment (Selman & Byrne, 1974). This chapter attempts a further clarification of the latter area of interest.

In theory, the process of learning to view the social world (including the self) from the perspective of another has frequently been considered a necessary condition for the development of sociomoral conceptions. Piaget (1932) held that a child could not manifest autonomous (advanced) morality until he had begun to decenter his point of view to include the perspectives of others. Prior to this initial decentering, Piaget argued, a child could not conceive of differential intentions behind actions or of the potential subjectivity of rules. More recently, Kohlberg wrote that "all morally relevant rules and institutions are . . . interpreted through processes of role taking (social perspective taking) directed by concern about both welfare and justice" (Kohlberg, 1971). Neither of the above theorists, however, distinguished between different developmental levels of social perspective-taking ability, and in consequence neither showed how a particular stage of moral reasoning could be based on a particular level of social perspective taking.

Recently, however, some empirical research has been directed to the study of the ability to take another's perspective and its relation to the development of advanced moral conceptualization. This research has been of two types. The first has hypothesized and generally found empirical correlations between subjects' performances on various operational measures of social perspective-taking ability and on moral judgment tasks (Dilling, 1967; Hardeman, 1967; Selman, 1971a; Stuart, 1967). Selman (1971a), for example, has shown that progress to conventional moral reasoning as defined by Kohlberg's Stages 3 and 4 is associated with social perspective-taking skills, such as those measured by Flavell's tasks (Flavell et al., 1968).

The second line of research assumes that moral development, defined as the development of justice conception, is also, by definition, "moral perspective taking", and that empirical correlations are not needed to prove that which is true by definition. This research (e.g., Moir, 1974) has therefore turned to the examination of the developmental patterns among moral and nonmoral perspective-taking tasks in order to determine empirically such questions as whether the child's perspective-taking structure is more easily applied to moral than to nonmoral (e.g., communication skills) contexts in the course of development. However, this approach sees moral judgment as nothing more than perspective taking in a moral context; it does not see perspective taking as a separate process that is necessary but not sufficient for moral reasoning. Our position maintains that although a given level of moral reasoning may imply a given level of social perspective taking, the reverse does not obtain; therefore, each perspective-taking level is seen as a necessary but not sufficient condition for its parallel level of moral reasoning. We shall attempt to show in this chapter exactly how a given level of justice conception implies a given level of social perspective-taking ability.

In particular, our emphasis is on the social perspective taking and moral reasoning of young children, ages 4–10 years. Therefore, we shall draw on Damon's (1973, in press) stage definitions of moral reasoning, which are an attempt to clarify and sharpen, with regard to the earliest moral stages, the structural analysis of moral development first posited by Piaget (1932) and subsequently revised and expanded by Kohlberg (1969). Table 2 presents a brief synopsis of Damon's moral stage definitions.

Our work is based on the following assertions:

1. That the child's reasoning about justice develops through a sequence of ordered stages, with each stage representing a progressive reorganization of the prior stage.

2. That each of these stages can be further broken down into two substages: an "emergent" (A) substage, which represents a reorganization of the child's conceptions of social and moral realities (norms, values, and customs), and a "consolidated" (B) substage, which represents a subsequent reorganization of the child's conception of justice.

3. That the necessary condition for the transition from the emergent to the consolidated form of each stage of justice reasoning is the application of a new level of social perspective-taking ability to the child's justice reasoning.

These assertions imply that social perspective taking has a distinct structure separate from moral reasoning, that certain levels of perspective taking are necessary structures for certain levels of moral reasoning, but that perspective taking is not sufficient to describe the structure of all moral reasoning.

Adequate empirical research to test the above hypotheses must entail a major effort, both longitudinal and cross cultural. The thrust of this chapter is deductive rather than inductive, theoretical rather than empirical. Induction and deduction, however, can never be truly dissociated, and we shall refer to data in this chapter in the form of protocols of children's reasoning. However, our data are used in a qualitative way to help explicate and describe theoretical relations between the concepts.

The data come from interviews with children between the ages of 4 and 10 years old on two types of social dilemmas. To exemplify levels of social perspective taking, children's responses to social dilemmas developed by Selman (1974) are used to study perspective-taking levels as applied to interpersonal relations. Each sociointerpersonal dilemma confronts the child with questions concerning his or her conception of persons (e.g., motivation, personality) and relationships (e.g., friendship, trust) between persons. A typical perspective-taking dilemma used in this study follows:

Two boys are trying to figure out what to get a friend for his birthday. Greg has already bought some checkers for Mike, but Tom can't decide whether to get Mike a football or a little toy truck. The boys see Mike across the street and decide to hint around to see what he'd like for his birthday.

Greg and Tom ask Mike about trucks and football, but nothing seems to interest him. He's very sad because his dog, Pepper, has been lost for two weeks. When Greg suggests that Mike could get a new dog, Mike says he doesn't even like to look at other dogs because they make him miss Pepper so much. He runs off home, nearly crying.

## TABLE 2
### Early Stages of Justice Conceptions

---

Stage 0
  Substage 0-A
    Justice choices derive from the subject's wish for an act to occur. Reasons for
    choices and the choices themselves are undifferentiated: reasons simply assert the
    choices and do not attempt to justify them  (e.g., I should get more because I want
    more).
  Substage 0-B
    Justice choices still derive from the self's desires. However, justifications for these
    choices refer to observable, external realities (e.g., physical characteristics of per-
    sons). Such justifications, however, are invoked in a fluctuating, after the fact
    manner.

Stage 1
  Substage 1-A
    Justice choices derive from considerations of (a)social realities (e.g., an act is right
    because it is rewarded and wrong because it is punished) and (b) equality in
    actions (e.g., everyone should get the same). Justifications are consistent but uni-
    lateral and inflexible.
  Substage 1-B
    Justice choices derive from (a) subject's view of actor's intentions (good or bad),
    and (b) considerations of reciprocity (e.g., persons should be paid back in kind for
    doing good or bad things). Justifications are consistent but unilateral and inflexible.

Stage 2
  Substage 2-A
    A moral relativity develops out of the understanding that different persons can
    have different, yet valid, justifications for similar acts. Moral choices attempt
    quantitative compromises between competing claims.
  Substage 2-B
    Subject's prescriptions are made on the basis of his or her view of competing
    claims in their relation to each other. Subject begins to coordinate consideration of
    equality and reciprocity.

---

> Greg and Tom are left with the dilemma of what to get Mike. On their way to the toy store,
> they pass a store with a sign in the window "Puppies For Sale." There are only two dogs left.
> Tom has to make up his mind whether to get Mike a puppy before the last two are sold.

To exemplify justice reasoning, we have used sociomoral dilemmas that pose
the subject with a problem concerning either punitive or positive justice. Punitive
justice measures test for conceptions of transgression, rules, obligation, and
punishment; positive justice measures test for concepts of how rewards and
resources may be distributed fairly. In each case, the subject is asked for his
judgment of what constitutes a good solution to the dilemma. This response is then

extensively probed in order to obtain a full sample of his moral reasoning. A typical moral dilemma used in this study follows:

> Holly is an eight-year old girl who likes to climb trees. She is the best tree-climber in the neighborhood. One day while climbing down from a tall tree, she falls off the bottom branch but doesn't hurt herself. Her father sees her fall. He is upset and asks her to promise not to climb trees any more. Holly promises.
>
> Later that day, Holly meets Shawn. Shawn's kitten is caught up a tree and can't get down. Something has to be done right away or the kitten may fall. Holly is the only one who climbs trees well enough to reach the kitten, but she remembers her promise to her father.

Both types of dilemmas (perspective taking and justice) have been presented through audiovisual film strips.

To clarify the distinction between these two types of social–cognitive tasks, the puppy dilemma focuses on the child's perspective-taking ability as it influences his prediction of what the characters in the situation will do and think (hence social), whereas the kitten dilemma elicits from the child a prescription of what the character in the situation ought to do (hence moral).[2] We shall use the sociointerpersonal dilemma (puppy) to exemplify levels of social perspective taking distinct from a moral context and the sociomoral dilemma (kitten) to exemplify stages of justice conception in relation to levels of social perspective taking.

Specifically, we believe that the structural changes in social perspective taking that occur at each social perspective-taking level are reflected in changes in justice conception at each of the B substages (see Table 2). Accordingly, each A substage is a point in transition, maintaining the social perspective-taking structure of the earlier B justice level, yet at the same time integrating new social conceptions with the child's justice reasoning. Table 3 illustrates this theoretical assertion.

The aim of this chapter is to focus on the structural and developmental relations between social perspective-taking Levels 0, 1, and 2 and the parallel justice Substages 0-B, 1-B, and 2-B, respectively. Part II of this paper elaborates on this thesis.

## LEVEL-BY-LEVEL ANALYSIS OF THE DEVELOPMENT OF PERSPECTIVE-TAKING AND JUSTICE CONCEPTIONS IN YOUNG CHILDREN

### Moral Reasoning Prior to the Advent of Social Perspective Taking: Substage O-A

Young children, even as they begin to distinguish self from other and self's visual perspective from other's (Masangkay et al., 1974), still lack a conception of selves as having subjective viewpoints, minds, or reasons for actions.

---

[2]Any given social dilemma may be viewed prescriptively, that is, from an obligatory or moral perspective. (For example, "Is it morally right for Tom to give Mike the puppy?") However, probe questions for the sociointerpersonal dilemmas asked specifically for reasoning of a nonmoral nature.

**TABLE 3**
**Developmental Relation between Perspective-Taking**
**Levels and Justice Substages**

| Levels of social perspective taking | Justice concepts substages |
|---|---|
| – | 0-A |
| 0 is necessary for | 0-B |
| | 1-A |
| 1 is necessary for | 1-B |
| | 2-A |
| 2 is necessary for | 2-B |
| | 3-A |
| 3 is necessary for | 3-B |
| | 4-A etc. |

An example of the young child's lack of a conception of persons as having subjective viewpoints comes from the following exchange between the first author and his 2½-year-old son; an example of a form of exchange that occurred frequently over a period of several months.

Son:     I want to go down the hill.
Father:  You can't go down. No one will be able to watch you. Stay here.
Son:     I don't want to stay here. I want to go down.
Father:  No, son, you can't.
Son:     Say *yes,* daddy!, don't say *no*!

This interchange exemplifies that this young child does not conceive of persons as subjects, that is, does not conceptualize persons as having covert states. For an older child, by saying "yes," I would mean (intend) "yes." My son's command to change my response (no to yes) disregarded the fact that my mind would not be changed even if my words were.

Justice reasoning at Substage 0-A is also highly egocentric. The child views his moral judgments not as his own subjective evaluations but as descriptive statements about his likes and dislikes. The notion of different and, therefore, conflicting judgments about the same act or situation has yet to be entertained by the child. Accordingly, the child does not differentiate his judgments from his desires, nor does he see the need to justify his judgments by reference to any criteria beyond those desires:

Dana (4 years, 10 months):
Say you were the father. How much would you punish Holly? *Six spankings.* You'd give her six spankings? *Yeah.* Why would you do that? *Because I just want to.* Suppose you decided to spank her 100 times, would that be O.K.? *No.* Why not? *'Cause I don't want it to be O.K.*

Maria (4 years, 1 month):
Do you think the father should punish Holly for what she did? *No.* Why not? *She doesn't like it when he sends her to her room.* Why doesn't she like it? *It makes her cry. . . .* Do you ever get sent to your room when you're naughty? *(Shakes her head emphatically to indicate "No.")* Well, why don't you? *Because I don't want to go to my room.*

At this substage, the child's reasons for his justice choices are merely reassertions of his desire for the choice to occur, rather than justifications (reasons for) of that choice. The judgments are made as if there were only one way of viewing a social situation, and as if that way were held by all viewers. It follows that the child at Substage 0-A implicitly (without reflection) assumes that his judgments will be acceptable to all parties concerned. Because the child does not recognize the possibility of different viewpoints, neither does he recognize the possibility that a solution that serves the self's desires may be in conflict with the desires of others. Substage 0-A reasoning is egocentric and time bound; it does not incorporate issues beyond the immediate wishes of the self. Most characteristically, Substage 0-A judgments confuse justice choices and justifications with statements of egocentric desire.

## The Beginning of Social Perspective Taking in the Moral Realm: The Incorporation of Perspective Taking Level 0 into Substages 0-B and 1-A Moral Reasoning

Social perspective taking at Level 0, although primitive, has its positive aspects. At this level, the child separates the attitude or viewpoint of self and other. For example, the child may realize that another may be sad even if he, himself, is happy. Even though the child separates viewpoints, however, he assumes that in similar situations, others will feel or act as he would in that situation (Selman, 1971b). Prior to Level 0, there is no differentiation of perspectives. At Level 0, although the child recognizes that there are two perspectives on a situation, they are assumed to be identical. A beginning conception of subjectivity emerges, but it is contaminated by a confusion of the self's subjectivity with the subjectivity of other. Social perspective taking at Level 0 has predominantly been found in our data in the reasoning of children at ages 4–6 years:

Abby (5 years, 1 month):
Do you think Tom will get Mike a new puppy? *Yes. He'll be happy. He's sad now but he'll be happy.* But Mike says he never wants to see another puppy. *Dogs are fun. I like puppies.* And so why will Tom get him a puppy? *Puppies are fun. I like puppies.*

Abby does not seem aware of the possibility that Tom might possibly not share her attitude toward a new puppy but she does seem aware that he has a perspective.

The child at justice Substage 0-B begins seeing the necessity of justifying his judgments on the basis of criteria more universal than his own desires. By his reference to external, observable physical characteristics—criteria that are outside himself and therefore not purely subjective—the child introduces an element of objectivity into his justifications. Such reference to objective justification implies the awareness of separate social perspectives—an awareness available to the child at social perspective-taking Level 0.

Brian (4 years, 10 months):
Who gets the most cake for desert in your family? *Me.* Why is that? *Because I'm the fastest runner.*

In fact, this child has probably misrepresented the truth in order to justify this judgment; for it is doubtful that he is the fastest runner in his family and equally dubious that he receives the largest share of the cake. Nonetheless, he has perceived the need to justify his judgments on the basis of a seemingly objective criterion, that is, the fastest should get the most. His attempt here is to employ reasons that may be shared by others, whereas at Substage 0-A there is no such attempt. "Because I want it" is no longer seen as reason enough; there is now a sense that such reasoning is futile in convincing another of his position. In other words, at Substage 0-B there is a beginning awareness on the part of the child that to be morally right his or her wishes in some sense need to be shared by others, and that he or she must therefore refer to some external criterion in order to convince another that he or she is right. However, this awareness is both made possible and at the same time limited by the constraints of Level 0 social perspective taking. For, although the child at Level 0 is aware of the perspective of another, he or she cannot accurately construct it nor appreciate its differences from the perspective of the self. The basic operating assumption at Substage 0-B is that what is right for the child will be right for all others:

Alan (6 years, 3 months):
What do you think Holly will do, save the kitten or keep her promise? *She will save the kitten because she doesn't want the kitten to die.* How will her father feel when he finds out? *Happy, he likes kittens.* What would you do if you were Holly? *Save the kitten so it won't get hurt.* What if Holly doesn't like kittens. What will she do? *She won't get it.* What if her father punishes her if she gets the kitten down? *Then she will leave it up there.* Why? *Because she doesn't want to get in trouble.* How will she feel? *Good, she listened to her father.*

Alan, above, is unable to perceive differences between Holly's perspective on the situation and the perspective of Holly's father. He focuses (or centers) on the act of rescuing the kitten and justifies the act by referring to the kitten's life. In doing so, Alan assumes that all the participants should agree on the course of action. When the interviewer refocuses Alan to the punitive aspects of breaking the promise to father, however, Alan orients to the father's viewpoint, and chooses to leave the kitten in the tree. This time Alan justifies on the basis of avoiding trouble, still maintaining a consensus among characters. There is no awareness of inconsistency and no appreciation of potential differences in separate points of view.

The advance in justice reasoning from Substage 0-B to Substage 1-A does not imply a parallel social perspective-taking advance.[3] The Substage 1-A justice conception derives from the child's reflection on relations within social reality. The child considers acts that are punished or have other bad consequences as wrong and acts that result in good consequences as right. Similarly, he or she sees that bigger, stronger people command resources and authority in the world and considers it just that they should.

> Adrian (6 years, 0 months):
> Which is worse, a daughter breaking a promise to her father, or a father breaking a promise to a daughter? *A daughter breaking a promise to her father.* Why is that? *A father is stronger and can slap.* Why isn't it bad for Holly's father to break his promise? *Because nobody can spank him.*

> Bill (6 years, 11 months):
> Which is worse, Holly telling on her brother or her brother telling on Holly? *They're both the same.* How about if it were Holly against her father. . . . *It's worse for Holly. It's her father. Besides, she could get in trouble.*

Although the child at Substage 1-A recognizes that egocentric assertions (Substage 0-B) are not shared and therefore cannot function as moral judgments, he or she is still bound to his or her own view of social reality. The child does not consider that others may have a different view of social reality, and that the valuing and relating of such disparate views is the function of prescriptive moral judgments. In other words, the child at Substage 1-A conceives of justice judgments as objective statements about an external social reality perceived in the same way by all viewers, rather than as the subjective evaluations of individual moral agents.

## The Development of Subjective Perspective Taking and Its Consequence for the Understanding of Intentionality in the Moral Realm

At Level 1 social perspective taking comes clear recognition that the self's perspective is separate from other's and is therefore unique. At this level the child realizes that self and other may view the same social situation in very different ways and that similar actions may reflect disparate reasons. The child focuses on the uniqueness of the covert, psychological, or subjective nature of others, rather than on other's overt actions. Social perspective taking discovery involves a new awareness of the thoughts, feelings, and intentions of others as distinct from the self's:

> Brenda (6 years, 2 months):
> Do you think Tom will get him a dog? *No. If he says he doesn't want a dog, that means he*

---

[3]Elsewhere, Damon (in press) has discussed the transition from the B substage to the following A substage in terms of the development of logical operations. However, as these advances are not directly explainable in terms of social perspective taking, they are not included here.

*doesn't want a dog. Just because Tom thinks he wants a dog doesn't mean Mike wants one. Will Mike and Tom be friends if Tom gives Mike a puppy? Well, Mike will be kind of angry: he doesn't want a dog.*

Brenda is able to differentiate the subjective perspectives of the two boys and to focus on the viewpoints underlying their actions. However, her belief that Mike will be angry at Tom implies that she is unable to realize that Mike may understand that Tom was thinking about Mike when he bought the puppy. This marks the limiting characteristic of Level 1 reasoning.

From the new realization, however, comes an understanding in the moral realm that the similar social acts of different actors can stem from different subjective intentions. It follows that some of these intentions may be considered "good," others "bad." The basis of advance at Substage 1-B is this understanding of intentionality. The child realizes that the intention behind an act cannot be inferred directly from the act itself: he or she sees that two persons may intend something very different by the same act. The child at Substage 1-B can reason that acts are not right or wrong in themselves, but that acts intending good are right and those intending bad are wrong. In this light, the child begins to distinguish between what persons have the right to do and what they have the power to do—and thus to distinguish moral prescriptions from social descriptions. He or she is able for the first time to evaluate the judgments of adults and authorities and to consider their judgments wrong when he disagrees:

Tom (6 years, 8 months):
Should the father punish her for climbing the tree? *He could, but it wouldn't be right.* Why not? *Because she wasn't doing anything wrong. She was trying to save the kitty.*

Sarah (7 years, 4 months):
Do you think Holly's father would understand if she told him why she climbed the tree? *Yes. Because she got the kitten down instead of just climbing up on trees, just climbing it for fun.*

Children at justice Substage 1-A feel that the father's right to punish depends on his status as father, whereas those at Substage 1-B view that right as contingent on their own understanding on the wrongness of the act. Likewise, although children at both substages may state that the father of a family deserves special consideration in the distribution of shares of goods, their justifications will differ. Substage 1-A children may justify such special consideration by the fact that the father is bigger, is the head of the family, or is "boss." Those at Substage 1-B give the father his due because he provides for the family, has cared for them in the past, etc.—all acts that reflect the father's good intentions toward his family, and that in the mind of the Substage 1-B child entitle him to larger shares in return. Children at Substage 1-B therefore conceive of justice as a payback for good or bad deeds, as they see that deeds imply intent as well as action. Such concepts as "deserving" and "earning" have entered into moral calculations.

Nonetheless, the Substage 1-B child still justifies his or her judgments on the basis of what he or she thinks the actors' intentions to be—and treats those intentions as if they are an objective reality to which all subjects must agree. And although the subject recognizes that the implication of two persons' having unique perspectives is that the two persons may see the same act differently and judge it differently, he or she views the two persons as existing atomistically, each arriving at independent views of right and wrong, uninfluenced by the judgment of the other. This is because the child at Substage 1-B can consider only one point of view at a time. He or she has yet to recognize the need for coordinating two conflicting perspectives in arriving at judgment of right or wrong. Although he or she is aware that another's evaluation of an act may differ from his or her own, the child has no means by which to coordinate their opposing views. Therefore, instead of mediating between two opposing views or modifying one in light of the other, the child at this level simply chooses between the two. One view then becomes absolutely right, the other(s) absolutely wrong. At Substage 1-B this absolutistic quality permeates the child's moral justifications.

The child at justice Substage 2-A makes important advances but does not yet employ Level 2 social perspective taking. The Substage 2-A child sees that there can be conflicting views concerning right and wrong (as could the Substage 1-B child), and furthermore that each of these views may be justifiable according to some criterion. Justice choices are no longer judged on a single dimension (e.g., good–bad) but can reflect the complexity of conflicting reasons supporting the various choices. However, the Substage 2-A child is still unable to coordinate the various possible claims to justice, because he or she cannot yet see the various points of view in relation to one another. He or she therefore mediates between the conflicting judgments through compromise instead of attempting to decide which judgment is best for the current situation:

Tom (10 years, 0 months):
Was climbing the tree to save the kitten's life actually right or wrong? *Well, from her father's point of view it was wrong. But from her point of view it was right. So it wasn't really right or wrong. Well, maybe it was a little more wrong.*

Joan (8 years, 4 months):
Does Holly deserve to be punished for what she did? *Half and half. Because she was saving the kitten's life, but she did break her promise not to climb trees. And so maybe she should get in a little trouble, but not a lot of trouble.*

When the child's attempt to weigh and balance between conflicting views of two persons fails, he or she resorts to an ethical relativism of sorts. The relativistic statements of the Substage 2-A child (such as "It would be right for him but wrong for me") are significant attempts to deal with conflicting views of self and other. However, these attempts fail to truly take the other's perspective into account despite the fact that they may consider the other's reasons:

Amy (7 years, 8 months):
Should Holly climb the tree? Would it be right? *If she wants to she can. To her it's right. To her father it's wrong. So she can do what she thinks is right.*

This relativism fails to consider the judgments and views of self and other in their relation to each other and continues to view them as atomistic selves, each judging independently of the other. For the child at Substage 2-A does not yet understand a further implication of the fact that another is capable of interpreting and evaluating a situation differently than the self—namely, that the other is likewise capable of interpreting and evaluating the self's judgments as well.

In the above example, Amy does not reflect on the fact that Holly can consider her father's perception of her own judgment in arriving at judgment of right or wrong.


## The Coordination of Social Perspectives at Level 2
## and the Partial Resolution of Conflicting Claims
## at Moral Substage 2-B

The major advance of Level 2 social perspective taking is the child's ability to see the viewpoints of persons (who may, of course, be self and other) in relation to one another. The perspectives are now seen to exist in a state of reciprocal influence rather than as independent assessments of objective information in the world. For the first time the child recognizes that his or her judgments and actions are open to scrutiny and evaluation by others, and his or her view of other is influenced by the realization that others can view the self as a subject just as the self can view others as a subject (hence, self-reflective perspective taking). Level 2 perspective taking usually emerges after age 8 years:

Carl (8 years, 3 months):
*Mike doesn't know what he's talking about. He just says he doesn't want a puppy, but he doesn't mean it.* How do you know that? *Well if I were Mike, I would feel bad too, but later I'd realize that I really want the new puppy.*

If Tom gets Mike the puppy, will Mike be angry at Tom? *No, because Mike will realize why Tom did it. He knows Tom thought he would want a puppy.*

The above statement exemplifies the major discovery at Level 2, that the self is aware that other can consider the self's point of view, and that this, in turn, influences the self's perspective on other.

The justice reasoning of Substage 2-B is distinguished by the child's ability to coordinate the perspectives of two persons (his or her own and another's, or those of two others) and to view those perspectives in their relation to one another. At Substage 2-B the process of mediation is incorporated in the making of a noncompromising judgment. The child now begins to see that his or her judgment is in part a function of knowledge and that it will be evaluated by another. It is therefore necessary for him or her to anticipate potential conflicts and to resolve them by making judgments that take the other's perspective into account. Justice reasoning at Substage 2-B is based on a new level of interpersonal reciprocity. When the self is considered both as self and as other, fairness can become an agreement between two parties as to what constitutes a fair arrangement between them. Substage 2-B reasoning defines justice as the process by which opposing views of right and wrong are reconciled and coordinated. This process has its roots in the child's recognition that his or her judgments and actions are open to the scrutiny and evaluation of others. At Substage 2-B there exists an imperative for the self to take the perspective of other in addition to his own in making a moral judgment.

> Ann (8 years, 1 month):
> Do you think that Holly should climb the tree? *No.* Why not? *She might think she should be-cause she is saving the kitten, but she can't.* Why can't she? *Because of her father. She is afraid her father would think she didn't care about him.* Why does that matter? *Well he has feelings too.*

> Tom (10 years, 0 months):
> *You should take the other's person's opinion. Like say you're about to step on an ant, and you get in the ant's shoes and you wouldn't want to be killed or something; so I wouldn't really step on the ant.*

In the first example, Ann is not only aware of both her own and her father's intentions and feelings, but she is also aware that her actions are evaluated on the basis of her father's awareness of her intentions. Hence the recipricol nature of her reasoning about the *relation* between social perspectives. In the second example, the child changes places with the other (the ant) and looking back on himself as he would view himself if he were the ant recognizes that his decision to kill the ant would be unacceptable from the ant's viewpoint. And so he decides that it would be wrong to step on the ant.

Behind this imperative to take another's perspective lies the recognition that if self and other are truly to be viewed as subjects, each with his or her own perspective, then their judgments and evaluations of the same social situation may conflict; hence the necessity for some coordination of their perspectives. At Substage 2-B self and other can no longer be viewed as atomistic subjects, each judging a situation independently, ignoring the potential conflict between their judgments. Such relativistic statements as ''It would be right for him and wrong for me,'' which were common at Substage 2-A, are therefore no longer evident at Substage 2-B. For now one's own judgments are seen to be, in part, a function of one's knowledge that they will be evaluated by others. If self expects his judgment to have relevance to another and to be accepted by him or her, then self will have to consider other's perspective when making his or her own judgment.

Still missing at Substage 2-B is the ability to see the reciprocal relations between two individuals from outside the dyad, from a third party position. The perspectives reciprocally taken at Substage 2-B are concretely those of self and other, or of two others. The claims of each are not seen as analyzable by a third party who can orient to the two claims mutually and simultaneously. For example, if an adult gets a child to agree to trade the child's 5 dollars for the adult's candy bar, this is seen as ''fair'' at Substage 2-B—as long as the two parties (child and adult) agree to the fairness of the arrangement.

It is not until social perspective-taking Level 3 that the subject is potentially able to step outside of the concrete dyad and view the interaction from a third-person point of view. At this point a judgment can be made concerning the unfairness of the two-party arrangement. The 5 dollar–candy bar trade is unfair because an impartial observer would judge the adult to be "taking advantage" of a child. This is the skill of mutual perspective taking, however, and is rarely found in children younger than 10 years old.

## SUMMARY

We have presented a description of the concomitant growth of children's justice reasoning and social perspective taking through a sequence of defined stages. Each justice stage consists of an organization of values, standards, and beliefs that enables the child to conceive of certain specified moral problems. At justice Stage 0, the problem is what the child wants, and how best to get it. At justice Stage 1, the problem is that others make demands, wield authority, and claim rights and that the self is obligated to recognize such claims. At justice Stage 2, the problem becomes the resolution of conflicting (although often equally justifiable) interpretations of how to define the rights and claims of both self and others.

Although each justice stage is structured around a common problem, each substage within that stage represents a distinct means of resolving the common problem. The hypotheses presented in this chapter assert that the B substages represent resolutions of moral problems that are based on the child's conception of justice; and, furthermore, that each level of justice conception implies the attainment of a new level of social perspective-taking ability and the application of this ability to the moral domain.

However, any given level of perspective taking is only a necessary condition for the parallel level of justice reasoning. It is not a sufficient condition. Within the theoretical framework presented here, it becomes possible to be at an advanced level of social perspective taking and still be retarded in one's moral thinking. In fact, recent research by Hickey (1972) indicates that delinquents have social perspective-taking equivalent to their nondelinquent peers but that their level of moral reasoning is at significantly lower stages.

Extrapolating the thesis of our paper to the analysis of current national concerns and the implications for adult perspective taking and level of moral judgment, it seems clear that perspective taking is a "neutral" social cognitive capacity and that higher levels of perspective taking can be used for good or evil, for decency or deception. Because politicians can exhibit high levels of perspective taking does not mean that they apply this ability to their moral judgments. Our analysis shows that each higher level of perspective taking is an important component of more mature moral thought and action. However, no level of perspective taking, no matter how advanced, bears with it an obligation to employ it in the service of justice. It is only when such a sense of obligation is considered and deferred to that perspective taking becomes prescriptive and determines the level of moral judgment.

## ACKNOWLEDGMENTS

Preparation of this manuscript was in part supported by a Spencer Foundation Grant to Robert Selman. We are grateful to the personnel of the Weston, Mass. Public Schools and the Child Study Center of the University of California, Berkeley, for their cooperation in this project. The authors express their appreciation to Lawrence Kohlberg and Martin Hoffman for their critical comments of earlier drafts of this paper.

## REFERENCES

Damon, W. The early development of justice conceptions. Paper presented to the Society for Research in Child Development, Philadelphia, Pa., April, 1973.

Damon, W. Early conceptions of justice as related to the development operations reasoning. *Child Development,* in press.

Dilling, C. A study of moral orientation in relation to the Piagetian concept of egocentrism. Unpublished doctoral dissertation, Michigan State University, 1967.

Feffer, M., & Gourevitch, V. Cognitive aspects of role-taking in children. *Journal of Personality,* 1960, **20**, 383–396.

Flavell, J. H., Botkin, P. J., Fry, C. L., Wright, J. L., & Jarvis, P. E. *The development of role-taking and communication skills in children.* New York: Wiley, 1968.

Hardeman, A. M. Children's moral reasoning. Unpublished doctoral dissertation, Columbia University, 1967.

Hickey, J. Evaluation of a moral education program in prisons and reformatories. Unpublished doctoral dissertation, Boston University, 1972.

Kohlberg, L. Stage and sequence: The cognitive-developmental approach to socialization. In D. Goslind (Ed.), *Handbook of socialization: Theory and research.* New York: Rand-McNally, 1969.

Kohlberg, L. From is to ought. In T. Mischel (Ed.), *Cognitive development and epistemology.* New York: Academic Press, 1971.

Masangkay, Z. S., McCloskey, K., McIntyre, C., Sims-Knight, J., Vaughn, B., & Flavell, J. The early development of inferences about the visual percepts of others. *Child Development,* 1974, **45**(2), 357–366.

Mead, M. *Mind, self, and society.* Chicago: University of Chicago Press, 1934.

Moir, D. Egocentrism and the emergence of conventional morality in preadolescent girls. *Child Development,* **45**, 299–305.

Piaget, J. *The moral judgment of the child.* (1932). Glencoe, Ill.: Free Press, 1948.

Piaget, J. *Structuralism.* New York: Basic Books, 1970.

Rawls, J. *A theory of justice.* Cambridge, Massachusetts: Harvard University Press, 1971.

Selman, R. L. The relation of role taking to the development of moral judgment in children. *Child Development,* 1971, **42**(2), 79–92.   (a)

Selman, R. L. Taking another's perspective: Role-taking in early childhood. *Child Development,* 1971, **42**, 1721–1734.   (b)

Selman, R. L. Perspective taking levels and the analysis of conceptions of interpersonal relations. Unpublished manuscript, Harvard University, 1974.

Selman, R. L. The development of social-cognitive understanding: A guide to educational and clinical practice. In T. Lickona (Ed.), *Morality: Theory, research, and social issues.* New York: Holt, Rinehart & Winston (in press).

Selman, R. L., & Byrne, D. A structural analysis of role-taking levels in middle childhood. *Child Development,* **45**, 803–806.

Stuart, R. B. Decentration in the development of children's concepts of moral and causal judgment. *Journal of Genetic Psychology,* 1967. **111**, 59–68.

# 4

# Recent Research on an Objective Test of Moral Judgment: How the Important Issues of a Moral Dilemma Are Defined

James R. Rest

*University of Minnesota*

A cognitive developmental approach to the study of morality assumes that as people develop they view moral dilemmas differently. The different conceptual frameworks for interpreting social interrelationships and responsibilities are described in terms of stages (see Kohlberg, 1971; Rest & Kohlberg, 1975). Each moral judgment stage has distinctive ways of defining the relevant elements of a social problem and the most important issues in making a decision about what to do.

Almost all research based on Kohlberg's stage typology has used the method of assessment devised in his 1958 dissertation or a somewhat modified version of it. The assessment requires a subject to react to a hypothetical moral dilemma, indicating what ought to be done and justifying this course of action. The interviewer tries to elicit and probe the subject's views without interjecting or suggesting any thinking different from the subject's own spontaneous thinking. This research therefore has focused on a subject's thinking *de novo* about a moral dilemma. Important as this kind of moral judging is, it is not the only important kind of moral judgment.

People also make judgments about the moral judgments of others. When a person is faced with a moral dilemma, he often seeks the advice of others instead of acting on his own immediate solution to the dilemma. In taking or not taking another's advice a person is making judgments about another's judgments. In public debate over moral–political issues, a person is hardly ever aware of a dilemma without also hearing someone's moral judgment of it.

Democratic political process involves reacting to the judgments of candidates for office and presumably voting for candidates whose judgments meet approval.

People are influenced not only by the conclusions that another person advises but also by the way that another person defines the problem. In public policy matters, such attention often centers on defining the "crucial issue" of a problem. Consider, for example, one of the major social–moral problems of our time, which is variously referred to as the "busing issue," "states' rights," "racial prejudice," or "equal opportunity." The particular definition of the crucial issue that one accepts is a very important moral judgment and is of interest in its own right.

For a number of years my colleagues and I have been studying how people choose the important issues of moral dilemmas. A procedure called the "Defining Issues Test" (DIT) requires a subject to read a hypothetical moral dilemma and then to select from among 12 statements those that are the most important issues in making a decision about the case. Each issue statement represents a stage characteristic of Kohlberg's stage typology (see Rest & Kohlberg, 1975). As a subject ranks the issue statements in terms of their importance in making a decision about the moral dilemma, he or she is indicating in effect the importance of various stage-characteristic ways of viewing moral dilemmas.

A major theoretical interest in this research has been to see whether a test of this sort (which is essentially a recognition task rather than a production task) demonstrates the properties theoretically expected of the construct, moral judgment. Recent discussions of different data gathering procedures for moral judgment suggest that there may be various facets of moral judgment development that different procedures assess (Rest, 1973, 1975). Several studies have indicated a difference between Kohlberg's interview assessment and other means of assessment (Rest, 1973; Rest, Turiel, & Kohlberg, 1969). In summary, I have been interested in the developmental character of the way people choose the important issues of moral dilemmas.

A major methodological interest in these studies has been to see whether a standardized, objectively scorable measure of moral judgment may be devised. Kohlberg's method of moral judgment assessment produces material that is not strictly comparable from subject to subject; the assessments are vulnerable to interviewer and scorer biases and scoring the material involves complex interpretations and rather great inferential leaps from the data. The test–retest reliability in several studies has been poor (Blatt & Kohlberg, 1975; Guilliland, 1971; Turiel, 1966). Correlations of Kohlberg's measure with other sets of moral dilemmas that use a similar interview method and similar scoring guides have been only moderate (Gilligan, Kohlberg, Lerner, & Belenky, 1975; Lockwood, 1974). Moreover, as with any free-response method, it is unclear to what extent differences in verbal expressiveness and other test-taking sets influence stage scores. Furthermore, Kohlberg's measure is very time consuming. The methodological advantages of the Defining Issues Test format are the following: it is highly structured so that the information from each subject is comparable; it minimizes variance in stage scores caused by individual differences in verbal expressivity; it is objectively scored (can be computerized), saving time and minimizing scorer bias; and, because each test item and subject response is discrete and can be analyzed separately, each part of the test can be checked for reliability and its contribution to trends. The test therefore lends itself to progressive refinement.

The test has been administered to thousands of subjects in at least four countries. This paper summarizes the major findings of several studies (for details, the reader should consult the reports of the individual studies) and discusses several points of contention typically raised about this research. Before the studies are discussed, however, a little more description of the DIT will be given.

## THE DEFINING ISSUES TEST

A subject reads a moral dilemma and is presented with 12 "issues" or considerations bearing upon that situation. For instance, for the moral dilemma of whether a husband, Heinz, should steal an exorbitantly priced drug for his dying wife (one of Kohlberg's standard dilemmas), the subject is asked to consider such issues as "Whether or not a community's laws are going to be upheld," "Isn't it only natural for a loving husband to care so much for his wife that he'd steal?" "Is Heinz willing to risk getting shot as a burglar to going to jail for the chance that stealing the drug might help?" "What values are going to be the basis for governing human interactions?" For each of six stories the subject evaluates a set of 12 issues and is asked to indicate how important each issue is in deciding what ought to be done. Subjects rate each issue on a Likert scale of importance ("most," "much," "some," "little," "no") in deciding what ought to be done; also, subjects rank their first four choices of the most important issues.

Each issue was designed to exemplify some distinctive characteristic of a stage. Items were written for Stages 2, 3, 4, 5A, 5B, and 6. Subjects capable of taking the tests (ninth grade and beyond) were too advanced for Stage 1 items. The division into Stages 5A and 5B followed more recent conceptions of the stages, as did the inclusion of antiestablishment (A) items (see stage discussions, Rest & Kohlberg, 1975). The issue statements were written to display the following characteristics:

1. The underlying stage structure of the item was emphasized so that higher stage statements appeared stark and abstract instead of lending themselves to interpretation as fancier ways of stating a lower stage idea. For example,

instead of a statement, "The value of life is more important than property," we have the statement, "What values are going to be the basis for governing human interactions?" The first statement could have appealed to subjects at many stages, whereas the second one could not. Expressing an "issue" in bipolar terms as a question (e.g., whether . . . or not . . .) helped accomplish this.

2. Among items representing the stages were nonsense items that used high-sounding phrases (e.g., "What is the value of death prior to society's perspective on personal values"). Such distractor items gave a check on the tendency of subjects to choose on the basis of complex, abstruse verbiage rather than on meaning.

3. Care was taken to match issues from various stages on word length, complexity of syntax, and use of technical or unusual terms.

4. In each set of considerations several items of a stage were presented so that if one example of a stage's orientation was not suitable to a particular subject, there were still other examples of that orientation from which to choose.

There are many ways of summarizing the ranking and rating data. These arise from various combinations of summing the ratings or rankings, of different weightings of items, of different weightings of stage scores, etc. In his doctoral dissertation, Cooper (1972) has considered dozens of these possibilities. He has found that (a) the ranking data are more reliable than rating data on test–retest; (b) that factor analyses indicate that Stages 5A, 5B, and 6 cluster together and therefore can most economically be treated simply as a single set of issues at the "principled" level of morality; and (c) that although different sets of weights can be given to ranks, and although a subject's developmental level can be represented in terms of his usage of each stage or in terms of an overall composite score (such as Kohlberg's Moral Maturity Quotient, a single composite score), nevertheless all these various indices produce nearly the same results in terms of age trends and correlations with other measures. Following Cooper's analysis, the following method of constructing an index is recommended for its simplicity: (a) give weights of 4, 3, 2, and 1 to the issues ranked first, second, third, and fourth, respectively; (b) sum the weights attributed to principled issues (items keyed as 5A, 5B, and 6) over all six stories; (c) express the result in terms of the percentage of weights attributed to the principled stages. This number (designated $P$) can range from 00 to 95 and is interpreted as the relative importance a subject gives to morally principled considerations in making moral judgments. Kohlberg has stated that principled morality (his Level III) is a "critical break" in his stages of moral judgment (Kohlberg, 1969, p. 395).

Test–retest stability (2 weeks) for a group of 28 ninth graders for the $P$ score was .81 (Pearson correlation).

## AGE TRENDS AND GROUP DIFFERENCES

In a first study (Rest, Cooper, Coder, Masanz, & Anderson, 1974) of the DIT, groups of 40 each of junior high school (age 14 years), senior high school (age 17, 18 years), college juniors and seniors, and graduate students were given the test. The graduate student group consisted of 25 seminarians and 15 doctoral students in political science and moral philosophy. The presumption was that these four groups represented an order of increasing advancement in moral judgment (i.e., is it not reasonable to assume that moral philosophy doctoral students are more advanced in moral judgment than junior high school students?). Table 1 shows the $P$ scores of the four groups as well as the stage scores of Stages 2, 3, and 4. Note that although scores of Stages 2, 3, and 4 decrease the more advanced groups are reached, it is $P$ that shows the clearest differentiation among the groups.

One-way analysis of variance on $P$ across the four major groups of 40 subjects each gives $F$ values far exceeding the .01 level of statistical signifi-

**TABLE 1**
**Group Differences on the DIT Indices**

| Student group | | Stage ($P$) | | | |
|---|---|---|---|---|---|
| | | 2 | 3 | 4 | 5 and 6 |
| Junior high $n = 40$ | $\bar{X}^a$ | 11.6 | 20.5 | 35.2 | 32.7 |
| Senior high $n = 40$ | $\bar{X}$ | 9.6 | 22.3 | 30.7 | 37.4 |
| College $n = 40$ | $\bar{X}$ | 5.5 | 14.6 | 24.9 | 54.9 |
| Graduate school $n = 40$ | $\bar{X}$ | 3.5 | 13.0 | 18.4 | 65.1 |
| Seminarians ($n = 25$) | $\bar{X}$ | 4.7 | 15.5 | 17.9 | 61.9 |
| Political science and philosophy majors ($n = 15$) | $\bar{X}$ | 2.2 | 8.8 | 18.8 | 70.3 |

$^a$ $\bar{X}$ is the average percentage of ranks (weighted 4 for first rank, 3 for second rank, 2 for third rank, 1 for fourth rank) given to the "issues" of each stage, respectively. One-way analysis of variance between groups on the $P$ score produced an $F = 48.5$ ($F$ at the .01 level of significance $> 3.95$).

cance. Another way of expressing the increase of $P$ across the student groups is to correlate $P$ with age. (The Defining Issues Test is not a strictly linear function of age, however, for the seminarians are older but not the "most expert" group, which somewhat attenuates this correlation.) The correlation of the $P$ index with age is .62. This finding has been replicated in another sample consisting of students from junior high school, senior high school, college, and graduate school: the correlation of $P$ with age is .67 in the second sample.

Quite a few studies have used the DIT since these first studies, and although the purpose of the subsequent studies has not been to investigate age trends of the DIT, nevertheless the average $P$ scores of these samples can be examined to see how closely they fit in with the first study. Table 2 lists 10 additional samples involving over 1000 subjects.

As can be seen from Table 2, the $P$ scores of the various samples are consistent with the scores in Table 1 with the exception of Sample 6 in Table 2. The scores of these college students seem unusually low: they have as low an appreciation for principled moral thinking as the junior high group. White (1973) gives corroborating evidence, however, that the moral judgment of this college population is predominantly at the conventional level in that their average moral maturity score from Kohlberg's assessment method is 369 (a mix of Stages 3 and 4). The scores of the junior high students in Table 2 are somewhat lower than the junior high group in Table 1, but there is a difference in the general academic achievement level in the schools, the junior highs in Table 1 having the advantage. The adult group (Sample 10 in Table 2) seems to have a $P$ average comparable to college freshmen and sophomores. It should be pointed out that this adult sample is not claimed to be representative of adults in general (see Coder, 1975) but is probably more advanced.

## RELATION TO KOHLBERG'S SCALE

Written responses to four moral dilemmas and stage scores using Kohlberg's scale were available on 47 subjects from the original samples. This subgroup was heterogeneous, consisting of 16 high school students, 19 college students, and 12 adults/graduate students. Subjects were ranked by stage type by the global rating method and this was correlated with their Defining Issues Test $P$ score. The correlation is .68, not high enough to regard the two measures as equivalent tests; nevertheless this correlation is the highest correlation of Kohlberg's measure with any other measure that we are aware of for a sample of at least this size.

A quick qualitative impression of the relation between spontaneously produced, free-response answers and the subject's score on the Defining Issues Test and the Comprehension Test can be gained from the following free responses to the "Heinz" story:

**TABLE 2**
$P$ **Scores of the DIT for Ten Additional Samples**

|  | Average $P$ score for group |
|---|---|
| Junior high samples | |
| 1. Lower-middle class ninth graders from inner city schools ($n$ = 417) (Rest, Ahlgren & Mackey, 1973) | 20.0 |
| 2. Another lower-middle class of ninth graders from inner city schools ($n$ = 61) (Rest, Ahlgren, & Mackey, 1973) | 22.7 |
| | |
| Senior high samples | |
| 3. High school seniors and juniors in special summer social studies program ($n$ = 18) (Rest, Ahlgren, & Mackey, 1973) | 37.0 |
| 4. Upper-middle special class high school senior girls in private Catholic school ($n$ = 33) (Masanz, 1975) | |
| | |
| College samples | |
| 5. Junior college subjects in philosophy courses in Midwest ($n$ = 101) (Panowitsch, 1975) | 38.3 |
| 6. College students in southern U.S. college ($n$ = 161) (White, 1973) | 24.5 |
| 7. College freshmen in New Zealand University ($n$ = 146) (McGeorge, 1973) | 43.0 |
| 8. College freshmen in Midwest liberal arts college ($n$ = 72) (Bransford, 1973) | 46.6 |
| 9. College seniors from the same liberal arts college ($n$ = 60) (Bransford, 1973) | 54.0 |
| | |
| Adults | |
| 10. Upper-middle class adults in religious education class, age 23–49 years ($n$ = 85) (Coder, 1975) | 45.3[a] |

[a]The scores for these samples used an earlier version of the DIT, which is highly correlated with the present DIT.

Subjects with low Defining Issues Test scores and low Comprehension scores:

    1. If Heinz were to steal the drug he could get in much trouble. He should return to the druggist and reason with him. Try to get the druggist to realize that if there were a few living testimonies for his drug that his drug would be more popular.

    2. That's a very big decision. I really don't know what I'd do in a situation as such. For someone you love risk becomes a pretty big thing. You'd do anything sometimes for someone you love, not actually thinking of the consequences.

Subjects with high Defining Issues Test and high Comprehension scores:

    3. There is conflict here between moral principles. If morality is viewed in such a way that it only enjoins one not to do harm, then Heinz should not steal—but morality is, or should be, more than that—a broader conception would include doing good as well as resisting evil. Under such a broader conception, the worth of the life of Heinz's wife outweighs the value of the money.

    4. The benefit which will be gained in saving the woman's life is very great compared to the burden of the loss by the druggist. Heinz may repay him anonymously or publicly at some future time. Then the economic loss of the druggist would be regained, and he would suffer no morally relevant burden. The burden of the death of Heinz's wife, however, cannot be removed at some future time. [ The crucial question is] whether or not the psychic, i.e., emotional and spiritual, burden to the druggist as an individual will be as great as the psychic benefit to Heinz and his wife.

## CORRELATION WITH COGNITIVE CAPACITY MEASURES

Do subjects pick higher stage "issues" because they appreciate their greater adequacy as conceptual frameworks, or do subjects select high-stage issues without understanding them, merely selecting them because of a test-taking set to pick more complex-sounding items? Correlating the DIT with an independent measure of comprehension indicates whether appreciation for high-stage issue statements goes along with understanding.

The comprehension test employed in the DIT studies first asks a subject to read a paragraph and then to read four statements; then the subject is to choose which of the four statements most closely recapitulates the main idea of the paragraph. Here is an example:

Obeying the law is not as important as obeying your conscience. A person must decide for himself what he feels is right and good, and hold himself to those ideals, or else he is being untrue to himself. One's conscience often demands more of a person than the law. In Heinz's case, if the law is different from what Heinz thinks is right, he should still live up to the values that he believes in.

1. As long as Heinz feels he's right, he can do as he pleases. Your own conscience is more important than the law.
2. Heinz should do what he feels is right and break the law because he loves his wife and that is more important than the law.
3. A person must act according to the set of standards he has chosen for himself throughout his life even if these standards conflict with the law.
4. A person must guide his behavior according to the values he was taught to believe are right. Your conscience tells you whether or not something is right and good.

Fifteen sets of paragraphs and statements were used, each designed to test comprehension of social–moral concepts, such as conscience as an internal standard, social contract, legitimized authority, or due process of law. Subjects who picked the keyed answer most often were considered to have high comprehension. As corroboration of the *a priori* key, the graduate students in political science and moral philosophy most often agreed with the key and had higher comprehension scores than the junior high students, senior high students, college students, and seminarians.

Comprehension correlated with the DIT at .63. The high correlation between comprehension and the DIT was replicated with another student sample (.67) and also with an adult sample (.52). Further corroborating evidence that high scores on the DIT reflect greater cognitive capacity comes from its correlations with IQ-type measures: the DIT correlates significantly with the Differential Abilities Test and the Iowa Test of Basic Skills for ninth graders (in the .30's and .40's—see Cooper, 1972) and the DIT correlates .42 with the IQ Quick Test for Adults (Coder, 1975).

The correlation between comprehension and the DIT was further examined by controlling for age (taking only the ninth graders) and also statistically partialling out their mutual correlations with the Differential Abilities Test, the Iowa Test for Basic Skills, father's education, and father's occupation. The partial correlation between comprehension and DIT remained highly significant (in the .50's) even after attenuation by statistically partialling out these other variables. This would be expected because the comprehension measure was more closely related to the moral domain than IQ tests.

## CORRELATION WITH ATTITUDES

There are two reasons for seeking correlations of DIT with attitudes. One is to seek evidence that moral judgment is not just a value-neutral intellectualizing skill or style, but that it relates to value commitments as well as to purely cognitive capacities. The DIT is expected to correlate with certain value positions that are required by a high-stage perspective but that may seem paradoxical from a lower stage perspective. In other words, moral judgment is expected to correlate with those attitude tests that key on stage characteristics, but not with all attitude tests (see Kohlberg, 1969, p. 390). In our studies, two attitude tests were used. One test (the "law and order" test) comprises 15 controversial public policy issues, such as the following:

> Under present laws it is possible for someone to escape punishment on the grounds of legal technicalities even though the person may have confessed to performing the crime. Are you in favor of a tougher policy for treating criminals?

(Subjects check Likert scale from "strongly agree" to "strongly disagree.") Items were written regarding wire tapping, civil disobedience, youth protest, etc. Responses were keyed as "law and order" that advocated excessive powers to authorities or support of the existing social system at the disproportionate expense of civil rights or individual welfare (See Rest et al., 1974). The second attitude test, libertarian democracy (libertarian), was one of several scales devised by Patrick (1971) for use in studying democratic political orientation. It was composed of such items as the following:

> If a person wanted to make a speech in this city favoring communism, he should be allowed to speak.

The subject is asked to indicate his endorsement on a five-point scale ranging from "strongly agree" to "strongly disagree." The libertarian scale measures support of civil liberties under unfavorable circumstances. Both the authoritarian and libertarian scales were chosen because on theoretical grounds their items seemed to be sensitive to the important division between the "law and order" orientation of Stage 4 and the principled morality of Stages 5 and 6.

A second reason for seeking evidence of association between the DIT and attitude measures is in the interest of relating responses to hypothetical situations with responses to actual, current value controversies. The DIT and the comprehension test employ hypothetical dilemmas that are quite distant from actual decision making of subjects. The question naturally arises of what they have to do with real life. Some researchers, interested in relating moral judgment to some public behavior that has some effect on the flow of real-life events, have sought correlations of moral judgment with such behavioral measures as cheating on school exams or on games, obeying an authority, and helping a person in distress (see Kohlberg, 1969, pp. 394–396, for discussion of several studies). Usually a statistically significant relationship is found, but of only moderate magnitude ($r$'s in the .30's and .40's). It seems that there is an arena of "real-life" behavior more closely related to moral judgment tests; namely, behavior involving taking a stance on a value issue—whether speaking out publicly, voting in an election, or discussing with co-workers and friends. As people participate in moral discussion and publicly support and defend certain sides of an issue, they are making public moral judgments that have influencing effects on others. Too often, moral judgment researchers have overlooked this "real-life" behavior, perhaps because it is most notable in older age groups than are typically studied or because verbal behavior seems less "real" in some sense.

The DIT correlation with the law and order scale was −.60 and with libertarianism was .63 for the original sample. This relationship was also replicated in two other samples (another student sample and an adult sample).

## CHANGES IN DIT SCORES

Panowitsch (1975) has been studying changes in DIT scores associated with taking a college course in logic or in ethics. Panowitsch hypothesized that there would be greater DIT change associated with a course giving specific attention to moral issues than with a course not giving specific attention to moral issues. Supposedly, the greater change would have come about in an ethics class that gave concentrated exposure, practice, and instruction in moral problem solving. Moreover, subjects choosing an ethics course might have been more motivated to develop their moral problem-solving capacities. Table 3 shows DIT change associated with an ethics class compared to change in a logic class.

Whereas the logic class emphasizes clearer thinking in general (in a very formal way), the ethics class emphasizes more adequate thinking in the specifically moral domain, and the DIT seems to be selectively sensitive to this. Panowitsch (1975) is also currently following up the ethics class to determine whether their gains remain after a longer time lapse and is also comparing the pre- and posttest changes associated with other classes. This work is particularly pertinent to researchers who are contemplating using the DIT to evaluate various educational programs and curricula. It suggests that unless the experience is specifically focused on moral issues and problem solving, there will not be much change in DIT scores over a period of a few months.

### TABLE 3
#### DIT Changes for Ethics and Logic Classes[a]

| | Pretest mean | Posttest mean | t-test value | Two tailed probability |
|---|---|---|---|---|
| Ethics (n = 60) | 38.7 | 44.0 | 3.44 | >.001 |
| Logic (n = 41) | 38.2 | 38.7 | .31 | .76 |

[a] From Panowitsch (1975).

## FAKING HIGH AND FAKING LOW ON THE DIT

McGeorge (1973) administered the DIT twice to college students. In a "fake good" condition subjects were instructed:

Please assist us by trying to fill in the questionnaire so that it records the highest most mature level of social and ethical judgment possible. Fill in the questionnaire as someone concerned only with the very highest principles of justice would fill it in.

In a "fake bad" condition, subjects were instructed:

Please assist us by trying to fill in the questionnaire so that it records the lowest, most immature level of social and ethical judgment possible. Fill in the questionnaire as someone with no sense of justice and no concern for other people would fill it in.

The standard condition asked subjects to fill in the DIT "to show what you yourself really think about the problems raised." Table 4 shows five groups given various combinations of instructions and their average $P$ scores.

Clearly, McGeorge's study indicates that subjects can fake downward but not upward on the DIT.

## DISCUSSION

### The DIT as a Developmental Measure

When subjects are presented with different ways of defining the most important issue in moral dilemmas, not all subjects choose the same issues as the most important ones. These differences in judgment seem to be fairly stable for individual subjects over a short time. Furthermore, the differences in judgment seemed to be largely developmental according to evidence coming from several sources. For one, when groups of students are studied (from junior high, senior high, college, and graduate school), the assumption has been that these groups differ in their relative advance in thinking about moral problems. Therefore, one question is whether the Defining Issues Test can differentiate the four criterion groups. The $P$ score has done this quite clearly: the presumably more advanced students attribute more importance to higher stage statements. This differentiation among groups has also been expressed as a correlation of the $P$ score with chronological age. It should be emphasized, however, that high $P$ scores need not invariably go along with chronological age. In fact, in one adult sample, the $P$ score does not correlate with age ($r = -.10$, nonsignificant) although the $P$ score in this sample does correlate with IQ $[r = .42$, significant beyond the .01 level—see R. Coder (1975), for discussion and detail$]$ and also correlates meaningfully with moral comprehension and attitudes. Age *per se* is expected to correlate with $P$ scores only when

**TABLE 4**
Group Differences in $P$ Scores[a,b]

| Group | Testing 1 | Testing 2 | $t$ test[c] |
|---|---|---|---|
| Good–standard ($n = 22$) | 24.77 | 27.36 | 1.29 |
| Standard–good ($n = 23$) | 26.39 | 23.74 | 1.98 |
| Bad–standard ($n = 29$) | 16.21 | 26.10 | 5.28[d] |
| Standard–bad ($n = 25$) | 26.60 | 10.04 | 11.64[d] |
| Standard–standard ($n = 47$) | 24.55 | 25.48 | 1.13 |

[a] From McGeorge (1973).
[b] $P$ scores are expressed as raw scores rather than as percents as in Tables 1 and 2.
[c] $t$ test for correlated data.
[d] $p < .001$.

it is reasonable to expect that developmental advance is taking place over time. It is easier to make this assumption with student groups (supposedly in their "formative years") than with an adult sample. And, of course, it is not predicted that merely with the passage of time all the junior high subjects will have high $P$ scores as do the graduate students, for this is no more likely than that all the junior high subjects will become moral philosophy doctoral students. The key point is that it is reasonable to assume *prima facie* that moral philosophy doctoral students are more advanced in their moral thinking than junior high school subjects, and therefore a developmental test should differentiate these groups (and the groups inbetween). In order to insure strict comparability of groups at different ages it is necessary to conduct a longitudinal study, which of course is not the first kind of study possible. The logic of using different student groups is more like that of using different criterion groups than like that of a longitudinal study.

Additional evidence that differences on the Defining Issues Test are developmental came from the correlations with other measures usually assumed to correlate with development. The $P$ score showed substantial correlations with Kohlberg's measure of moral judgment development, with the Comprehension of Social–Moral Concepts Test, and with the Differential Abilities Test. These correlations suggest that as subjects develop cognitively they come to define moral dilemmas more complexly and come to place great importance on principled moral thinking than do the less cognitively advanced subjects. The particularly high association between the comprehension test and the Defining Issues Test indicates that the subjects who demonstrate the capacity to understand the more complicated moral concepts are the subjects who also tend to attribute more importance to them.

It can be asked whether socioeconomic status may not better account for the variance in the Defining Issues Test than "development." The most direct test of this comes from correlations in a ninth-grade sample in which the $P$ score is correlated with SES indices (father's occupation and father's education) and is also correlated with other developmental indices (Comprehension of Social–Moral Concepts Test and Differential Abilities Test). The $P$ score is clearly more highly correlated with the developmental indices (significant at least beyond .05 level in every case) than with the SES indices (nonsignificant in every case). Moreoover, if the SES levels of the different student groups tested in Sample 1 are considered, there is not much difference in SES level between them. Specific SES data are available for the junior high students and they are solidly in the middle-class range; the senior high students have come from the same community and hence presumably have comparable SES backgrounds; the College of Education students and the seminarians can by their career choices be classified also in the middle SES range; the doctoral students can be classified slightly above the others but because they constitute only 15 subjects of the sample, the trends obtained cannot be as well accounted for in terms of SES differences (see Rest *et al.*, 1974).

## The Special Interest in Principled Morality

It will be noted that the subjects in this study are older than those typically studied by Piaget and Kohlberg. My selection of this age range stems from a special interest in the conventional—principled morality shift. A group of subjects has been studied whose moral judgments are likely to span this particular part of moral judgment development. The differences between a conventional framework for making moral judgments and a principled framework are discussed in some detail elsewhere (Rest & Kohlberg, 1975). Briefly, conventional thinking has attained the perspective that "no man is an island" and that certain expectations and social norms must be maintained in order for an individual to relate positively with others and for group living to be orderly. The basis of moral obligation and rights according to conventional thinking is the maintenance of one's social system and loyalty to established institutions and social relationships. In contrast, principled thinking appreciates the need for social structure and stabilized expectations among people but also appreciates that societies and social relationships can be arranged in many possible ways and that each way, in effect, maximizes certain values and minimizes certain others. Therefore, there must be a rationale for choosing among these possibilities. Principled moral judgment goes beyond conventional thinking in appealing to second-order principles as the basis of moral obligation and rights. Principled thinking is a developmental advance over conventional thinking in not only seeing the need for social structure but also in seeing institutions and social arrangements as embodiments or implementations of human values.

One aspect of principled thinking is that people in leadership roles are not seen as a different breed of humankind, nor as infallible, but are seen as individuals having certain prerogatives in order to perform certain functions in society's division of labor. Accordingly, one can criticize or question the job performance of an "authority" (as with anybody else's job performance) without being disloyal to the whole group. Moreover, the prerogatives of authority are limited to the necessities of the role. This less exalted view of authority contrasts with the more exalted concept of authority of conventional thinking, which regards loyalty and support of authority as a sign of loyalty and support for the whole social system. Another aspect of principled thinking is its functional view of social norms. One has a moral obligation to abide by social norms insofar as they serve human values. In contrast, conventional thinking views adherence to established norms as the essence of moral obligation. From these theoretical contrasts between principled and conventional moral judgment it is obvious why a relationship between principled moral judgment and libertarianism and the law and order attitude measures has been hypothesized here.

We regard the development of principled thinking as especially important for its social–political implications and also in the individual's own personality development. From society's perspective, principled moral judgment is presupposed in the functioning of a democracy: the electorate supposedly plays a role in law making as well as law maintenance. The difference between conventional moral thinking and principled moral thinking is crucial in people's judgment of many current public policy issues. Of the various ways that moral judgment may relate to "real behavior," one of the most important and most promising is the relation of principled thinking to such behavior as voting, taking a stance on social issues, supporting certain political candidates, engaging in value discussions, understanding various points of view, and making value judgments in one's community, club, business, etc. My special interest therefore stands somewhat in contrast to researchers more interested in early moral judgment development and its relation to such "real-life" behaviors as cheating in school, confessing to one's mother, or touching a forbidden toy.

From the perspective of the individual's own personality development, the distinction between conventional moral judgment and principled moral judgment has special importance also. Erikson (1968) and others have discussed how ideology comes to play a central role as a person shifts from a conformist, other-directed personality organization to an autonomous organization based on an integrated set of values. Achieving clarity on the basic terms of social cooperation (i.e., why one has moral obligations and under what conditions one has an obligation) can be expected to play an important part in the development of autonomy. A measure of principled moral judgment is therefore expected to contribute to this research in the future. For the present study the choice of this older age group has seemed especially appropriate assuming, with Erikson, that in adolescence subjects are more interested in social and moral topics, will give these matters serious thought, and are more likely to find the questionnaire meaningful than younger subjects.

It is interesting to note that aside from the research initiated by Kohlberg, most other researchers who have studied the development of moral and political thinking in younger subjects have found a ceiling effect on their measures in early adolescence. Adelson and O'Neil (1966), Hess and Torney (1967), National Assessment of Educational Progress—Citizenship (1971) and Piaget (1932), to name a few, have all found that the upper limits of development on their measures are reached somewhere between 12 and 17 years of age. In contrast, adolescent subjects are in the lower range of DIT scores. I believe that the developmental characteristics that Kohlberg has examined are more complex and do greater justice to the subtlety of adult thought than these other developmental indices.

## Objective Tests for Studying Moral Judgment

Is it appropriate to study moral judgment by a standardized test with structured responses? The two fundamental methods for assessing moral judgment are (a) having the subject talk or write about his moral thinking in a free-response mode and then having a scorer use some standardized scoring system by which to classify the response, and (b) presenting the subject with a set of standardized alternatives representing the scoring categories and having the subject choose among them. The essential difference is who does the categorizing, the scorer or the subject. The first method has the advantage of allowing the subject to tell what his thinking is like in his own way and allows inductive formulation of scoring categories after the subject has provided the information. In order to find out what people actually say without prejudging the case, it seems that this is a necessary first step. Many hours of interviewing preceded the formulation of items of the DIT and the formulation of stage characteristics on which the items are keyed (Rest & Kohlberg, 1975). I believe that items of an objective test should be based on recurrent type of responses given in the free-response mode. However, after recurrent response types have been identified and a scoring system has been devised, and when the purpose of data collection is not to experiment with the scoring characteristics but to provide assessments of moral judgment development, then the advantages of the free-response method are diminished and there are decided advantages to an objective, standardized format.

It has been argued that it is too soon to attempt assessment of moral judgment with an objective test. This issue can be considered by observing that many previous studies have used stage-prototypic statements—that is, have used statements that are designed to exemplify the thought structure of a particular stage of moral judgment (Rest, 1969, 1973; Rest, Turiel, & Kohlberg, 1969; Turiel, 1966). The use of prototypic statements assumes (a) that stage characteristics can be specified; (b) that a statement can be written which distinctively exemplifies stage characteristics; and (c) that subjects who are advanced enough in their own development can appropriately recognize stage characteristics in statements. The additional assumption the DIT makes that goes beyond these previous studies is that subjects can meaningfully rank statements. Those who argue that DIT research is premature either must claim that studies using prototypic statements have also been premature or must show why having subjects rank statements is such a crucial extension of established precedents. I agree that it is premature for researchers to work only on measurement problems and to abandon efforts to clarify stage theory and further definition of stage characteristics. The task ahead involves theoretical work as well as work on purely psychometric problems. I have argued elsewhere, however (Rest, 1975), that further theoretical clarifications may well depend on developing more focused methods of data collection and sharper tools of analysis than available in the current free-response and scoring methods (see also Flavell & Wohlwill, 1969). The assessment of cognitive structure is more complicated than just obtaining some sample of a person's thinking and classifying the person as being in some stage. It is evident that slight variances in test question or stimuli often affect the subject's response. In other words, if assessment is not carried out under standardized conditions, then score differences between subjects may be caused by developmental differences or to different test conditions. Furthermore, the classification of a subject as being "in a stage" has many problems and there is some evidence to indicate that this procedure is not always the best way to index development (Rest, 1975), even if it is recognized that there are qualitatively different structures of cognition. Given the long way that moral judgment research must go both theoretically and methodologically, it seems to me that researchers cannot afford to throw away the new type of data base that the DIT has provided but must see if it can be used to break through some of the logjams in the moral judgment area.

Studies now underway include a longitudinal study and cross-cultural study of the DIT. A number of researchers are studying the correlations of the DIT with other attitude and personality measures. Perhaps a dozen or more educational projects are currently using the DIT as an evaluation measure. Also, work is in progress on item analyses, different scaling techniques, developing internal checks on random responding, and the revision of the "first-generation" DIT into a more refined instrument.

# REFERENCES

Adelson, J., & O'Neil, R. P. The growth of political ideas in adolescence: the sense of community, *Journal of Personality & Social Psychology*, 1956, **IV**, 295–306.

Blatt, M., & Kohlberg, L. The effects of classroom discussion on the development of moral judgment. In L. Kohlberg and E. Turiel (Eds.), *Moralization: the cognitive-developmental approach*. New York: Holt, Rinehart and Winston, 1975, in preparation.

Bransford, C. Moral development in college students. Unpublished manuscript, St. Olaf College, 1973.

Carroll, J. Children's judgments of statements exemplifying different moral stages. Unpublished doctoral dissertation, University of Minnesota, 1974.

Coder, R. Moral judgment in adults. Unpublished doctoral dissertation, University of Minnesota, 1975.

Cooper, D. The analysis of an objective measure of moral development. Unpublished doctoral dissertation, University of Minnesota, 1972.

Erikson, E. H. *Identity: Youth and crisis*. New York: Norton, 1968.

Flavell, J., & Wohlwill, J. Formal and functional aspects of cognitive development. In D. Elkind and J. Flavell (Eds.), *Studies in cognitive development*. London and New York: Oxford University Press, 1969.

Gilligan, C., Kohlberg, L., Lerner, J., & Belenky, M. Moral reasoning about sexual dilemmas. In L. Kohlberg and E. Turiel (Eds.), *Moralization: The cognitive developmental approach*. New York: Holt, Rinehart and Winston, 1975, in press.

Guilliland, S. F. Effects of sensitivity groups on moral judgment. Unpublished doctoral dissertation, Boston University, 1971.

Hess, R. D., & Torney, J. *The development of political attitudes in children*. Chicago: Aldine, 1967.

Kohlberg, L. Stage and sequence: The cognitive-developmental approach to socialization. In D. Goslin (Ed.), *Handbook of socialization theory and research*. New York: Rand-McNally, 1969.

Kohlberg, L. From is to ought. In T. Mischel (Ed.), *Cognitive development and epistemology*. New York: Academic Press, 1971.

Lockwood, A. L. Stage of moral development and reasoning about public policy issues. In L. Kohlberg & E. Turiel (Eds.), *Moralization: The cognitive developmental approach*. New York: Holt, Rinehart and Winston, 1975, in preparation.

Masanz, JoAnna. Moral judgment of high school girls. Unpublished master's dissertation, University of Minnesota, 1975, research in progress.

McGeorge, C. The fakability of the Defining Issues Test of moral development. Unpublished manuscript, Univer. of Canterbury, New Zealand, 1973.

National Assessment of Educational Progress-Citizenship: National Results. Report 2-1. Denver, Colorado: Educational Commission of the States, 1971.

Panowitsch, H. Change and stability in the defining issues test. Unpublished doctoral dissertation, University of Minnesota, 1975, research in progress.

Piaget, J. *The moral judgment of the child* (1932). New York: Free Press, 1948.

Patrick, J. Political education and democratic political orientations of ninth grade students across four community types. Unpublished manuscript, Indiana University, 1971.

Rest, J. R. Hierarchies of comprehension and preference in a developmental stage model of moral thinking. Unpublished doctoral dissertation, University of Chicago, 1969.

Rest, J. R. The hierarchical nature of stages of moral judgment. *Journal of Personality*, **41**(1), 86–109, 1973.

Rest, J. R. New approaches in the assessment of moral judgment. In T. Lickona (Ed.), *Morality: Theory, research, and social issues*, New York: Holt, Rinehart and Winston, 1975, in press.

Rest, J. R., Ahlgren, A., & Mackey, J. Report on Minneapolis Police Resource Team Project. Unpublished manuscript, University of Minnesota, 1973.

Rest, J. R., Cooper, D., Coder, R., Masanz, J., & Anderson, D. Judging the important issues in moral dilemmas—an objective measure of development. *Developmental Psychology*, 1974 ✗ **10**(4), 491–501.

Rest, J. R., & Kohlberg, L. A study of patterns of comprehension and preference of moral stages. In L. Kohlberg and E. Turiel (Eds.) *Moralization: the cognitive developmental approach.* New York: Holt, Rinehart and Winston, 1975, in press.

Rest, J. R., Turiel, E., & Kohlberg, L. Level of moral development as a determinant of preference and comprehension of moral judgment made by others. *Journal of Personality*, 1969, **37**, 225–252.

Turiel, E. An experimental test of the sequentiality of developmental stages in the child's moral judgment. *Journal of Personality & Social Psychology*, 1966, **3**, 611–618.

White, C. The development of moral judgment in college students: An objective measure and its relation to life history variables. Unpublished doctoral dissertation, University of Georgia, 1973.

# 5

## "You Will Be Well Advised to Watch What We Do Instead of What We Say"

James H. Bryan

*Northwestern University*

"You will be well advised to watch what we do instead of what we say," said Attorney General John N. Mitchell, July 1, 1969, in "what must stand as the most astonishing admission of high level duplicity in government history"; so wrote Richard Harris (1970, p. 225). Perhaps if astonishment can be extinguished as can other emotions, none of us can feel much of it in this year. Whether it can or not, however, it can be asked whether Mitchell's admission of hypocrisy, or Harris' astonishment at it, is astounding. This chapter is concerned with presenting data and speculations concerning the impact of hypocrisy on the observing child and adult. In effect, the focus is on the public's responses to acts of hypocrisy by others.

It is likely that the public, including children, are often exposed to hypocritical others. This society, and the individuals who comprise it, is often characterized as one that maintains pluralistic and competing values. Obligations to self, family, and the commonwealth are many and often may not be served with equal dedication (Darley & Latané, 1970). Indeed, their very multitude may provide justifications for the violation of any particular standard preached (Rokeach, 1973). Second, as Campbell (1963) has indicated, the cost of action is probably much greater than the cost of talk, this being particularly true of moral behavior. It is likely, for example, that the preaching of altruism to a child is much easier than the modeling of such behavior, the latter often being determined and constrained by situations and moods not likely to affect simple statements of virtue. Indeed, it is repeatedly noted among fund raisers that more pledges are made than met.

Although references to hypocrisy can often be noted in the popular press, there are very little systematically gathered data concerning the impact of such duplicity. This is somewhat surprising for several reasons. Long recognized is the fact that tutorials and examples are two powerful means of socialization (Campbell, 1963). Whatever the processes that mediate such learning experiences, there is little question that behavioral examples and verbal instructions can show powerful influences over the conduct of children. Although there are literally hundreds of studies on the effects of each technique of influence, investigations of their combined effects are lacking. Do they show an additive relationship, as suggested by Campbell (1963), or do words and deeds interact? If they interact, do discrepancies in moral preachings and practices produce conflict in the observer, devaluation of the hypocrite, states of anomie, or psychopathology?

The few speculations concerning the impact of hypocrisy on the audience lead to the assumption that severe consequences to the observer might well result from such moral inconsistency. Drug usage by adolescents has been cited as one outcropping of the individual's observance of hypocrisy (Joint Commission on Mental Health of Children, 1973). Others have suggested that hypocrisy may well lead to antisocial behavior by children of tender ages, this behavior being reflected by thefts, on the one hand, and depression of prosocial behavior, on the other (Rosenhan et al., 1968). Only minor injustice will be done to the theory of double-bind communications in suggesting that hypocrisy may produce an extreme form of pathology of thought and speech, although I must agree with Brown (1973) when he concludes that if the theory is correct, we would all be schizophrenics. As yet, however, the presumed precursor to drug usage, thefts, and schizophrenia has received little attention by experimenting psychologists. Perhaps the most that can be said about our notions of the effects of hypocrisy on either the hypocrite or his audience is that hypocrisy will produce an uncomfortable state in one who experiences it, and that hypocrisy is bad, disruptive to both the social order and to personal adjustment. Why it is bad, in what manner it offends the integrity of either its practitioner or its observer, are questions left unexplored. The term "hypocrisy," or its synonyms, carries much pejorative weight but little else. Moreover, the question concerning the independent effects of such modalities of communications has been left unanswered. Do preachings and practices have independent focuses of influence, and if so, what are they? Do they combine in influence, either additively or interactionally, in affecting other domains of behavior, and if so, what behaviors are so affected? It is to these general questions that much of my research over the past several years has been addressed.

Buying the sense of commonsense, I and such colleagues as Mark Barnett, Una Gault, Elizabeth Midlarsky, Bob Prentky, and Nancy Walbek set about to explore the impact of percepts and precepts and their discrepancies, on individuals who might be exposed to them. Before going into the results of these many studies, I would like to briefly describe some definitions and the conceptual limits of the phenomena that had captured our interest. I suppose that reasonable consensus can be reached as to what constitutes the act of hypocrisy; that is, it is "simulation; a feigning to be what one is not; the acting of a false part; a deception as to real character and feeling, especially in regard to morals and religion. . ." (Whitehall, 1950, p. 849). There also appears to be an assumption that hypocrisy cannot be demonstrated under conditions of coercion, or that hypocritical acts can be manifested only under conditions of personal liberty. Intimidation or threats may produce behavioral and verbal discrepancies, but such discrepancies are in violation of the free will and the assumption is made that once such external constraints are removed, so will be the discrepancy. Any false appearances thus generated reflect the elements of coercion, not of the self. In effect, then, "hypocrisy" typically refers to the verbal expressions of moral beliefs that are not, in fact, behaviorally enacted under conditions of personal liberty.

Before proceeding, a distinction between hypocrisy and double standards should be made. It seems to me that the critical features that distinguish the two is that the hypocrite expresses a belief or standard, by one means or another, the behavioral directives of which to others are, at best, vague, and that others' conformity or lack thereof to that norm is not a product of coercion. "Double standards" refer to the specification of particular rules of conduct to others, but not the self, within a given and specific context and are often accompanied with implicit elements of intimidation. In effect, the parent directing the 5-year-old child to bed at 8 p.m. or punishing him for a sexual liaison with the blonde next door, while not going to bed and enjoying sexual liaisons himself, reflects the operation of a double standard, not of hypocrisy. The hypocritical act, to get back to our example, reflects the verbalization of the general rule, applicable to self and others, that it is good to be in bed and celibate, while acting contrarily to those principles.

In initiating experiments on hypocrisy, a value or norm was sought that would be likely to be accepted by most observers. Implicitly, the assumption was made that reactions to hypocrisy would be more likely manifested when the subject himself held or was aware of the value being violated. To study the effects of discrepancies in practices and preachings on children, a norm that is learned at a very young age was sought. Altruism was selected as the theme for the scenario.

Children, as well as adults, agree that helping needy others is a virtue rather than a vice and, by and large, the multitude of addendums that constrain adult helping are not likely to constrain helping by children. Additionally, this virtue can be easily exhorted and behaviorally transgressed within the experimental setting. Moreover, the study of altruism, as so many papers and symposiums attest, is of importance in its own right. The altruistic response can not only tell of the effects of hypocrisy but shed light on both practical problems of socialization and on more esoteric theoretical ones, such as the nature of reinforcements.

The basic experimental design used here has changed little over the years. Children are exposed to one of six types of exemplars. Sometimes the exemplars are adults, sometimes peers; it appears to make little difference to children. In effect, some children are exposed to a model who preaches charity and demonstrates charitable behavior, that is, a saint. Others are exposed to a model who preaches greed and, consistent to his beliefs, practices it as well, that is, a sinner. For control purposes, some children are exposed to a nonpreacher who practices charity, and others to a nonpreacher who practices greed. Of particular interest is the preacher of greed and practitioner of charity, and the preacher of charity who behaves selfishly.

The children are brought into a trailer, exposed to the model, typically a videotaped one but occasionally a live one, and then left alone to play a bowling game, win money and, if he or she so desires, to donate some of the money to the March of Dimes.

This research has thus focused on the impact of simple exhortations involving the theme of altruism; behavioral enactments, either being congruent or incongruent with such exhortations; and the discrepancy between the two, in affecting both children and adults. Clearly the richness of the parent–child interaction in their attempts to come to terms in the moral domain has not been captured; instead, the focus has been on the impact of behaviors that can reasonably be thought to provide cues to the child as to the appropriate course of conduct. Three types of responses are of particular import: the child's own donation and theft behavior under anonymous conditions; the child's evaluations of the model that he has viewed; and finally, his social communications to others about his experiences within the setting (Bryan, Redfield, & Mader, 1971; Bryan & Walbek, 1970a, b).

The original experiments were addressed toward determining whether inconsistency or hypocrisy would alter the child's behavior by either depressing his willingness to help others or increasing his disposition toward exploiting others. The basis of such expectations was an experiment conducted by Rosenhan, Frederick, and Burrowes (1968). In their experiment, the investigators did find that the imposition of discrepancy in self-reward standards between the model and the child, particularly under conditions where the model was self-indulgent but imposed strict standards on the child, led to a significantly greater incidence of theft behavior by the "victimized" children. Although those investigators suggested that the viewing child in the critical condition suffered from a crisis of hypocrisy, their experimental design seemed to be addressed more to double standards than to hypocrisy. My expectations concerning hypocrisy effects failed to be supported. Indeed, after studying somewhat over 1500 children from the suburbs of Skokie and Evanston, Illinois, the city of Denver, the schools of Southern California, and the surrounds of Princeton, I have yet to demonstrate that inconsistency in moral precepts and percepts regarding altruism is a sufficient condition in affecting the child's anonymous donation or theft behaviors. The futile search however has not been limited to my laboratory efforts, as Rushton (1973), working with English children, and Jones (1972), testing Australian children, also failed to find any such behavioral consequences.

This does not mean that children's altruistic behavior is not modified; it is. A consistent finding from laboratories too numerous to mention is that if a child views another person donate, he or she, like his or her adult counterparts, will also be more likely to donate (Bryan & London, 1970). The actions of the model thus affect the actions of the child. What of moral exhortations such as "It is good to give," "You should give," "Others will like you if you give," "Others will not like you if you don't give," and virtually any other simplistic exhortations one may wish to include? My results have consistently failed to find that such norm reminders affect the children's donations. It is not that such exhortations do not have an effect, or that children do not attend to them or they do not remember them. They do remember them and are affected by them; it is simply that their donations are not affected, at least immediately so.

It is interesting that recently Rushton (1973), employing children from England, has replicated the procedures of one of my early experiments and many of the results of all of my experiments. His results have differed from mine, however, in one important respect. Although children's donations have not been affected by the simple exhortations when assessed immediately after the experimental manipulations, they have been during a posttest some 2 months later. Children who have heard exhortations to give give more during this posttest than children exposed to other types of exhortations or normatively neutral materials. Although the explanation of this particular finding requires further research, one plausible hypothesis is that children are likely to communicate to others what they have heard from the model in the experiment, and it is possible that such communications have facilitated the children's subsequent dispositions to donate (Bryan & Walbek, 1970a; Stein & Bryan, 1972). There is some difficulty with this interpretation but it does remain a viable one. Whatever the explanation of the posttest result, it is quite clear from the results of these studies as well as those of others that moral exhortations does not immediately affect the altruistic behavior of children.

It can be reasonably argued that the impact of hypocrisy may be detected with a more sensitive measure. It is not farfetched to suppose, and there is abundant data (e.g., Bryan & Walbek, 1970a; Rosenhan & White, 1967) to support the supposition, that most children are quite reluctant to give up valued resources for the needy others. The lack of an hypocrisy effect may simply be because no child is likely to give up anything; the depression of generosity by hypocrisy will therefore be veiled. In effect, then, I asked whether children learn moral abhorrance to the hypocritical other and therefore devalue either an adult or a peer showing such moral inconsistency. I have therefore explored the impact of such duplicity on the children's judgments of the model. Some interesting effects have been found, but none that is attributable to inconsistency of precepts and percepts. With children up to the age of 10 years, it has been found that children's judgments of the model appear to reflect a simple additive function. Figures 1 and 2 demonstrate the results of two studies. Essentially, if the model says good things, he gains some interpersonal or judgmental credits. Credits can be incremented if he does good things or subtracted if he either does or says bad things. The child does not devalue the exemplar, however, on the basis of his inconsistency *per se*.

Although the figures present data drawn from children's responses to rating scales, other methods of evaluation have been used. For example, Schwartz and Bryan (1971) have found that children's selection of a balloon with either the model's name or the experimenter's name imprinted on it correlated reasonably well with their responses to a rating scale. Additionally, we have conducted very open-ended interviews with children after exposing them simply to a hypocritical model. Neither method of measurement indicated any sensitivity of the child to the hypocrisy manifested by the model.

For the reader who may feel patronizing toward children, several comparable experiments conducted with high school and college age subjects should be

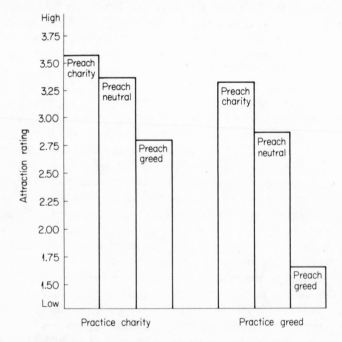

**FIG. 1**    Mean attraction ratings of model: model practices, $F = 29.19$, $p < .01$. (From Bryan & Walbek, 1970a)

mentioned (Bryan, Barnett, & Gault, 1971, unpublished manuscript). The experiments have generally followed the same experimental design, usually have focused on the topic of altruism, and have concerned themselves with interpersonal judgments of the model. Studies in our laboratory have consistently failed to reveal that adults are at all sensitive to the hypocrite. They remember what is said, they remember what is done, yet they do not devalue or attribute negative characteristics to the model. Figures 3 and 4 depict the results obtained by Bryan *et al.* (1971). Figure 3 presents the mean evaluation ratings of the model by college students on a semantic differential scale consisting of eight items. Figure 4 represents high school students' judgments of the model as measured by the same scale. Although older subjects' judgments do not conform entirely to those of the 8 year old, they are more wary of the preacher of charity; there simply is no devaluation of the hypocrite. Neither the adult nor the child demonstrates sensitivity to hypocrisy displayed by others.

There was yet another domain of behavior, however, that was of concern. That was the impact of hypocrisy or, in fact, of exhortations and behaviors on the social communications of children. Walbek, Stein, and I (Bryan & Walbek, 1970a; Stein & Bryan, 1972) conducted several experiments addressed to this concern. We attempted to assess these consequences by asking the child to leave a message for another child by speaking into a mike, which unknown to

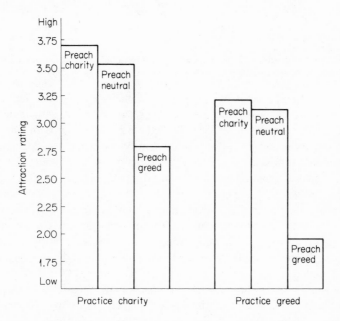

**FIG. 2**   Mean attraction ratings of model: model practices, $F = 11.49$, $p < .01$. (From Bryan & Walbek, 1970a)

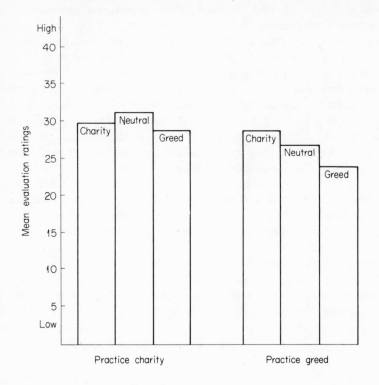

**FIG. 3** Mean evaluations ratings of model by Northwestern University students, 1971: model practices, $F = 9.90$, $df = 1/48$, $p < .01$. (From Bryan, Barnett, & Gault, 1971.)

him, was attached to a tape recorder. We then released our tapes to two independent judges who rated the messages the child left with regard to the emphasis placed on the desirability of donating to the March of Dimes. The model's hypocrisy did not affect the content of the messages. Moreover, and perhaps more surprisingly, neither did the actions of the model. If they had seen the model act charitably, they were no more likely to preach charity than if they had witnessed the model retain his winnings.

It must be remembered, however, that it is exactly the model's actions that provoke the child himself to donate. The model's actions do not appear to trigger children's cognitions concerning charity, at least by this method of assessment. What does affect the children's preachings is the preachings of the model. Children who hear either exhortations commending charity or those commending greed, are more likely to preach charity than those subjects who hear normatively neutral material. A subsequent study by Walbek (1969) suggests that most children within the donation context will preach charity, even when they have not heard exhortations, except when they hear normatively neutral material. Apparently the neutral material suppresses preachings.

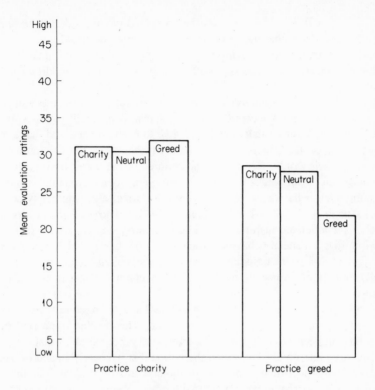

**FIG. 4** Mean evaluations ratings of model by high school students, 1971: model practices, $F = 6.65$, $df = 1/48$, $p < .01$; model exhortation, n.s.; practices × exhortation, $F = 3.26$, $df = 2/48$, $p < .05$. (From Bryan, Barnett, & Gault, 1971.)

Although it is possible to look at the influence of the model's actions and preachings on the child's behavior and communications, it is also possible to look at the relationship of the child's behavior to his preachings. In effect, one can ask whether the child's behavior is consistent with his moral exhortations.

Not surprisingly, the preachings of the children showed considerable variation in terms of the themes struck. Some made simple pleas, such as ''You should give to the March of Dimes, it goes to a very, very good cause.'' Others communicated the consequences of giving or not giving: ''If crippled children didn't get any money, they could probably never get uncrippled,'' ''Sometime if you give peoples a lot, poor peoples a lot of money, sometime they might write back and send you more money back. So don't forget, please give them more money and maybe if you give them more money they could be just like us, and maybe happier than us, and have more fun than us down there. So please help them, them poor peoples,'' and finally one that essentially went; if you don't give, the people are going to get out of the hospital and burn your houses down. Although there were reasonable differences among children in the degree to and the style in which they exhorted other children to give, it is probably safe to say that their exhortations were not correlated with their own behavior. Children who had witnessed a nongiving model would preach charity but, in fact, practice selfishness. In effect, then, hypocritical children had been produced.

Let me then briefly summarize what these particular experiments suggest. It is clear that children do accept the norm of social responsibility at least insofar as they verbally indicate that one should give to needy others, and judge others on the basis of the others' endorsement of the norm through either their behavior or their words. Reminding the children of the norm, however, fails to elicit altruistic behavior, although it does elicit social communications encouraging such behavior by others. What does affect altruistic behavior is the model's actions. Finally, I have consistently failed to find that hypocritical models have a deleterious effect on children's altruistic behavior, a facilitating effect on their antisocial behavior, or any effect on their social communications or judgments of peers or adults. Likewise, the college age student appears equally impervious to such hypocrisy, their claims and pretensions to the contrary.

To this point, the experiments described have been concerned with the impact of "pure" hypocrisy on the observer. That is, the hypocrisy of the model has not been produced in conjunction with other variables that may be of consequence. Essentially I accepted the notion that hypocrisy in and of itself is not a critically important condition to either child or student, but that it is possible that hypocrisy in conjunction with other variables may show influence. Taking a lead from the editorialists, I have tested the notion that labeling another a hypocrite may revolve around the labeler's moods as well as the qualities of the hypocrite. Several experiments have been undertaken in which an attempt is made to introduce a personal theme into the scenario.

Although I initially hoped to exploit anger toward the potential hypocrite, I ended with the manipulation of disgust. In effect, the hypothesis was that if the observer had had a previously unpleasant interaction with the model, he would be more likely to label the model a hypocrite if reality so justified it. Notice that we did not expect this manipulation to sensitize the subject; most subjects tested did recognize that the actor percepts and precepts did not correspond. Instead, it was expected that the unpleasant interpersonal interaction would facilitate the observer's willingness to name call.

The experimental design was as follows. Before the usual six types of models were presented, the model and the judge interacted for a 2- or 3-minute period in a waiting room. The interaction was arranged so that the subject arrived in the room after the model only to find that the one remaining chair was covered by both the model's shoes and, apparently from the shoes, mud. The judge remained standing. Additionally, in what appeared to be a very effective manipulation, the model, just before leaving the waiting room, started coughing. He terminated this pseudo-seizure by spitting into a wastepaper basket. Some strong spontaneous responses from the subjects indicated to us that this latter behavior was particularly disgusting. The subject then witnessed one of the six types of models typically employed in our experiments. The manipulation checks did indicate that the subjects thought that the spitting model was less desirable than the model who did not; they did remember what the model said and did and therefore did notice the discrepancies in percepts and precepts, yet there was no evidence from two separate experiments that subjects were likely to devalue the hypocrite more than the nonhypocrite or that they were more likely to devalue the hypocrite when disgusted than when not. The hypothesis that an unpleasant interaction with the hypocrite would increment veridical labeling of that person as a hypocrite was not supported.

A second line of research involving hypocrisy and additional variables in interaction in affecting responses to a hypocrite recently began. Two experiments addressed to the impact of the model's consistency on his subsequent ability to influence the child's altruistic behavior by means of social approval were conducted (Midlarsky, Bryan, & Brickman, 1973). In effect, the questions of whether the often presumed two most powerful sources of socialization, modeling and reinforcement, might interact in affecting the child's generosity was posed.

There are a multitude of experiments demonstrating that children do respond to grunts, nods, and smiles of adults, particularly strange ones (Stevenson, 1965). What is less explored are those conditions that may limit or constrain the effectiveness of such approval, and what is totally unexplored are the conditions under which positive social approval becomes outright aversive to the recipient so that it inhibits rather than increases the probability of the response in question. Intuitively, this does appear to occur as people have all probably at one time or another been embarrassed by praise.

On the basis of the work of Insko and his colleagues (Cialdini & Insko, 1969; Insko & Butzine, 1967), it was predicted that a source who was not well regarded and who attempted to reinforce a response that was inconsistent with his own position might, through his verbal reinforcements, inhibit rather than increment the criterial response by the child. The two experiments were conducted with sixth-grade girls residing in Denver and with black and white boys and girls residing in Evanston. The design of both experiments was quite similar and was a 2 × 3 factorial. The child either did or did not receive verbal approval from the model whenever the child donated and witnessed the model either donate, retain, or fail to claim his own winnings. The procedures employed in the initial experiment were as follows. Children were brought into the experimental trailer and watched the model play the bowling game and either donate some of her winnings, keep all of her winnings, or fail to claim her rewards. Children were then exhorted by the model to give to charity with the following statement: "Now it is your turn [to play the bowling game]. But before you begin, let me remind you about poor children. Please think about them as you are playing, and about how very much they would love to receive the prizes that these chips can buy. It would make them very happy to get toys and candy, because it is so easy for a needy child to feel really forgotten. Let us let them know that we remember them.'' In the first experiment, children were further pressured to give during the first ten trials. Following these ten trials, the model either gave them social approval (e.g., ''Boy, you're really nice to do that'') or said nothing on each occasion the child donated.

Of primary interest for purposes of the analysis was the amount of winnings the children donated during the ten-reinforcement/no-reinforcement trials. Table 1 presents the results. As can be seen, the children were influenced by both the model's actions and his social reinforcements. Of particular interest, however, was the fact that children, exposed to a model who himself would not donate and then subsequently attempted to influence the child's donations by means of social approval, were quick to stop donating. As predicted, therefore, the inconsistent model's social approval of the child's donation behavior served to inhibit that behavior, and the consistent model's social approval facilitated altruistic behavior.

Experiment II attempted to replicate, clarify, and extend the generality of these findings in several ways. Younger children were employed, boys as well as girls, and children both black and white were incorporated into the study. Additionally, we were interested in whether approval from the inconsistent model would, in fact, inhibit the motor actions involved in donations rather than simply the amount given (although these indexes are typically highly correlated). We predicted that approval from such a model would inhibit the child's donation acts as soon as he became aware of the contingencies involved. In effect, we predicted that the children would act in such a manner as to ''turn off'' praise from the inconsistent model. Finally, the high pressure tactics employed in the initial experiment were eliminated.

**TABLE 1**
**Mean Amount Donated[a, b]**

| Model's reinforcement to subject | Model's actions | | |
|---|---|---|---|
| | Charitable | Neutral | Greed |
| Social approval | 17.67 | 16 | 6 |
| No social approval | 13 | 13.92 | 9.08 |

[a] Interaction, $F = 14.19, p < .01$; model's actions, $F = 70.40$, $p < .01$; reinforcement $F = 4.08, p < .05$.

[b] From Midlarsky, Bryan, and Brickman (1973).

As in the previous experiment, analysis of variance of the results indicated that the model's actions and reinforcements interacted with the trials to affect the child's donation. Indeed, with the inconsistent model, children stopped donating quite quickly following their experiences with such reinforcement. It was only in this condition, in fact, that the number of children donating on the first trial exceeded the number of such children donating on each of the remaining 11 trials. Apparently the aversive approver "turned off" children very rapidly. These two studies therefore suggested that praise might not only be faint, but that it could be outright obnoxious. The transformation of praise to punishment could be accomplished by inconsistency by the approver.

There are limitations to the generality of these results that should, alas, be pointed out. First, just what elements of the inconsistency facilitate this important transformation have not been determined. Does praise become punishment when the model reinforces an action that he or she fails to commit, or does Dr. Jekyll become Mr. Hyde only when he exhorts one position, fails to enact it, and then reinforces the child for just those behaviors he exhorts but does not enact? Whatever the important configuration of the inconsistency, however, the processes by which the effects are produced are not well understood.

Initially, it was assumed that, by and large, children would act as if they were telling the model to "get lost"; yet a questionnaire failed to find that the children either devalued or otherwise harbored antagonisms toward the aversive approver. Whether the effect was mediated by some other cognitive mechanisms that were independent of interpersonal attraction, such as feelings of inequity or reactance, or whether the effect was not cognitively mediated at all, remain to be determined. Although the aversive approval effect is reliable, the process by which it is produced was obscure. Additionally, it should be noted that in these two experiments, concern was with the child's public rather than private donation behavior. Donations were always made in the presence of the model; therefore, in the current jargon, compliance rather than internalized behavior was being assessed. Finally, it should be noted that in one previous experiment an aversive approval effect was not found (Bryan et al., 1971). In that experiment, the model demonstrated his inconsistency on a task that was quite different from the game subsequently operated by the child. Therefore, the aversive approval effect might only emerge for a narrowly relevant range of responses, responses that could easily be categorized by the child as containing the same elements, goals, or procedures, which had or had not been demonstrated by the exemplar.

After the caveats, however, important implications are suggested by the results of the aversive approval experiments. These two experiments indicate that an adult's inconsistency may produce a decrement in his subsequent ability to exert positive influence in the domain of the moral behavior at issue.

Inconsistency may well attenuate his ability to exercise one of the two most powerful means of socialization, that of social reinforcement. To predict the impact of reinforcement independent of the prior modeling of moral behavior by the socialization agent, be it parent, peer, or teacher, may be more hazardous than has heretofore been recognized. At least in relation to the development of altruistic behavior, the parent who models selfishness may be better advised to do nothing than to attempt to reinforce altruism, if teaching altruism is his aim.

Aside from the relatively reliable data concerning the aversive approval effect, attempts to demonstrate a hypocricy effect have continually failed. The data repeatedly suggest that discrepancies in an individual's moral preachings and practices do not lead to a devaluation of that individual, and that the impact of the moral preachings has focuses that differ from that of moral action. Prosocial behavior breeds similar behavior from both child and adult, whereas moral exhortations generate a lip-service morality, at least in the short run. This is not to say that all forms of tutorials are ineffective in producing altruistic behavior by children. Indeed, Grusec and her colleagues have presented impressive evidence that some form of instructions, for example verbal descriptions of the donation act, will be as effective as behavioral enactments, particularly for girls (Grusec & Skubiski, 1970). However, the power of simple moral exhortations to extract self-sacrifice from the child seems quite limited. If such reflect a more general case, it would seem critical that socialization agents, particularly those who have little personal interaction with the child (e.g., television, Boy Scout manuals, the moral lecturer) be particularly wary as to the degree of behavioral influence his or her verbalized morality might exert over the young child.

The results of the many studies of hypocrisy, at least under conditions in which the individual observer has no personal or vested interest, has repeatedly failed to demonstrate that such discrepancies in percepts and precepts (be they evidence with regard to altruism or cheating on tests) affect children's or adults' behaviors, social communications, or evaluations of the sinner. It would seem, however, on an a priori basis, that hypocrisy would be extremely damaging to both the individual actor and the public welfare. The political events of the past year further attest to this belief. It is perhaps on this basis that various methodological issues have been raised regarding these redundant failures. For example, it may well be true that if an increased sample size is employed, effects will be found; that if different exhortations are spoken, outcroppings of the hypocrisy will be evident; that if the timing of the exhortations is somehow altered, surely impacts will be noted; and that if older subjects, or different sex subjects, or different models are utilized, effects will be evident. Surely, hypocrisy will be found to have effects; perhaps the aversive approval findings are a first lead to them, but these effects seem to be surprisingly elusive. I have tried many exhortations; others have changed their timing within the experiment; I have used children and models of various ages and sexes and yet the results seem quite consistent. Although it may well be that the right combination of manipulations and subjects has not been paired, it must also be considered that the subjects themselves may also be resistant to the labeling of, or indifferent to, or indeed tolerant of, such duplicity by either peer or adult, with or without power, live or televized. And if this is so, the question must arise as to why this is so, particularly in light of the presumed moral abhorrance of the public to such actions by others.

It is true that for many children the encoding of the elements that define the hypocritical act, that is, the words and the deeds, is difficult. A minority of children cannot recall both what the hypocritical model said and what he did. Interestingly, it is not that the communication modes differ; children do not appear to remember actions better than words, or vice versa. Instead, their recall of the hypocrite is such as to produce a thematic harmony, usually by attributing socially desirable attributes to the hypocrite. That is, if either the model's words or deeds suggest an inclination toward charitable action, both his words and deeds will be remembered as implying a charitable person. At least for the young child, and perhaps this is where they depart radically from the adult observer, behavior is not criterial or more important than exhortations in determining their interpersonal judgments. However, the fact remains that hypocrisy lacks effects for even those children who do correctly recall the elements defining the hypocrisy.

One likely candidate for the explanation of this lack of effect is a shopworn one, and that is that children receive very little training, either from the media or from their parents, regarding hypocrisy. For example, Thorndike and Lorge (1944) presented information indicating that in those books designed for third to eighth graders, the terms "hypocrisy" and "hypocrite" appeared once in 4½ million words and the term "hypocritical" but three times. It does not appear to be a topic of great moment. Moreover, there is increasing evidence that the recognition of objects and, by extrapolation, phenomena is intimately related to frequency of word usage, and the age at which the learning of the label occurred (Carroll & White, 1972a, b; Loftus & Suppes, 1972). In the light of this evidence, it is unlikely that children's literature is an important training agent.

Second, if it is assumed that hypocrisy is generally the verbalization of commonly held values in combination with the failure to motorically match such statements, then, by and large, one important element of hypocrisy is an act of omission rather than one of commission. Clearly, this is the case within these experiments. As Staub (1971) has pointed out, socializing agents are likely to spend considerably more time or effort in training their children about the do not's than about the do's. Acts of omission are probably not as likely as those of commission to draw either the attention or the wrath of the parent or his surrogate. If such acts are not noticed, then hypocrisy will be unnoticed as well.

Perhaps John Milton has best summarized these findings when he wrote in *Paradise Lost*: "For neither man nor angel can discern hypocrisy, the only evil that walks invisible, except to God alone." Perhaps, in answer to my original question, it is Harris' astonishment, not Mitchell's hypocrisy, that is astounding. And if this is so, it is time that the particular and specific effects of moral preachings and moral behavior on the observing child are investigated. The "inter-substitutability," to use Campbell's (1963) term, of various modes of social influence is not at all apparent. It seems instead that moral exhortations may affect very different response modalities than do demonstrated moral behaviors.

## ACKNOWLEDGMENTS

Parts of this study were supported by the National Institute of Child Health and Human Development under research grant HD 03234 to James H. Bryan. Thanks are due to Tanis Bryan and Robert Prentky for their many helpful suggestions concerning the substance and style of this article.

## REFERENCES

Brown, R. Schizophrenia, language, and reality. *American Psychologist*, 1973, **28**, 395–403.

Bryan, J. H., Barnett, M., & Gault, U. The impact of words and deeds about altruism upon viewer's judgments of the model. Unpublished manuscript, Northwestern University, 1971.

Bryan, J. H., & London, P. Altruistic behavior by children. *Psychological Bulletin*, 1970, **73**, 200–211.

Bryan, J. H., Redfield, J., & Mader, S. Words and deeds about altruism and the subsequent reinforcement power of the model. *Child Development*, 1971, **42**, 1501–1508.

Bryan, J. H., & Walbek, N. H. Preaching and practicing generosity: Children's actions and reactions. *Child Development*, 1970, **41**, 329–353 (a).

Bryan, J. H., & Walbek, N. H. The impact of words and deeds concerning altruism upon children. *Child Development*, 1970b, **41**, 747–757 (b).

Campbell, D. T. Social attitudes and other acquired behavioral dispositions. In S. Koch (Ed.), *Study of science*, Vol. 6. New York: McGraw-Hill, 1963. Pp. 94–172.

Carroll, J. B., & White, M. N. Word frequency and age of acquisition as determinants of picture-naming latency. *Research Bulletin*, 72–10, Princeton, New Jersey: Educational Testing Service, 1972. (a)

Carroll, J. B., & White, M. N. Age-of-acquisition norms for 220 picturable nouns. *Research Bulletin*, 72–58, Princeton, New Jersey: Educational Testing Service, 1972. (b)

Cialdini, R. B., & Insko, C. A. Attitudinal verbal reinforcement as a function of informational consistency: A further test of the two-factor theory. *Journal of Personality & Social Psychology*, 1969, **12**, 342–350.

Darley, J. M., & Latané, B. Norms and normative behavior: Field studies of social interdependence. In J. Macaulay & L. Berkowitz (Eds.), *Altruism and helping behavior*. New York: Academic Press, 1970.

Grusec, J. E., & Skubiski, L. Model nurturance, demand characteristics of the modeling experiment and altruism. *Journal of Personality & Social Psychology*, 1970, **14**, 352–359.

Gurin, G., Veroff, J., & Feld, S. *Americans view their mental health*. New York: Basic Books, 1960.

Harris, R. *Justice: The crisis of law, order, and freedom in America*. New York: Dutton, 1970.

Insko, C. A., & Butzine, K. W. Rapport, awareness and verbal reinforcement of attitude. *Journal of Personality & Social Psychology*, 1967, **6**, 225–228.

Joint Commission on Mental Health of Children. *Mental health: From infancy through adolescence.* New York: Harper & Row, 1973.

Jones, W. T. Hypocrisy as an epi-phenomen: The effect upon subjects' donations and ratings of a model if cognitive cues about hypocrisy are supplied when there is discrepancy between the model's speech and action. Unpublished M.A. Thesis, University of New South Wales, Australia, 1972.

Loftus, E. F., & Suppes, P. Structural variables that determine the speed of retrieving words from long-term memory. *Journal of Verbal Learning & Verbal Behavior,* 1972, **11**, 770–777.

Midlarsky, E., Bryan, J. H., & Brickman, P. Aversive approval: Interactive effects of modeling and reinforcement on altruistic behavior. *Child Development,* 1973, **44**, 321–329.

Milton, J. *Paradise lost.* Cambridge, England: Cambridge University Press, September, 1972.

Rokeach, M. Value therapy: A new approach to the modification of health seeking and health avoiding behavior. Paper presented at the annual meeting of the American Public Health Association, San Francisco, 1973.

Rosenhan, D., Frederick, F., & Burrowes, A. Preaching and practicing: Effects of channel discrepancy on norm internalization. *Child Development,* 1968, **39**, 291–301.

Rosenhan, D., & White, G. M. Observation and rehearsal as determinants of prosocial behavior. *Journal of Personality & Social Psychology,* 1967, **5**, 424–431.

Rushton, J. P. Generosity in children: Immediate and long term effects of modeling, preaching, and moral judgments. Unpublished manuscript, London School of Economics and Political Science, University of London, 1973. (*Journal of Personality & Social Psychology,* in press.)

Schwartz, T., & Bryan, J. H. Imitation and judgments of children with language deficits. *Exceptional Children,* 1971, **38**, 157–158.

Staub, E. Helping a person in distress: The influence of implicit and explicit "rules" of conduct on children and adults. *Journal of Personality & Social Psychology,* 1971, **17**, 137–144.

Stein, G. M., & Bryan, J. H. The effect of a television model upon rule adoption behavior of children. *Child Development,* 1972, **43**, 268–273.

Stevenson, G. W. Social reinforcement of children's behavior. In L. P. Lipsett & C. C. Spiker (Eds.), *Advances in child development and behavior,* Vol. 2. New York: Academic Press, 1965.

Thorndike, E. L., & Lorge, I. *The teacher's word book of 30,000 words.* New York: Columbia University Press, 1944.

Walbek, N. H. Charitable cognitions and actions: A study of the concurrent elicitation of children's altruistic thoughts and deeds. Unpublished master's thesis, Northwestern University, 1969.

Whitehall, H. (Ed.) *Webster's new twentieth century dictionary of the english language.* New York: The World Publishing Company, 1950.

# 6
# To Rear a Prosocial Child: Reasoning, Learning by Doing, and Learning by Teaching Others

Ervin Staub

*University of Massachusetts*

In this chapter I will discuss several socializing influences that are likely to be important for children's learning to behave prosocially. Almost certainly, it is a pattern of child rearing practices and other socializing influences, rather than a single influence, that leads to a tendency by children to help others, share with others, and cooperate with others. What are the elements in this pattern, and what is learned when various socializing influences affect children? How do they come to increase prosocial behavior? In the following, theoretical considerations are first presented and then relevant research by my colleagues and me is described. This is followed by a discussion of some basic research and theoretical issues.

Before discussing potentially important socializing influences I would like to elaborate on the meaning of a "tendency to behave prosocially." It is not yet established that various forms of prosocial behavior are interrelated. Although no strong attempts have been made to study the interrelationship among different forms of prosocial behavior, when multiple dependent measures have been used in experiments, the correlation among these dependent measures, representing different forms of prosocial behavior, tended to be low. In my view, internal processes and "internal contents"—such as values, plans, skills, and the capacity for empathy—that may mediate or determine prosocial behavior may be fairly specific to certain kinds of prosocial behavior or may be relatively general, relevant to a variety of prosocial behaviors. For example, some people may have prosocial values or empathic tendencies that are activated by many conditions, whereas other people may react only to some conditions, depending on what they have previously learned. Even if a prosocial tendency is fairly general, the costs of different types of prosocial behavior still vary, these costs affecting the likelihood that prosocial values and other internal contents or processes will gain expression in behavior. In addition, conflicts among various personal tendencies or goals must be considered. The goal of helping someone in need may conflict with the goal of gaining approval or the need to achieve on a task; alternately these goals may all be satisfied in the same way, increasing the likelihood of prosocial action (Schwartz, Feldman, Brown, & Heingartner, 1969; Staub, 1974).

A specific situation in which prosocial action is appropriate or is needed may call into play different goals to different degrees. If fairly detailed information about the characteristics of individuals is obtained and the characteristics of a situation are sufficiently considered, both the kind of goals it may activate and the costs associated with as well as the possibilities of rewards resulting from prosocial behavior, the ability to predict prosocial behavior may greatly improve. As this discussion implies, high correlations across varied situations among different forms of prosocial behavior are not necessarily expected.

Some suggestive support for these notions and for individual differences in "prosocial orientation" were found in a study that Sumru Erkut, Dan Jaquette, and I conducted at Harvard (described in Staub, 1974). These findings showed that responses to sounds of distress and help for the distressed person in the course of subsequent interaction with him were affected by a combination of the characteristics of the situation and the personality characteristics of the subjects. Subjects with a more advanced level of moral reasoning (Kohlberg, 1969) or those who tended to ascribe responsibility to themselves for others' welfare (Schwartz, 1970) helped more, but only when they felt less need to work on their task uninterruptedly; that is, when they were less concerned about disapproval for interrupting their work. Also, goals or values that conflicted with helping, such as ambition, reduced helping. Finally, subjects who were characterized by prosocial tendencies as measured by a number of tests (they had a more general prosocial orientation) tended to be more generally helpful and were relatively unaffected by situational variation.

In another study conducted in collaboration with Dennis Krebs, we found positive relationships among different kinds of prosocial behaviors even without the elaborate interactive approach of the above study. We administered a large number of personality tests to 43 Harvard freshmen and measured several forms of their prosocial behavior. Their willingness to help an experimenter, their cooperation with another "subject" in a prisoner's dilemma game, their willingness to work—both by addressing envelopes and making telephone calls—to collect money for a charity, and various other prosocial actions were studied. Apart from the test of cooperation on the prisoner's dilemma, which was negatively related or unrelated to other measures, the measures of prosocial behavior were positively and significantly related to each other.

To return to child-rearing practices, I should like to mention several that are likely to be extremely important for children learning to behave prosocially before I introduce those that are emphasized in this paper. Perhaps the most important one, possibly a condition for children developing concern about other people, is a warm, affectionate, nurturant relationship between the parent and the child.

[ Several theoretical approaches suggest the importance of parental nurturance for moral development (Mowrer, 1950; Sears, Maccoby, & Levin, 1957). In one experiment, nurturance has enhanced a prosocial behavior, children helping another child in response to sounds of distress from another room (Staub, 1971a). In another experiment, nurturance has enhanced the degree to which children come to imitate a prosocial model and, later, behave prosocially] (Yarrow, Scott, & Waxler, 1973).

Another very important influence is modeling, or parental example. Parental nurturance may, in fact, be considered a particularly important form of modeling with positive behavior directed at the child. However, the models that parents provide in their interactions with other people are also very important.

A third important influence is likely to be parental control. Unless parents are able to guide the child's behavior so that the child acts in a manner that the parents advocate, it is unlikely that children will learn the behavioral tendency that the parents advocate or internalize related values. The reasons for the importance of nurturance, modeling, and control and some of the relevant research evidence have recently been discussed elsewhere (Staub, 1975).

## REASONING AND INDUCTION

Research findings on the effect of child-rearing practices on moral development showed that the use of reasoning by the parent with the child, explaining why what the child did was wrong and why he should act in certain ways, is related to various indices of moral development, such as internalized values, confession upon wrongdoing, and sometimes resistance to temptation (Hoffman, 1970; Maccoby, 1968; Sears et al., 1957). Hoffman (1970) argued that one type of reasoning by the parent, pointing out to children the consequences of their behavior on others, including its effect on the parent, was the most important antecedent of internalized moral values and corresponding behavior. Hoffman and his associates found that parental "induction," as he called this child-rearing practice, was associated both with the use of internalized moral values and peer ratings of consideration for others among seventh graders (Hoffman & Saltzstein, 1967) and with positive social behavior among pre-school children (Hoffman, 1963).

I have long believed that verbal information communicated to people is likely to affect their subsequent behavior, given certain conditions that help them take the information seriously, that is, help them learn from it. Induction seemed a particularly important form of information, and I wondered whether, if it were employed in an experimental setting, induction would increase later prosocial behavior. In an early experiment I attempted to explore this question, using "positive induction" with children. Hoffman and his associates studied the effects of parents' pointing out to children the negative consequences that their undesirable behavior had on others. I attempted to enhance prosocial behavior by pointing out the positive consequences of helping. In this study, with kindergarten children (Staub, 1971b), the effects of role playing were explored. Pairs of children enacted a series of scenes in which one child needed help and another provided help; they then exchanged roles. The effects of induction were also examined: the positive consequences of such helpful acts were pointed out to children, either in conjunction with role playing or by itself. Then the effects of these treatments on children's subsequent sharing and helping behavior were evaluated. The complicated findings suggested that role playing could increase both helping and sharing behavior. However, induction had no effect on sharing with and helping another child. It actually decreased prosocial behavior on a third measure, helping an adult pick up paper clips that she had dropped.

These negative findings raise some questions about the effects that induction may have and the conditions that may be necessary for induction to enhance prosocial behavior. First, parental induction may lead to an increased ability to perceive how another person feels, when this is not obvious, and to anticipate how certain events may make another person feel, the probable negative or positive consequences of various experiences. As a result, induction may increase role taking, the ability to view an event from another person's point of view.

Second, induction may increase the probability of empathy—of vicariously experiencing another person's feelings—or of anticipatory empathy, the experiencing of feelings that another person is likely to have upon the occurrence of certain events, including one's own actions. One reason for this may be that the experience of induction leads to a certain way of interpreting others' experience and the impact of events on other people. Having been exposed to induction statements, a person may come to interpret others' distress as bad and others' wellbeing as good (and may also come to feel a sense of responsibility to minimize others' distress and to enhance others' welfare). Another way that induction may come to enhance empathy with others is conditioning. It is often the case that when other people experience positive or negative feelings this is associated with one's own experience of parallel feelings. When parents are upset, their emotional state itself, or negative behavior that they direct at the child which may accompany their negative emotions, is likely to generate parallel feelings in the child. The same may hold for positive feelings.

Other children's feelings may also result in parallel feelings, particularly if one has contributed to those feelings by one's actions. Through association between others' feelings and one's own, others' feelings, real or anticipated, may become conditional stimuli that can evoke similar feelings in an observer. Aronfreed's (1968) view of the effect of verbalization on children's behavior emphasizes this conditioning aspect; self-verbalizations later guide behavior because they come to function as conditioned stimuli for various effects. However, recent research findings strongly suggest that conditioning is mediated by the manner in which people interpret experience (Bandura, 1971). Induction, with or without conditioning experiences, is likely to affect the manner in which children interpret and evaluate others' needs and their welfare, their interpretation affecting their emotional reactions, which in turn motivate action.

Current cognitive theories of emotion, and related findings (Arnold, 1960; Lazarus, Averill, & Option, 1969; Schachter & Singer, 1962) also emphasize that the manner in which stimuli (such as others' distress or welfare) are interpreted or assessed is likely to determine the feelings that those events generate (see also Staub, 1975).

What conditions are necessary for induction to increase later prosocial behavior? The frequent use of induction statements may focus attention on others' feelings. It is likely, however, that more than verbal communication is necessary for induction to enhance the likelihood of either prosocial behavior or of children using induction type thinking to guide their own behavior. It is likely that parents must exercise control over the child so that the child engages in action that is implied by the induction statements (or refrains from action that harms others). If conditions in the environment lead children to actually behave prosocially, then their appreciation of the positive consequences of their behavior that is enhanced by induction may make it more reinforcing to expend effort and energy or to sacrifice valued resources for others.

First, as a result of the repeated experience by the child of induction statements associated with his own prosocial behavior, empathic emotions may later be generated by anothers' need that motivates prosocial action.

Second, positive induction statements may enhance the child's feeling of importance; they point to the beneficial effect that the child can or will have on other people. A feeling that one is important to others is likely to be reinforcing, and may motivate prosocial action (White, 1959). From another theoretical point of view, under certain circumstances at least, induction may be regarded as a minimally coercive influence in getting children to behave prosocially and may increase the likelihood that they regard the prosocial behavior that they engage in as self-determined. The findings about the effects of insufficient reward on behavior seem applicable (Festinger & Freedman, 1964). However, this is probably not true under all circumstances; sometimes induction may lead to psychological reactance (Brehm, 1966; Staub, 1971b, 1975).

Finally, induction statements are also likely to be effective if they are associated with various reinforcing events, increasing the probability of their later use by the child and thus the likelihood that they will guide his behavior.

## RESPONSIBILITY ASSIGNMENT
## AND ENGAGING IN RESPONSIBLE ACTION

I recently suggested elsewhere (Staub, 1975) that an important influence that leads to children learning to behave prosocially is the focusing of responsibility by parents and other socializing agents on children to engage in behavior that enhances others' welfare. Responsibility "assignment" may be structured, when children have regularly occurring duties that contribute to others' welfare (taking care of younger siblings, contributing in various ways to the welfare of the family, or even taking care of a pet) or it may be relatively unstructured, when the parents expect that the child will share toys with others and will respond to others who need help or sympathy in the course of on-going events.

Some tentative data that responsibility assignment might be important in enhancing prosocial behavior came from several sources. Young children who were asked to "take charge" were more likely to respond to sounds of distress by another child in an adjoining room (Staub, 1970a). Whiting and Whiting (1969) found that children in cultures where they had responsibilities that contributed to the maintenance of the family—the tending of animals, the care of younger siblings, and so on—were also more helpful in other ways than those in cultures where they had fewer or less important responsibilities. Finally, older siblings, who in general appear less sure of themselves in social situations (Hartup, 1970), nonetheless tended to initiate more helping behavior in response to sounds of other children's distress (Staub, 1970a, 1971b, 1971c). This might well have been the result of greater demand on them that they assume responsibility for others' welfare, particularly for the welfare of their younger siblings.

How may responsibility assignment enhance later prosocial behavior? A distinction may again be drawn between parents verbally focusing responsibility on the child, versus also exercising sufficient control to ensure that the child actually behaves prosocially; that is, between responsibility focusing and the actual participation in responsible action. Focusing responsibility on children may, by itself, make children aware of (knowledgeable about) parental (and/or societal) values. When children are also led to engage in responsible action of sufficient magnitude or frequency, minimally this may lead to the learning of a societal norm (Staub, 1972), i.e., that it is expected of people to do things for others, that to do so is regarded by other people as an obligation, and that one can expect rewards for doing so and punishment for not doing so.

Under certain conditions children may also "internalize" this value and the norm derived from it. By "internalization" I mean that they have a set of cognitions that they employ under appropriate conditions and thus guide their own behavior, and that they experience self-reinforcement and self-punishment as a function of their behavior. Internalization may be promoted by a variety of circumstances; I shall only mention two of them here. One may be that children are provided with cognitions (beliefs, value statements, inductions) promoting prosocial behavior. In the course of engaging in prosocial behavior they may come to use these statements to guide and evaluate their behavior, and later on such self-verbalization may initiate prosocial action, as discussed in the previous section. Second, when positive consequences of the behavior are made clear to the child (by his or her being able to observe them), the reinforcing effect of being able to affect others' welfare may make prosocial behavior intrinsically reinforcing. Therefore, simply engaging in prosocial behavior (of sufficient duration and magnitude, under relatively noncoercive conditions, with some awareness of the consequences) may enhance the tendency to behave prosocially.

## INDIRECT LEARNING OF PROSOCIAL BEHAVIOR

Both in the home and in schools, children are usually the "target" of instruction, whether they are taught cognitive or social skills, or values. However, rather than instruction being directly aimed at them, children may learn while acting as collaborators of socializing agents. One form of collaboration, suggested above, may be when children collaborate with adults in accomplishing important goals, such as maintaining and furthering the welfare of the family or of other individuals. Another type of collaboration, a form of indirect instruction, may be when children are taught skills and values in order to teach others and subsequently do teach others what they have learned.

In an experiment that we conducted, children acted as confederates: they engaged in a variety of play activities, as well as activities in the course of which they needed help, this way providing subjects with opportunities to help. Subsequently, they initiated more help in response to sounds of another child in distress than the subjects whom we tried to teach directly to respond with help to the need of the confederate (Staub, 1975; Staub & Buswell, unpublished research). More generally, reports from active programs around the country in which older children tutored younger ones (R. Lippitt, 1968; P. Lippitt, 1969; Thelen, 1969) suggest that important positive personality changes might result from acting as a tutor. However, experimental data about any aspect of such programs are scant.

Why and how does indirect instruction in prosocial behavior lead to learning? First, as mentioned above, direct instruction may activate psychological reactance (Brehm, 1966), an opposition to the curtailment or threat of curtailment of behavioral freedom. Morally relevant behaviors carry the implications "ought" and "ought not." When in the course of direct instruction, as in the case of verbal instruction, and even during induction and certain forms of modeling, a parent or teacher attempts to communicate the desirability of prosocial action, he automatically invokes cultural norms and standards that make such behavior obligatory, thus limiting perceived freedom and perhaps producing reactance. This is less likely to happen in the case of indirect instruction. Teaching others prosocial behavior or prosocial values, in contrast to being taught them, may enhance the acceptance by the teacher of the content of the material taught, or the values implied. Several attitude change experiments have shown that people who are asked to advocate a position are more likely to accept that position or to change their attitude in the direction of that position, than are people who hear someone else advocate the position or are exposed to it in other ways (Sears & Abeles, 1969). A teacher may simply get more involved with the material that he teaches, may think about it more, and may come to feel that what he or she teaches is part of him- or herself. In addition, being a teacher puts children into a position of importance. Teaching others may be regarded as a privilege, an indication of trust, and being a teacher may be regarded as a role of importance. Therefore, under appropriate conditions (when the activity is supervised by a warm and rewarding rather than a cold and punitive adult, when the material is not too difficult to learn and teach, and when the interaction with the child who is taught is positive) teaching others is likely to be a rewarding experience.

Because of this reinforcing and self-enhancing context, when children teach others prosocial behavior or values the content of what they teach may come to be accepted and valued by them. There is also another aspect to this, however. Usually, a person who is taught something benefits from what he learns. Teaching others may therefore be regarded as a form of prosocial behavior regardless of its content. Because both beneficial consequences to another person and the reinforcing experience to the teacher are inherent in teaching, through the association between them children may learn in the course of teaching others that benefiting others will be or can be reinforcing. Teaching others may thus enhance prosocial behavior even when the content of the teaching is not a prosocial behavior or prosocial value.

## THE RESEARCH

Three experiments have been conducted thus far to test the effects of indirect instruction, positive induction, and participation in responsible action on subsequent prosocial behavior. A further goal of this research has been to try to evaluate the usefulness of a variety of measures of prosocial behavior.

### Experiment 1

In the first experiment, the influence of children acting as teachers of other children was explored on several measures of prosocial behavior (Staub, Leavy, & Shortsleeves, 1975). This experiment was conducted with fifth- and sixth-grade girls as subjects, and has a 2 × 2 design. Some children were taught three first-aid skills (which we regarded as a prosocial activity) and then practiced these skills. The stated purpose of this was to enable them in the future to help people who needed help. Other children learned a presumably nonprosocial activity, making a puzzle, and then practiced that activity. The stated purpose was to enable children to make toys for themselves, because this might be enjoyable for them. These children were therefore instructed directly in learning either a prosocial or a nonprosocial activity. Following the instruction they spent 15 minutes practicing these skills. Two other groups of children were taught indirectly; they were asked to learn either first aid or puzzle making so that they could teach these skills to younger children. The instruction was couched in terms of how they were to teach the first-aid skills or puzzle making to the younger children. Children in these two groups then spent 15 minutes teaching these skills to a second- or third-grade girl. During the practice or teaching periods the experimenter was "doing her work" behind a room divider with a concealed one-way mirror on it and noted some characteristics of the interaction between "teacher" and "pupil."

Following the practice or teaching period (and after the younger child was sent back to the classroom) the subjects received five 10-cent gift certificates for their participation. After an intervening conversation with the experimenter they were told that they might want to donate some of their gift certificates to buy toys for poor children. The subjects could put their gift certificates into a box that was in the corridor outside the room on the way back to the classroom. Four days after this another experimenter came to the school, told the children that he worked at a local hospital, and asked them to help decide what toys to buy for children in the hospital by rating their preference for several different toys. Then he mentioned that children could do something for these children themselves and asked them to write down, on a sheet of paper, how many hours in the course of 1 week they would be willing to spend in visiting children in their homes who were previously hospitalized and were now convalescing. Finally, he said that there was something else that children could do right away; they could write letters to hospitalized children. He gave each child four envelopes and stationery, and a list with the first names of children and the reason for their hospitalization. The subjects were told that they could put the letters into a box, which was left in their classroom, and that the letters would be picked up in 3 days.

The analysis of the data showed that the treatments did not affect the number of gift certificates that children donated. The treatments had complex effects on the number of hours that children said they were willing to visit convalescing

### TABLE 1
#### Average Number of Letters Written
#### by Subjects

|              | Teaching | Not teaching |
|--------------|----------|--------------|
| First aid    | .89      | .37          |
| Puzzle making| 2.12     | .12          |

children, with a highly significant three-way interaction between whether they taught or not, what the content of their activity was, and which experimenter directed their training session. I would like to focus here on the effect of treatments on the number of letters that children wrote to hospitalized children. There were several significant effects here, and this measure of prosocial behavior is, in my opinion, a meaningful and promising one.

Children who taught other children wrote substantially more letters to hospitalized children than children who did not teach ($p < .01$; $\bar{X}$ teachers = 1.5; $\bar{X}$ nonteachers = .31, Table 1). There was also a marginally significant interaction between teaching and the content of the activity, first aid versus puzzle making ($p < .07$). Contrary to the original expectations, children who taught younger children to make a puzzle wrote more letters than those who taught them first-aid skills ($t = 2.16$; $df = 23$, $p < .05$; $\bar{X} = 2.12$ versus .89) with no difference among children who did not teach ($t < 1$). Finally, children who participated under the guidance of one of the experimenters wrote significantly more letters than those who participated under the guidance of the other one ($p < .04$). These are referred to as more effective (ME) and less effective (LE) experimenters.

There were several additional interesting findings. The experimenters' ratings of the teachers' responsiveness to the younger child was significantly positively related to the number of letters that teachers wrote ($r = .68$, $p < .05$) but negatively related to the number of gift certificates they donated ($r = -.52$, $p < .10$). "Responsiveness" in teaching refers to such things as proceeding at a speed that the younger child could follow, responding to questions, and considering the younger child's feelings. Responsiveness by the teacher was also related to responsiveness by the child she taught ($r = .55$, $p < .10$). The experimenter effect on letter writing appeared, in part, to be mediated by the effect of the experimenter on the responsiveness of the teacher ($p < .10$), as well as on the responsiveness of the younger child to her teacher ($p < .03$). That is, both teachers and pupils who participated under the guidance of the ME experimenter were more responsive. Finally, donating gift certificates was unrelated to the other two measures, although the number of visiting hours and the number of letters children wrote were significantly related to each other ($r = .51$, $p < .01$).

The findings suggest that acting as teachers of others can increase prosocial behavior. Although I still consider it likely that teaching another child prosocial attitudes, values, and behavior is a means of learning them, the findings may be regarded as support for the view that teaching itself is a form of prosocial behavior regardless of its content, which, because it is inherently satisfying or rewarding to the teacher, leads to an increase in the subsequent probability that the teacher will engage in behavior that has beneficial consequences for others. One reason for this interpretation is that teaching significantly increased letter writing regardless of what children had taught. Another reason for this view is that the effect of teaching was greater when children had taught puzzle making rather than first aid. In retrospect, this may be explained by considering an unintended aspect of our procedure. In the puzzle-making condition the teachers have been told that the reason to teach the younger child to make puzzles is to enable her to make toys for herself, which may be enjoyable to do. Therefore, the teachers in this condition may have felt that their teaching has direct benefits, that it enhances the younger child's wellbeing. In contrast, teachers in the first-aid condition probably did not feel that they produced direct benefits, as they have benefited not the younger child, but the individuals whom the younger child may help at a later date. Therefore, in the puzzle-making group the satisfaction children may have experienced from their role and activities as teachers was probably associated with the feeling that they have produced more direct, and perhaps greater, benefits.

The effect of experimenters and probably the effect of teaching on letter writing were both mediated to some degree by the child's responsiveness to the younger child. Presumably, the children who were more responsive had a generally more positive, satisfying experience in teaching and thus learned more from it. The difference in the effect of the experimenters on children's responsiveness to each other, and on the number of letters that teachers wrote to hospitalized children, is important. It again emphasizes what we already know, that the manner in which a socializing agent relates to a child is of great importance. Although it is reasonable to speculate that the experimenters probably differed in warmth and nurturance, and perhaps in their own responsiveness to children, none of the data in the present research specifies the dimension on which the experimenters differed.

## Experiment 2

Another experiment (Staub & Fotta, 1975) was designed to explore the effect on prosocial behavior of induction combined with participation in responsible action, and the hypothesis that the combination of the two is necessary for induction to have an effect.

Fifth- and sixth-grade boys and girls participated in small groups in four 40-minute-long experimental sessions. In one experimental group they spent this time making puzzles for hospitalized children (responsible action) with a minimal explanation of why this would be beneficial. In a second experimental group they also made puzzles for hospitalized children. In addition, in the first two experimental sessions the experimenter pointed out various positive consequences that the puzzles were likely to have, whereas in the last two sessions she reported on the apparent actual benefits they produced by describing the hospitalized children's reactions to the delivery of some of the puzzles to them, and by reading letters from hospitalized children in which they described the beneficial consequences of the puzzles on them (responsible action with induction). In a third experimental group the children heard stories and made drawings about the content of the stories (neutral action), ostensibly to help the experimenter find out how well children liked this sort of activity. Finally, in a fourth group children made drawings but were told about other children who were making puzzles for hospitalized children, and that they might have the opportunity to do so themselves in the future. Then the same induction statements were delivered to these children in each experimental session that were delivered to the subjects in the responsible action with induction group. This condition, in addition to completing the design, served the purpose of finding out the effect of the probably not too infrequent experience that children have of being told why it is good to do something, without the necessity or the opportunity to actually engage in the behavior in question.

The effect of these treatments was evaluated immediately after the last treatment session by giving children gift certificates and asking them to donate some of them for the purchase of toys for poor children. About a week later the children were asked to indicate how many puzzles they would be willing to make for hospitalized children and then were also told that they could write letters to hospitalized children. The method of administering the measure of intention and the test of letter writing was similar to that of the first experiment described above, with the exception that children in this experiment received only two (rather than four) envelopes and stationery, although they were told that they could write as many letters as they wanted to.

An analysis of variance showed that the statements had only a slight, complex effect on donating gift certificates; there was a marginally significant three-way interaction among prosocial action, induction, and sex ($p < .10$). An analysis of variance of the second behavioral measure, the number of letters that children wrote, produced several significant findings, including a significant sex effect ($p < .02$), with girls writing more letters; a significant Responsible Action × Induction interaction ($p < .02$); and a marginally significant three-way interaction ($p < .10$). Table 2 shows the cell means.

It is clear from this table that the significant effects are almost exclusively the result of the larger number of letters that girls wrote in the responsible

TABLE 2
Average Number of Letters Written
by Each Subject[a]

| Sex | Treatment | Induction | No induction |
|-----|-----------|-----------|--------------|
| Girls | Neutral | .25 (12) | .45 (11) |
| Girls | Responsible | 1.45 (11) | .17 (12) |
| Boys | Neutral | .18 (11) | .40 (10) |
| Boys | Responsible | .08 (12) | .00 (12) |

[a]Sex, $F = 4.89$, $df = 1/83$, $p < .02$; induction (I) × responsible activity (RA), $F = 5.70$, $df = 1/85$, $p < .02$; I × RA × Sex, $F = 2.60$, $df = 1/83$, $p < .10$.

action with induction group than the subjects in the other treatment groups. On this measure we found what we expected, but only with girls. The combination of making puzzles for hospitalized children and having the consequences of this behavior pointed out to them enhanced girls' prosocial behavior.

Finally, analyses of variance of the intention data showed a significant three-way interaction effect on the number of puzzles that children intended to make ($p < .01$). The combined treatments increased girls' prosocial intentions, the number of puzzles they volunteered to make, in comparison to the other three treatments. In contrast, both responsible action and induction increased, by themselves, the number of puzzles that boys volunteered to make, in comparison to the control treatment, although their combination had only slightly elevated the mean number of intended puzzles.

The findings supported the hypothesis that the combination of engaging in a prosocial behavior and having the beneficial consequences of it pointed out to children would enhance subsequent prosocial behavior. This combination increased girls' prosocial behavior on two of the measures, writing letters to hospitalized children and expressing the intention to make puzzles for them. However, the treatments had only relatively minor effects on boys, increasing their prosocial intentions.

Several speculations can be advanced for this sex difference. First, past research findings suggest that girls are more responsive than boys to verbal communications about the desirability of certain attitudes (Hovland & Janis, 1959) or behavior (Staub, 1972). Second, boys may have been more sensitive to the pressure toward prosocial action inherent in the combined responsible action–induction procedure, reacting to this pressure with opposition. Unfortunately, very little is known about the characteristics of experimental treatments that make them too forceful for certain groups of subjects (Staub, 1972) and this interpretation remains speculative. Finally, the nature of the dependent measures probably contributed to the sex difference: for example, writing letters is probably a more congenial activity for 5th and 6th grade girls. Past research has mainly explored children's willingness to share, or children's responses to other children's physical distress, with very little research on other forms of helpful activities. At least in some areas of such activities girls may have less resistance to helping than boys and may therefore be more responsive to procedures that attempt to induce helping. Finally, the possibility that the difference has in part been caused by both girls and boys having participated in the experimental sessions under the guidance of female experimenters cannot be ignored. Some of these issues are further discussed in a later section.

A final point of importance is the lack of treatment effects, both in this and in the previous study, on children donating gift certificates for other children. As the treatments in both experiments affected letter writing to hospitalized children at least a week following the last experimental session, why did they not affect the willingness to donate gift certificates immediately after the children experienced the treatments? The findings from a series of experiments conducted in the last few years suggested a possible explanation (Staub, 1973). They showed that children who earned rewards through their own activities and, as a result, presumably felt that they deserved them, were less likely to share these rewards than children who received rewards without having earned them.

In one study, for example, children played a bowling game in which the scores were prearranged. All children "did well" on the game; they then either received candy because they earned it by their good performance, or they were given candy unrelated to their performance, "so that they could enjoy themselves during the next activity." In both groups children were told that they could eat their candy while listening to a taperecorded story, which was the next activity. Then another child was brought to the room and listened to the story together with the first one. The children who believed that they earned the candy shared less than those for whom getting candy was unrelated to performance on the bowling game.[1]

The children in the present study received gift certificates for their participation in and help with the project. They had good reason to believe that they earned and deserved the rewards, which might have decreased their willingness to part with them, particularly immediately after their participation, when the feeling that they deserved the rewards might have been most acute. Giving subjects the gift certificates for their participation at a later time, when this feeling of deserving might no longer be as acute, and then asking for a donation, might allow greater variation in sharing behavior, and demonstrate the effects of treatments. This was done in the next experiment.

## Experiment 3

In this experiment, the effects of both teaching other children and of the use of inductive statements on children's subsequent prosocial behavior were explored (Staub & Jancaterino, unpublished research, 1975). In exploring the effects of teaching, we intended to make several improvements. In the first experiment, the content of instruction varied in different experimental groups; in the present one the content was the same, puzzle making, but the reason for making the puzzle was varied. In one of the direct instruction (no teaching) groups children learned to make a puzzle so that they could make one for

---

[1]In this experiment, which consisted of several parts, there was also a second experimental manipulation. On the way to the experimental room, the second child, the "receiver," was either told that the other child had candy that he earned by doing very well on a bowling game, or that the other child had candy that he received for the two of them, so that they could enjoy themselves by eating the candy while listening to the taperecorded story. This manipulation of deserving also had significant effect: Receivers who believed that the candy was for the two of them got significantly more candy than those who believed that the other child earned the candy. The exchange of candy involved varied "transactions" between children, including offers by givers, requests by receivers, refusals of both requests and offers, and even receivers taking candy from the bowl that was at the side of the giver (Staub, 1973).

hospitalized children and then continued to work on the puzzle for a while (prosocial group). In another group children learned to make a puzzle for hospitalized children but were also given a list of induction statements to read and rehearse that pointed out the benefits that making puzzles for hospitalized children was likely to produce (prosocial-induction group). They were told that knowing the consequences of their behavior was likely to make it more enjoyable for children to help others. Then they spent some time working on the puzzle.[2] In a third group (not prosocial) children learned to make a puzzle, because, they were told, "it might be enjoyable for children to know how to make toys for themselves," and then spent some time working on the puzzle. In one of the teaching groups children learned to make a puzzle so that they could teach younger children to make puzzles for hospitalized children. Then they taught a younger child how to make the puzzle. In a second teaching group they did the same as in the first one, but also received and rehearsed the list of induction statements, to be used while teaching the younger child. They were told that knowing the consequences of their behavior would make it more enjoyable for the younger children to help hospitalized children, and that they would be more likely to help. In a third group the children taught the younger child how to make a puzzle because "it might be enjoyable for children to learn how to make their own toys." With subjects varying in sex, we had a $2 \times 3 \times 2$ design (teaching–not teaching; prosocial activity–nonprosocial activity with induction–not prosocial activity; and sex).

Following the treatment sessions, subjects' willingness to donate gift certificates was first tested. They either received the gift certificates 1 or 2 days after the treatment or several days afterwards, generally after 5–6 days, and then were asked to donate some of the gift certificates for a group of needy children.

Eleven days after the test of gift certificates children were administered the next posttest, the envelopes test. Each subject received two large manila envelopes and was told that he or she might want to fill the envelopes with picture stories and poems, cut out of magazines or copied from magazines and books, and other items. The children were told that these envelopes would be given to children who do not have families (orphans) and have few attractive objects or toys of their own. Finally, 2 weeks after the envelopes test, the subjects were administered the puzzle test. They received three large envelopes containing unmade puzzles of the same kind that they had previously worked on. When they received the puzzles, they were asked how many of these puzzles they thought they would make for hospitalized children (intentions measure). Then the puzzles that they actually made were collected in 3 days.

[2]This group primarily served as a control for the teaching–prosocial-induction group described below. In that group teachers read and rehearsed induction statements so that they could use them in teaching other children. Although reading and rehearsing induction statements to make the task more enjoyable might have appeared contrived to the children, we wanted to equate degree of familiarity with the induction statements, because that might have been an important determinant of whether children later used them or not, and what effect they would have.

Scores for both the envelopes test and the puzzles test were derived from the ratings of two independent raters of how much work the material that the children handed in represented, and in the case of the envelopes test, how much material sacrifice it involved. Agreement between the raters was over 90% in both cases.

Analyses of variance showed a significant effect of teaching on donating gift certificates ($p < .05$). Children who taught other children donated more gift certificates, regardless of what they taught. There was a highly significant sex effect ($p < .001$); girls donated more. The timing of the test of donation was varied, to explore the possibility that children who receive gift certificates later, when the feeling of deserving might be less acute, would share more. Correlations computed within each treatment group between the number of days that the donation test followed the treatment and the number of gift certificates that children donated showed that in the three nonteaching groups and in one of the teaching groups (prosocial–no induction) the relationship was negligible. However, in the other two teaching groups the longer the delay after the treatment session, the more gift certificates children donated (teaching–prosocial induction, $r = .37$, $df = 19$, $p < .10$; teaching–not prosocial, $r = .70$, $df = 19$, $p < .01$). This might be interpreted as support for the hypothesis that the treatments (e.g., teaching) enhanced children's donations when their feeling that the gift certificates were earned and deserved was less acute.

The other measures of helping were affected by treatments only in interaction with sex or children's "Quad" membership. "Quad" refers to the children's classroom; all subjects came from one of two open classrooms, with about 100 children in each. On all measures, girls helped more than boys, marginally significantly more on the envelopes test ($p < .10$) and substantially more on the intention to make puzzles ($p < .001$) and on the puzzles test ($p < .002$). In addition, on both the envelope ($p < .01$) and puzzle ($p < .01$) tests children who came from Quad 1 helped significantly more than children who came from Quad 2.

The treatments did not affect children's envelope scores. On the intention to make puzzles, there was a significant Teaching × Sex interaction ($p < .05$) and a significant Prosocial Treatment × Sex ($p < .05$) interaction. Girls were unaffected by either treatments, whereas boys who taught intended to make more puzzles than boys who did not teach ($\bar{X} = 3.42$ versus 2.07) and boys who were in the not-prosocial group intended to make fewer puzzles than boys in the prosocial–induction and prosocial groups. Finally, the analysis of variance of the puzzles scores showed a significant Prosocial Treatment by Quad membership interaction ($p < .05$). The pattern of means showed that in Quad 1 the prosocial treatment enhanced most strongly the amount that children worked on the puzzles for hospitalized children, while in Quad 2 the prosocial–induction treatment did so. One of the two treatment groups did elevate helping behavior in each Quad in comparison to the non-prosocial group.

Altogether, teaching enhanced the donation of gift certificates (particularly by children who received the gift certificates and were asked to donate not immediately after the treatment session but after some delay), and also enhanced boys' intentions to make puzzles. Both giving children a prosocial reason for making the puzzles and a prosocial reason (i.e., prosocial activity) combined with induction had some effect on subsequent behavior.

The extent to which the children's sex and the classroom that they came from affected prosocial behavior on all the measures was impressive. The sex effect was stronger than in most of our prior research. In this experiment we deviated from our previous practice of using experimenters of one sex, usually females, with all subjects. Instead, female experimenters conducted the treatment session with girls, and male experimenters conducted them with boys. Therefore the sex difference might, in part, be caused by the influence of the sex of the experimenter, which covaried with the sex of the subject. The finding of significant experimenter effects in the first experiment reported above, and the fact that additional analyses in this experiment showed that helping behavior varied not only according to the sex of the experimenter but to some extent as a function of which of the two male or two female experimenters conducted the session (although there were no Experimenter × Treatment interaction effects), combined with other researchers' findings about experimenter effects, strongly suggests the need for parametric research in this area. More must be learned about the differences in the effects of male experimenters (and/or socializing agents) with boys and girls, as well as differences in the effects of experimenters as a function of differences in the manner of their interaction with children. It is known that experimenter warmth or nurturance can have important effects on the subjects' later behavior, but it is not known exactly what the important components of warmth and nurturance are, nor is much known about the differential effects of the behavior of experimenters along other dimensions.

The difference in behavior related to Quad membership points to another important issue. The atmosphere established in a classroom, whether it is primarily cooperative or competitive, whether it is more or less friendly, and so on, can have important effects on the behavior of children independently of the socioeconomic and cultural composition of classrooms. In addition, the attitude on the part of teachers toward the children's participation in a project can have important effects. I believe that at least part of the reason for the Quad differences was a difference in teachers' attitudes. As the experiment progressed, we encountered difficulties in securing the continued cooperation of the teachers. These difficulties appeared mainly in Quad 2. The results might very well reflect the attitude that these teachers communicated to the children. It was also interesting that on our first measure, the donation of gift certificates, there was no significant Quad effect. On the other measures, which came later in time, after these conflicts became apparent, there were significant Quad effects.

A related issue to that of the influence of teachers is how our subjects perceive what we do, what they tell each other about it, and what meaning a project acquires and what attitude develops toward it. The shared evaluation of a project that probably inevitably develops may be as powerful a determinant of the children's behavior in it as anything specific that we do. It is important to learn about such shared evaluation among children, but it is difficult to do so. We administered to the subjects in this last experiment an elaborate, as yet unanalyzed, questionnaire about their beliefs and attitudes toward our project, but I am not too hopeful about the "yield." Our young subjects tended to be nice to us and to tell us what they thought we would like to hear, or what they thought would not get them into trouble, in explaining the reasons for their behavior. We also interviewed a group of subjects after the experiment, and perhaps the interview will provide some useful information about their thoughts. Can we develop a reasonable methodology to learn about the information that is exchanged in the "child culture," about the beliefs and attitudes of children?

## GENERAL DISCUSSION
## AND ISSUES IN PROSOCIAL DEVELOPMENT

Teaching others, induction, and participation in prosocial behavior all had effects on some form of later prosocial behavior, if not by themselves then in combination with each other. Teaching others enhanced the number of letters that girls wrote to hospitalized children in one experiment, and the number of gift certificates that children donated to needy children in another experiment; it also increased boys' intentions to make puzzles for hospitalized children. Induction in combination with participation in prosocial behavior substantially increased the number of letters that girls wrote to hospitalized children. By itself it increased, in two experiments, boys' expressed intention to make puzzles for hospitalized children. It also enhanced, in combination with prosocial behavior, the amount that subjects from one Quad (but not from another) worked in making puzzles for hospitalized children. Finally, participation in prosocial behavior, making puzzles during four 40-minute periods, affected subsequent prosocial behavior primarily in combination with induction; by itself, it only enhanced boys' intention to make puzzles for hospitalized children.

It may be useful to stress the distinction between studying influences on the on-going behavior of children, their prosocial behavior in specific settings, and attempting to bring about durable and generalized increases in their prosocial behavior. In an extensive series of experiments exploring influences on the reaction of children and adults to sounds of distress from the adjoining room,

we found that a variety of social-situational influences and personality characteristics had significant and often substantial effects on helping. The number of
other children present and their age (Staub, 1970a); an adult focusing responsibility for action on a child (Staub, 1970b); implicit rules of appropriate
behavior that children apparently follow; and explicit rules of what behavior is
permissible and appropriate that an experimenter communicated to children and
adults all affected helping behavior in response to sounds of distress (Staub,
1971c; 1974). The behavior of another person in the same situation—what
this other person said, how he or she verbally defined the meaning of distress
cues, and what he or she did—and the nature of the physical situation, the
opportunity to escape from it without having to face the person in need or not
being able to do so (Staub, 1974), as well as personality characteristics of
adult subjects (Staub, 1974) also affected subsequent attempts to help a
distressed person in an adjoining room. Not surprisingly, exposure to a helping
model, and perhaps more surprisingly simply interaction with a nurturant adult,
increased this form of helping (Staub, 1971a).

In all these studies the influence of the experimental treatments on the
subjects' behavior in the same setting, shortly after or concurrent with the
treatment variation, was explored. This research provided extensive information about the determinants of behavior in specific instances. The treatment
procedures evoked norms, either prosocial or other kinds; they probably
strongly affected the perceived consequences to oneself for helping and not
helping; and they possibly activated empathy and internalized values or norms.
However, when the concern is with having children learn to be empathic, and
learn values and norms, and to internalize them so that at later times these
values and norms will be activated and affect their behavior, a problem of a
different kind, and probably of a different magnitude, arises.

A basic issue, raised in a different way in the theoretical discussion at the
beginning, is the conditions that must exist in order to produce learning that
enhances prosocial behavior and the degree to which it is possible to create
such conditions in experimental settings. I have suggested above, and have
discussed elsewhere (Staub, 1975), the need for parents to exercise control, so
that children actually behave in a manner consistent with parental demands.
Another way this has been stated is that participation in prosocial behavior of
sufficient intensity and duration may itself enhance later prosocial behavior,
and that induction or verbalization to children may only be effective when it
accompanies "doing." Some support for the latter part of this statement has
been found with girls. Only when circumstances lead children to apply
induction to themselves and associate it with their own behavior is induction
likely to lead to learning to behave prosocially.

The conditions of the usual psychological experiment, in which an experimenter administers some "treatment" for a brief period of time, may primarily
lead to an awareness of what is the desirable or expected behavior in that
setting, leading to the expectancy that social and material rewards, or social

and material punishments, are a function of certain types of behavior. Because of the brevity and specificity of training, only limited temporal duration of the treatment effects, and limited generalization can be expected. The more aspects of the situation are changed, such as the setting, the type of help demanded, the person who is in charge, and so on, the less likely is it that the specific learning produced will manifest itself. A "good" experiment, therefore, in which different experimenters are used in training and testing, decreases the probability of enduring and generalized effects.

The situation is different with parents, teachers, and other agents of socialization, with whom the child has a long-lasting relationship. They can guide the child's behavior according to certain principles that are applied across a number of different types of behavior, so that the child may be induced, with consistent application of principles and consistent discipline, to apply the principle to a relatively wide range of activity. Therefore, the likelihood that he or she learns the principle (for example, concern with others welfare) and that he or she comes to guide his or her own behavior according to the principle may be much greater.

The statements that I am making can obviously have only relative validity. In the experiments that I described we have found, and in other research other experimenters have found, durable and sometimes generalized effects of treatments. In terms of the likelihood that durable and generalized learning can be found from the treatment procedures, however, these statements have validity. It is also the case, of course, that parents are often inconsistent, that they often reward and punish behavior not according to its consistency with a principle, value, or norm but according to the convenience or inconvenience of the child's behavior to themselves. Also, the manner in which parents enforce behavior, if they do, can be such that it does not lead to self-guidance by the child. What I am arguing is the necessity for a period of supervision of the child's behavior, a period of application of certain practices, before learning in the form of self-guidance, self-reinforcement, and self-punishment, empathic reactions, and tendencies to interpret events in certain ways rather than others will ensue.

In addition to the nature of the training or learning conditions, the nature of our measures of learning, their meaning to children, and their relationship to each other need further clarification. Almost exclusively past research on prosocial behavior has used two kinds of dependent measures: giving up material objects (usually received by children just beforehand as rewards, and thus involving the issue of "deserving" that was raised before) for persons who are normally not present, and helping a presumably physically distressed person. We have also conducted some experiments in which sharing behavior in the course of interaction with another person has been explored (Staub & Sherk, 1970; Staub, 1973). Although there are many indications that children and adults consider it important to help a physically distressed person, the meaning to children of other forms of helping behavior and their probably varying attitudes toward different types of prosocial behavior are not well established.

First, the degree to which an activity appears interesting or boring, worthwhile or trivial, may vary. If the activity is generally viewed by children as trivial (if it is inappropriate for their age, they regard it as childish and it is therefore discrepant with their self-concept to engage in such an activity), the frequency of the behavior may be low and the behavior therefore insensitive in showing treatment effects. The frequency of filling envelopes with desirable objects has been low in this study perhaps because children do not value this activity. In addition, however, the children's feeling toward and desire to help others with different characteristics and having different types and degrees of needs may greatly vary (e.g., hospitalized children, who presumably could be very similar to themselves and have one kind of need, versus "needy," poor children, who may be quite dissimilar and/or have a different kind of need). Parametric studies of base-rates of different types of prosocial behavior at different ages (Green & Schneider, 1974) are important. Studies exploring what children think and feel about helping in general, helping others with different types of needs and different characteristics, and helping in different ways, and the relationship of children's thoughts to their actions will also be extremely useful. They will enable researchers to improve tests of prosocial behavior (to select measures appropriate for their purposes), to improve tests of generalizations (select measures that are related to each other on meaningful dimensions), and to both better predict and better understand children's prosocial behavior. Some of the information gained from the studies described in this chapter may lend itself for these purposes.

There are several implications of the above discussion for further research. For example, in attempts to enhance prosocial behavior, relatively long-term treatment procedures may be desirable, such as a period of time during which children's acts and reasons for the behavior are associated, a period of time during which children are induced to follow the behavior of a model (White, 1972), and involvement in teaching others on repeated occasions rather than on a single occasion.

With regard to the use of reasoning to promote prosocial behavior, two strategies may contribute to learning; we are planning to explore in our research whether they do so or not. The first is involvement of children in elaborating the reasons for helping others, in thinking about and stating the positive consequences of action, in contrast to having reasons provided by the experimenter. The second is the use of verbalizations that will structure the meaning of a need so that its importance is apparent to children. Children often hear normative statements by adults about the desirability of helping, and possibly positive induction statements, used in a casual manner. The elaboration on the meaning of being an orphan, or being poor, or being hospitalized and the description of the condition of the child who is to be helped and of his feelings may be necessary before the elaboration of the positive consequences of helping behavior. It is possible that such verbal influences can be particularly effective if they provide children with a new perspective, so that they have an aspect of novelty and therefore interestingness.

I have stressed in this discussion the procedures and conditions that lead to learning and appropriate measures to evaluate the effect. We also need to concern ourselves, of course, with the principles by which learning takes place (Staub, 1975), as well as what it is that is learned, whether it is specific prosocial acts, the expectation of rewards for prosocial behavior, internalized values and role taking, or the tendency to react empathically to others' needs. Finally, the relationship between such products of learning and the conditions under which they lead to prosocial behavior (Staub, 1974), an issue that I briefly considered at the beginning of the introduction, must be the subject of continuing analysis.

## ACKNOWLEDGMENTS

The research reported here and the preparation of the manuscript were facilitated by National Institutes of Health Grant, MH 23886. This contribution was prepared while the author was a Visiting Professor in the Department of Psychology, Stanford University.

I am grateful to the administrators, teachers and students of the Amherst, Mass. schools, who by their kind cooperation made this research possible. I am particularly grateful to the principals of the schools where this research was conducted, Mr. Michael Greenebaum, Mr. John Dalton and Ms. Nancy Morrison, and to the Superintendant of the Amherst schools, Mr. Ronald Frizzle.

## REFERENCES

Arnold, M. *Emotion and personality*. New York: Columbia University Press, 1960.
Aronfreed, J. *Conduct and conscience*. New York: Academic Press, 1968.
Bandura, A. *Social learning theory*. New York: General Learning Press, 1971.
Brehm, J. W. *A theory of psychological reactance*. New York: Academic Press, 1966.
Festinger, L., & Freedman, J. L. Dissonance reduction and moral values. In P. Worchel & D. Byrne (Eds.), *Personality change*. New York: Wiley, 1964.
Green, F. P., & Schneider, F. W. Age differences in the behavior of boys on three measures of altruism. *Child Development*, 1974, **45**(1), 133.
Hartup, W. W. Peer interaction and social organization. In Mussen, P. N. (Ed.), *Carmichael's manual of child psychology*, New York: Wiley, 1970.
Hoffman, M. L. Parent discipline and the child's consideration for others. *Child Development*, 1963, **34**, 573–588.
Hoffman, M. L. Moral development. In Mussen, P. H. (Ed.), *Carmichael's manual of child development*. New York: Wiley, 1970.
Hoffman, M. L., & Saltzstein, H. D. Parent discipline and the child's moral development. *Journal of Personality & Social Psychology*, 1967, **5**, 45–47.
Hovland, C. L., & Janis, I. J. *Personality and persuasability*. New Haven: Yale University Press, 1959.
Kohlberg, L. Stage and sequence: The cognitive-developmental approach to socialization. In Goslin, (Ed.), *Handbook of socialization theory and research*. Chicago: Rand-McNally, 1969.
Lazarus, R. S., Averill, J. R. & Option, E. M., Jr. Towards a cognitive theory of emotion. In M. Arnold, (Ed.), *Feelings and emotions*. New York: Academic Press, 1969.
Lippitt, P. Children teach other children. *Instructor*, 1969, **78**, 41–42.
Lippitt, R. Improving the socialization process. In Clausen (Ed.), *Socialization and society*. Boston: Little, Brown, 1968.
Maccoby, E. E. The development of moral values and behavior in childhood. In Clausen (Ed.), *Socialization and society*. Boston: Little, Brown, 1968.

Mowrer, O. H. *Learning theory and personality dynamics*. New York: Ronald, 1950.

Schachter, S., & Singer, J. E. Cognitive, social and physiological determinants of emotional state. *Psychological Review*, 1962, **69**, 379–399.

Schwartz, S. H. Moral decision making and behavior. In Macauley & Berkowitz, (Eds.), *Altruism and helping behavior*. New York: Academic Press, 1970.

Schwartz, S. H., Feldman, K. A., Brown, M. E., & Heingartner, A. Some personality correlates of conduct in two situations of moral conflict. *Journal of Personality*, 1969, **37**, 41–57.

Sears, D. O., & Abeles, R. P. Attitudes and opinions. In D. H. Mussen & M. H. Rosenzweig (Eds.), *Annual review of psychology*. Palo Alto, California: Annual Reviews, 1969.

Sears, R. R., Maccoby, E. E., & Levin, H. *Patterns of child rearing*, New York: Harper, 1957.

Staub, E. A child in distress: The effects of focussing responsibility on children on their attempts to help. *Developmental Psychology*, 1970, **2**, 152–154.   (a)

Staub, E. A child in distress: the influences of age and number of witnesses on children's attempts to help. *Journal of Personality & Social Psychology*, 1970, **14**, 130–140.   (b)

Staub. E. A child in distress: The influence of modeling and nurturance on children's attempts to help. *Developmental Psychology*, 1971, **5**, 124–133.   (a)

Staub, E. The use of role playing and induction in children's learning of helping and sharing behavior. *Child Development*, 1971, **42**, 805–817.   (b)

Staub, E. Helping a person in distress: the influence of implicit and explicit "rules" on conduct on children and adults. *Journal of Personality & Social Psychology*, 1971c, **17**, 137–145. (c)

Staub, E. Instigation to goodness: The role of social norms and interpersonal influence. *Journal of Social Issues*, 1972, **28**, 131–151.

Staub, E. Children's sharing behavior: Success and failure, the norm of deserving and reciprocity. Paper presented at the symposium: "Helping and Sharing: Concepts of Altruism and Cooperation" at the meeting of the Society of Research in Child Development, Philadelphia, March 1973.

Staub, E. Helping a distressed person: Social, personality, and stimulus determinants. In L. Berkowitz (Ed.), *Advances in experimental social psychology*, Vol. 7. New York: Academic Press, 1974.

Staub, E. *The development of prosocial behavior in children*. New York: General Learning Press, 1975.

Staub, E., & Fotta, M. Participation in prosocial behavior and positive induction as means of children learning to be helpful. Unpublished manuscript, University of Massachusetts, Amherst, 1975.

Staub, E., & Jancaterino, W. Teaching others, participation in prosocial action and prosocial induction as means of children learning to be helpful. Unpublished research, University of Massachusetts, Amherst, 1975.

Staub, E., Leavy, R., & Shortsleeves, J. Teaching other children as a means of learning to be helpful. Unpublished manuscript, University of Massachusetts, Amherst, 1975.

Staub, E., & Sherk, L. Need for approval, children's sharing behavior and reciprocity in sharing. *Child Development*, 1970, **41**, 243–252.

Thelen, H. A. Tutoring by students. *School Review*, 1969, **77**, 229–244.

White, G. M. Immediate and deferred effects of model observation and guided and unguided rehearsal on donating and stealing. *Journal of Personality & Social Psychology*, 1972, **21**, 139–148.

White, R. W. Motivation reconsidered: The concept of competence. *Psychological Review*, 1959, **66**, 297–333.

Whiting, J. M. W., & Whiting, B. The behavior of children in six cultures. Unpublished manuscript, Harvard University, Cambridge, Massachusetts, 1969.

Yarrow, M. R., Scott, P. M., & Waxler, C. Z. Learning concern for others. *Developmental Psychology*, 1973, **8**, 240–261.

# 7
# The Development of Altruistic Motivation

Martin L. Hoffman
*University of Michigan*

After decades of neglect, research on altruism has suddenly burgeoned. The magnitude of the research effort is indicated by the appearance of four reviews in the past four years. The definition of ''altruism'' implicitly accepted by the researchers includes any purposive act on behalf of someone else that involves a net cost to the actor; the types of altruism studied include helping another in distress and sharing or making a donation to someone in need. The main focus has been on factors in the situation or in the person that momentarily govern the altruistic response. The research on children has been concerned mainly with age differences and creating various types of altruistic behavior in the laboratory, although there have also been several investigations of the contribution of child-rearing practices to the child's altruism.

The development of theory has not kept pace with the proliferation of empirical studies. The doctrinaire view in Western psychology continues to be one in which the human being is an essentially selfish animal. What appears to be altruism, according to this view, can always be explained ultimately in terms of the actor's self-serving egoistic needs. It seems just as reasonable to suppose, however, that in the course of human evolution there must have been selection for altruistic as well as selfish predispositions, because from the beginning group life has been necessary for survival. This is not to deny that helping another may often be egoistically motivated, nor that such essentially irrelevant personality characteristics as courage and independence may often play an important contributing role. The purpose of this chapter is to suggest, however, that humans may have a built-in predisposition for purely altruistic behavior, however fragile it may appear to be in the individualistic societies of the Western world, and to propose a theory to account for the development of such a motive in the individual.

The central idea of the theory is that empathy, or more specifically an empathic response to another person's distress, interacting with the observer's cognitive sense of the other, may provide the underlying basis for an altruistic motive—or at least for a component of altruistic motivation—that is independent of egoistic, self-serving motivation.

I shall now present a theoretical account of the development of this altruistic motivational component. In this account, the attempt is made to pull together what is known about the individual's affective response to another person's distress, on the one hand, and cognitive development and role taking, on the other.

"Empathy" refers to the involuntary, at times forceful experiencing of another person's emotional state. It is elicited either by expressive cues that directly reflect the other's feelings or by other kinds of cues that convey the affective impact of external events on him.

The various explanations for empathic distress boil down to two basic classical conditioning paradigms. One paradigm views empathy as developing early in infancy, with the bodily transfer of tension from the caretaker to the child. For example, when the mother experiences distress her body may stiffen with the result that the child (if he is being handled at that time) also experiences distress. Subsequently, the mother's facial and verbal expressions that initially accompanied her distress can serve as conditioned stimuli that evoke the distress response in the child. Furthermore, through stimulus generalization, similar expressions by other persons become capable of evoking distress in the child.

A second paradigm holds that the unpleasant affect accompanying one's own painful past experience is evoked by distress cues from another person that resemble the stimuli associated with the observer's experiences. A simple example is the child who cuts himself, feels the pain, and cries. Later on, he sees another child cut himself and cry. The sight of the blood, the sound of the cry, or any other distress cue from the other child associated with the observer's own prior experience of pain can now elicit the unpleasant affect that was initially a part of that experience.

In both paradigms the observer's empathic distress is attributed to the similarity between distress cues from another person and stimuli associated with his own actual distress experiences in the past. The process involved in the second paradigm is more important for our purposes, however. Because this process is neither confined to early infancy nor limited to distress originating in physically communicated tensions, it opens up the possibility of a multiplicity of distress experiences with which the child can empathize.

The possible contribution of empathy to altruism has long been noted in the literature. As early as 1924 Wilhelm Stern suggests that empathy contributes to such acts as attempting to comfort, help, or avenge a distressed person. Since then, a host of other writers, including Susan Isaacs, Anna Freud, Justin Aronfreed, and I, have stressed the connection between empathy and altruism. These writers have typically stressed the affective and reinforcing properties of empathy, to the relative neglect of the cognitive. It seems reasonable to suppose, however, that because cognitive processes help determine how even the simplest emotion is experienced the same must be true for such a complex emotional experience as empathy. It is likely, for example, that the actor experiences not only the feelings but also some of the perceptions, thoughts, and wishes of the distressed person, as well as images of his own past distress and the actions of himself and others that helped relieve it (images that may serve as cues to what may be done to help the other in the immediate situation). These cognitions have obvious ramifications for altruistic motivation and action. More fundamentally, because empathy is a response to cues about the affective state of others, it must depend to a great extent on the actor's cognitive development, especially his development of a sense of the other. I will now discuss, at length, the development of a sense of the other, following which an attempt will be made to combine it with empathy, to account for the development of altruistic motives.

The development of a cognitive sense of the other may be viewed as occurring in three broad steps. First, there is awareness of the other's existence as a separate physical entity from the self. The young infant apparently lacks such awareness. Objects, events, and people are not experienced as distinct from the self. The infant, for example, makes no distinction between sounds that he has produced and sounds that are independent of him. It is not until 6–8 months of age, according to Piaget, that he begins to organize the fleeting images making up his world into discrete objects and to experience them as separate from his biologically determined sensations; and it is not until a year later that he can maintain an internal image of an object for an appreciable length of time.

The main evidence for this conclusion comes from studies of object displacement and the general finding that infants do not seek an object that has been invisibly displaced (e.g., first hidden visibly in a container that is, in turn, hidden behind a screen and then brought out empty after releasing the object in the hidden place) until approximately 18 months. At this later age the child can retrieve a toy after several successive invisible displacements, which indicates that he can then evoke the image of an object even when there is nothing in sight to attest to its existence. From this pattern of behavior, Piaget and others infer that it is not until about 18 months that the child shows the beginning of true object permanence, that is, the beginning of a stable sense of the separate existence of physical objects even when they are outside of his immediate perceptual field. Recent research by Sylvia Bell, however, suggests that infants may attain a sense of the separate existence of persons, as opposed to objects, 6 or 7 months earlier, that is, by about 11 or 12 months of age.

Having attained a sense of the separate existence of persons, however, the child still has a highly limited sense of the other. He is bound up in his own point of view, which he regards as absolute; the world exists as he perceives it. Although aware of the other's existence as a physical entity, he does not yet know that others have inner states of their own, and he tends to attribute to them characteristics that belong to him. According to Piaget, it is not until about 7 or 8 years of age that his egocentrism begins to give way to the recognition that others have their own perspective. The role-taking research by and large supports Piaget's view. Its emphasis, however, has been heavily cognitive, that is, its dominant focus has been on the cognitive aspects of the other person's perspective; and the tests used have typically put a premium on the cognitive and verbal skills of the subject. The problem with this is that requiring cognitive or verbal operations beyond the child's capacity may mask his actual role-taking capability. It follows that to estimate how early in life the child can take another's role requires evidence from studies employing measures that are minimally complex cognitively. The following are two anecdotal illustrations of what I mean.

One incident I observed involved a very young child. Marcy, aged 20 months, was in the playroom of her home and wanted a toy with which her sister Sara was playing. She asked Sara for it, but Sara refused vehemently. Marcy then paused, as if reflecting on what to do, and then began to rock on Sara's favorite rocking horse (which Sara never allowed anyone to touch), yelling "Nice horsey! Nice horsey!" and keeping her eyes on Sara all the time. Sara came running angrily, whereupon Marcy immediately ran around Sara' directly to the toy and grabbed it. Without analyzing the full complexity of Marcy's behavior, one can infer from her actions that she had deliberately set about luring her sister away from the toy. Although not yet 2 years of age, she was capable of being aware of another person's inner states that were different from her own. Although her behavior was self-serving rather than altruistic, this child demonstrated that she could take another's role; yet had she been a subject in a typical role-taking experiment it is doubtful that she could have understood the instructions, much less performed the designated role-taking response.

The second example was in some respects less dramatic and depicted a cognitively less demanding type of behavior, but the child was only 15 months old and the context was more germane to altruism. The boy, Michael, was struggling with his friend Paul over a toy. Paul started to cry. Michael appeared concerned and let go of the toy so that Paul would have it, but Paul kept on crying. Michael paused, then gave his teddy bear to Paul but the crying continued. Michael paused again, then ran to the next room, returned with Paul's security blanket and offered it to Paul—whereupon he stopped crying.

Several aspects of this incident deserve comment. First, it seems clear that Michael first assumes that his own teddy, which often comforts him, will also comfort his friend. Second, its failure to do this serves as corrective feedback that leads Michael to consider alternatives. Third, in considering the processes underlying Michael's final, successful act, three possibilities stand out: (a) he is simply imitating an effective instrumental act observed in the past, that is, he has observed Paul being comforted with the blanket; this can tentatively be ruled out because his parents cannot recall his ever having such an opportunity; (b) in trying to think of what to do he remembers seeing another child being soothed by a blanket, and this reminds him of Paul's blanket—a more complex response that at first appears, because Paul's blanket is out of his perceptual field at the time; (c) Michael, as young as he is, can somehow reason by analogy that Paul will be comforted by something that he loves in the same way that Michael loves his own teddy.

I favor the last, although it does involve a complex response for a young child to make. Regardless of which, if any, of the three interpretations is correct, however, the incident suggests that a child not yet a year and a half old may be able, with a very general form of corrective feedback (Paul's continuing to cry when offered Michael's teddy), to assess the specific needs of another person that differ from his own. This is a far cry from the 5 or 6 years suggested by the laboratory research—a discrepancy too large to be explained strictly in terms of Michael's precocity. It is unclear what the crucial factors are—Michael's intense motivation, his familiarity with the other child and the physical surroundings, or the corrective feedback, which, although minimal, has been sufficient to disconfirm his initial, more primitive interpretation of the other's needs. (Although feedback is not present in the previously described incident involving Marcy, Michael is a few months younger, and perhaps this is enough to make the difference between needing feedback and not needing it.) Further study may identify which, if any, of these factors—none of which has as yet been investigated systematically—is the more crucial in situations of this kind. In any case, it appears that just as "person permanence" may precede "object permanence" by several months, certain forms of role taking in familiar and highly motivating natural settings may precede the more complex forms investigated in the laboratory by several years. The child who can take the role of a familiar person at home may behave egocentrically in complex role-taking tasks in the laboratory because he cannot utilize the available cues regarding the inner states of others and must therefore rely on his own perspective. In other words, the rudiments of role-taking competence may be present before the child is 2 years old—not long after he has attained person permanence—although role-taking performance varies with the cognitive and verbal complexity of the particular task.

The third broad step in development of a sense of the other pertains to the view of the other as having his own personal identity, that is, his own life circumstances and inner states beyond the immediate situation. This has been largely ignored in the literature. The closest to it is Erik Erikson's conception of ego identity, which pertains to the individual's sense of sameness in himself through time. In support of Erikson's view, it seems reasonable to suppose that at some point the child develops the cognitive capacity to integrate his own discrete inner experiences over time and to form a conception of himself as having different feelings and thoughts in different situations but being the same continuous person with his own past, present, and anticipated future.

There is very little relevant research. Lawrence Kohlberg has suggested that during the preoperational period (2–7 years) the child not only lacks the concept of conservation with respect to physical attributes, such as mass, weight, and number, but also with regard to qualitative attributes. Most 4-year-old children, for example, will agree that a cat can be a dog if it wants to or if its whiskers are cut off. By 6 or 7, however, children are firm in asserting that a cat cannot change its identity in spite of apparent perceptual changes. Kohlberg has also asked 4–8-year-old children if a pictured girl can be a boy if she wants to, if she plays boys' games, or if she wears boys' haircuts or clothes. He has found that "by age 6 or 7, most children were quite certain that a girl could not be a boy regardless of changes in appearance or behavior," in contrast to younger children, who are often thrown off by physical appearances and think that girls can change to boys in these ways. This finding suggests that the child has a sense of stabilization and continuity regarding gender by about 6 or 7 years of age.

The findings on racial identity are similar. Harold Proshansky, after reviewing the research literature, concludes that a firm sense of one's racial identity does not appear to be established until about 7 or 8 years of age. Although the 4- or 5-year-old child may often use racial terms to describe himself and others and show a preference for one race over another, Proshansky concludes from the research that the child's racial conception is more apparent than real, more a reflection of verbal fluency than a stable attainment of racial concepts.

Finally, Guardo and Bohan, in a developmental study of self-identity in middle-class white children, have found that 6- and 7-year-olds recognize their identity as humans and as males or females mainly in terms of their names, physical appearance, and behaviors—a finding that is consistent with the results for gender and racial identity. These children's sense of self-continuity from the past and into the future is still hazy, however. It is not until 8 or 9 years of age that more covert and personalized differences in feelings and attitudes make a contribution to their sense of identity, although even then most feel that their names, physical characteristics, and behaviors are the essential anchorage points of identity. Only one out of six thinks that the feeling of being a singular and personal individual is the main factor that provides for continuity across time.

It appears, then, that somewhere between 6 and 9 years marks the beginning of the child's conception of his or her own continuing identity. This emerging sense of one's own identity may be presumed to result, by early adolescence, in a broadening of one's view of others. That is, once the child has the cognitive capacity to see that his or her own life has coherence and continuity despite the fact that he or she reacts differently in different situations, he or she should soon be able to do the same with regard to others. The child can then not only take the role of others and assess their reactions in particular situations but also generalize from these interactions and construct a concept of the other's general life experience. In sum, the child's awareness that others are coordinate with self expands to include the notion that others, like self, have their own identity as persons that goes beyond the immediate situation. The child's perspective on others and his or her interpretation of their response in the immediate situation is thereby dramatically altered.

To summarize, I am suggesting three steps in the development of a cognitive sense of the other: (a) the sense of the other as a physical object; (b) the sense of the other as possessing inner states independent of the observer's; and (c) the sense of the other as having his own continuous identity as a person extending beyond the immediate situation. A theory of altruistic motivation is presented below that is essentially a developmental account of the synthesis of empathic distress and the cognitive sense of the other.

First, there is empathic distress alone. The neural capacity needed for a conditioned affective response such as this is minimal, because both classical and operant conditioning are known to be possible in the early weeks of life. It follows that the infant is capable of empathic distress long before he has developed a sense of self or a sense of the other. As a result of this lack of self–other differentiation, the child for at least most of the first year is presumably unclear as to who is experiencing any distress that he witnesses, and he often behaves as though he is experiencing it. That is, he sees the other's distress cues, and they automatically evoke an upset state in him. He may then seek comfort for his own distress.

This was recently illustrated by an 11-month-old child of a student of mine. On seeing another child fall and cry, she first stared at the victim, appearing as though she were about to cry herself, and then put her thumb in her mouth and buried her head in her mother's lap—her typical response after she had hurt herself and needed comforting.

This is obviously a very primitive response. The word "empathy" is used to describe it, but the child does not really put himself in the other's place and try to imagine what he is feeling. The response is rather a conditioned, passive, involuntary one—based on the "pull" of surface cues associated with elements of one's own past. If there is action, its dominant motivation is hedonistic: to eliminate discomfort in the self. Empathic distress is nevertheless basic in the early development of altruistic motivation precisely because it shows that a person may involuntarily and forcefully experience emotional states of others rather than simply the emotional states pertinent and appropriate to his or her own situation—that people are built in such a way that distress is often contingent not on a person's own but on someone else's painful experience.

A major change in the child's reaction to distress occurs when he or she begins to be capable of distinguishing between self and others. When confronted with another person in pain, he or she still experiences empathic distress, but because of this new cognitive capacity the child now knows that it is the other person and not the child who is in actual pain. The recognition that the other is actually experiencing the distress transforms the empathy with the victim—a parallel affective response—into sympathetic concern for the victim—a more reciprocal response.

Just how this transformation occurs is difficult to say. I suggest that initially the child continues to have global empathic distress reactions to another's pain but now his or her own unpleasant feelings, which are a part of that reaction, become fused with his or her rudimentary impression of the other person. Subsequently, with increasing self–other differentiation, the previously undifferentiated distress feeling and the desire for its termination become transferred to both the separate "self" and the separate "other" that emerge. That is, the properties of the whole become the properties of its emerging parts. As a consequence, the child's initial concern to relieve his or her own empathic distress becomes a sympathetic concern to relieve the distress of the other.

It also seems likely that the process of self–other differentiation is gradual and subject to occasional "regression," for example, when the child is fatigued or under tension. This means that in the early stages of differentiation he or she is only vaguely and momentarily aware of the other as distinct from the self. The child must therefore go through a period of responding to another's distress by feeling as though his or her dimly perceived self and the dimly perceived other are somehow simultaneously, or perhaps alternately, in distress. That is, the self and the other slip in and out of focus as the object whose distress he or she wishes to have terminated. Consider the child of a colleague of mine, whose typical response to his own distress, beginning late in his first year, was to suck his thumb with one hand and pull his ear with the other. At 13 months, on seeing a sad look on his father's face, he proceeded to look sad himself and to suck his thumb while pulling his father's ear!

An early period of subjectively overlapping concern such as this, in which the self and the other are experienced as "sharing" the distress, seems to provide a further basis for a positive orientation toward the emerging other. The gradual nature of self–other differentiation is important, therefore, because it gives the child the experience of simultaneously wanting to terminate the emerging other's distress as well as his own, providing a link between the initial hedonistic empathic distress response and the earliest trace of sympathetic distress. If the sense of the other were attained suddenly, the child would lack this experience; when he discovered that the pain is someone else's, he might simply react with relief (or even blame the other for his own empathic distress). All of this is not to deny that the child's response may continue to have a primitive, purely empathic component, or to deny that the child may also fear that the undesired event will happen to him. The important thing, however, is that the quasi-hedonistic motive to alleviate the child's "own" distress ("I want to get rid of my distress") gives way, at least in part, to the more prosocial motive to alleviate the other's distress ("I want to get rid of his distress") and this is an addition to the child's repertoire.

The transformation of empathic into sympathetic distress occurs in three stages, which are tied to the three levels of cognitive apprehension of the other—person permanence, role taking, and identity. At the level of person permanence the child knows the other is a separate physical entity. The child knows the other is the victim, and his or her empathic reaction is transformed by this knowledge into a genuine concern for the other. However, the child cannot yet distinguish between his own and the other's inner states (thoughts, perceptions, needs). Without thinking about it, he or she automatically assumes the other's states are identical to his or her own. Consequently, although the child can sense the other's distress, he or she does not understand what caused it nor knows what the other's needs are in the situation (except when they happen to coincide with his or her own). This lack of understanding is often evidenced in the child's efforts to help, which consist chiefly of giving the other what the child finds most comforting. In the example cited earlier, Michael's initial attempt to placate his friend is a case in point. I have also heard a description of a 13-month-old child who brought his own mother to comfort a crying friend, even though the latter's mother was equally available; and of another child the same age who offered his beloved doll to comfort an adult who looked sad. (At this age the child's helping behavior may also at times be quite transitory and the next moment he or she may strike the person he or she was just comforting.)

This first level of sympathetic distress is in some ways as primitive as the empathic distress described earlier—a passive, involuntary, and sometimes grossly inaccurate and transitory response to cues perceptually similar to those associated with the child's own past distress. It is a significant advance, however, because for the first time the child experiences a desire to help the other, although his or her effort to do so may be misguided because of cognitive limitations. This motive to help is aroused by the awareness of someone in distress, although its qualitative aspects, including the conception of the nature and intensity of the other's distress and the type of action needed to relieve it, depend on the child's level of cognitive development.

At the second developmental level, that of role taking, the child has begun to acquire a sense of others not only as physical entities but also as sources of feelings and thoughts in their own right. That is, he or she is no longer certain that the real world and his or her perception of it are the same thing. The child has begun to realize that others may at times have inner states that differ from his or her own, as well as different perspectives based on their own needs and interpretations of events, although he or she may be uncertain as to what their perspectives actually are. This advance, as mentioned in the discussion of role taking, is very likely the result of the child's cognitive development together with experiences in which his or her expectations that others have identical inner states are disconfirmed by corrective feedback from them.

A caution is necessary here. The literature on role taking stresses development of the capacity to grasp another's perspective when it differs from one's own. What is sometimes lost sight of is the fact that this is only done to make clear the nature of the child's progress away from egocentrism. In real life, when the child takes the perspective of others, he or she is apt to find that it is usually much like his or her own, except for minor variations. This is because all children have the same basic nervous system, they all have an increasing capacity for stimulus generalization on the basis of both conceptual and perceptual similarities, and they have many experiences in common during the long period of socialization. In the example discussed earlier, although Michael finds out that he and his friend differ as to the particular object they want in the situation, the basic feeling that he initially projects to his friend is shown by the final outcome to be veridical. That is, his assumption that his friend's basic emotional needs are the same as his own is confirmed. Therefore, while moving away from the automatic, egocentric assumption that the other's inner states are identical to his or her own, the child discovers both that others react as persons in their own right, and that their responses are often very similar to his or her own. The realization that the child's feelings resemble those experienced independently by others in similar situations must inevitably contribute to a sense of "oneness," which preserves and may even enhance his or her developing motivation to alleviate the other's distress.

The awareness that the other has inner states that are independent of his or her own has profound effects on the nature of the child's response to distress. Although the affective aspect of the distress aroused in the child remains essentially the same and although he or she may continue to project his or her own feelings to the victim as in the past, these reactions are now only part of a more conscious orientation to the other's state. Moreover, the child is aware of the guesswork involved and therefore uses other inputs besides his or her own empathic distress in formulating an idea of the other's needs and feelings, such inputs as specific information about which acts can alleviate the other's distress and which cannot. Initially he may engage in trial and error based on his own past experience and, like Michael in the example discussed above, may alter his behavior in response to corrective feedback in the situation. Eventually the trial and error and reality testing take place internally, and external feedback is no longer needed except perhaps in new and complex situations.

For the first time in our developmental account, then, the child begins to make an active effort to put him- or herself in the other's place, although he or she remains aware of the tentative and hypothetical nature of the inferences he or she makes. The child has now achieved genuine role taking. His or her motivation to relieve the other person's distress is far less egocentric than it has been and is based to a far greater degree on a veridical assessment of the other's needs. The child's attempts to help, as a result, are more sophisticated and appropriate.

Despite this obvious progress, the child's response at the second level is still confined to the other's distress in the immediate situation. This deficiency is overcome at the third level, owing to a significant new input: the child's emerging conception of others, as well as her- or himself, as continuous persons each with his or her own history and identity. By the time the child has reached the preadolescent years, he or she is presumably fully aware that others not only react to situations with feelings of pleasure and pain, but also that these feelings occur within the context of their larger pattern of life experiences. The child continues to react to their momentary distress but feels worse when he or she knows it is chronic. The child may also imagine their repeated experiences of distress even when these are not reflected in the immediate situation. In sum, being aware that others have inner states and a separate existence beyond the immediate situation enables the child to respond not only to their transitory, situation-specific distress, but also to what he or she imagines to be their general condition. (The transitory and the general are ordinarily consonant, but when they conflict the individual's response is determined by the latter, because it is the more inclusive and therefore more compelling index of the other's welfare—except when the cues of the transitory are so salient as to preempt his or her response.)

This third level of development, then, consists of the synthesis of empathic distress and a mental representation of the other's general plight, that is, his or her typical day-to-day level of distress or deprivation, the opportunities available or denied to him or her, his or her future prospects, and the like. If this representation of the other falls short of what the observer conceives to be a minimally acceptable standard of wellbeing (and if the observer's own life circumstances place her- or himself above this standard), this third level of the sympathetic distress response will typically be evoked, regardless of the other's apparent momentary state.

To summarize, the individual who progresses through these three stages may reach the point of being capable of a high level of sympathetic response to another person in distress. He or she can process all levels of information—including that gained through his or her own empathic reaction, immediate situational cues, and general knowledge about the other's life. The individual can act out in his or her own mind the emotions and experiences suggested by these sources of information and introspect on all of this. He or she may thus gain an understanding of the circumstances, feelings, and wishes of the other, have feelings of concern for him or her and wish to help, while all the time maintaining the sense that this is a separate person from him- or herself.

With further cognitive development the person may acquire the capacity to comprehend the plight not only of an individual but of an entire group or class of people to whom he or she is exposed, such as those who are economically impoverished, politically oppressed, socially outcast, victimized by war, or mentally retarded. Because the observer is part of a different group, his or her own distress experiences may not be quite like those of the less fortunate group. All distress experiences have much in common, however, and by this stage the individual has the capacity to generalize from one distress experience to another. It may therefore be assumed that most people have the cognitive and affective requisites for a generalized empathic distress (although the salience of others' misfortune may be necessary to activate this capacity). Possible exceptions are those rendered incapable of empathy by their socialization, or whose status in life has permitted only the most superficial contact with less fortunate people (consider Marie Antoinette's aprocryphal "Let them eat cake" response to the people who were clamoring for bread). In any case, the synthesis of empathic distress and the perceived plight of an unfortunate group results in the developmentally most advanced form of sympathetic distress.

So far nothing has been said about what happens when the observer sees him- or herself as the cause of the other's distress. Blaming oneself becomes possible developmentally once one has acquired the cognitive capacity to recognize the consequences of one's action for others and to be aware that one has choice and control over one's own behavior. The synthesis of sympathetic distress and awareness of being the cause of the other's distress may be called guilt, because it has both the affectively unpleasant and cognitive self-blaming components of the guilt experience.

Personal or true guilt might be experienced not only as the result of acts of commission but also because of inaction (things the person might have done to help the other but did not). Observing another in distress in situations where one might have helped, but for any number of reasons did not, might therefore be expected to add a component of guilt to the sympathetic distress response.

Eventually, with the capability of forseeing the consequences of one's action and inaction, anticipatory guilt also becomes a possibility. Guilt may also be added to the sympathetic distress response when the observer views the victim's plight as caused by the action or inaction of others with whom he or she identifies. Some of the white activists of the 1960s, for example, as suggested in the interviews obtained by Kenneth Keniston, appear to have experienced guilt because their parents or other members of their social class behave in an exploitative manner toward others.

Finally, guilt may be aroused by the sheer awareness of a marked contrast between the other's life condition and one's own. Such a marked contrast may make one's own relative well-being the focal point of attention, as in survivor guilt and the guilt over affluence evinced by some of the activists of the 1960s. Sympathetic distress may then no longer be a response to the other's plight alone, but to the other's plight in relation to one's own well-being. That is, the individual feels overwhelmed by the knowledge that others suffer far greater misfortunes than he or she, or that he or she enjoys pleasures that they are denied. In the absence of any justification for one's relative advantage, sympathetic distress may become transformed, at least in part, into a sense of guilt. I call this "existential guilt" to distinguish it from true guilt, because the person has done nothing wrong but feels culpable for circumstances of life beyond his or her control.

Guilt may, therefore, be important in any theoretical account of altruism that stresses sympathetic distress, because once the capacity for guilt over inaction, anticipatory guilt, and existential guilt are attained, all subsequent sympathetic distress reactions may contain a guilt component.

The focus of this presentation is on motives; a full treatment of the relation between motives and action is beyond its scope. This topic cannot be ignored, however, because the importance of motives for society ultimately lies in their influence on behavior. The assumption implicit in my formulation is that motives do relate to action—that empathic and sympathetic distress predispose the individual to act, although only in the latter case does he or she feel him- or herself to be acting on the other's behalf. Developmentally, this means that as the child acquires coping skills, he or she tends to use them in the service of these motives. At first, the child simply enacts behaviors that have alleviated his or her own distress in the past, as exemplified in my earlier illustrations of empathic distress and the lowest level of sympathetic distress. Eventually the child experiences doubt about the appropriateness of these acts for the other person; role taking and higher levels of cognitive processing begin to intervene between the motives and the act; and the child's response becomes more veridical in terms of the victim's needs. Presumably, there is also some sort of feedback or reinforcement process throughout, whereby acts that successfully alleviate the other's distress are retained and repeated in the future. The corrective feedback that often follows unsuccessful, inappropriate acts may lead to trial and error or the operation of higher level cognitive processes that, in turn, result in appropriate acts.

To date, there is only modest empirical support for the key point in this formulation—that sympathetic distress predisposes the person to act altruistically. In the intensive nursery school observations by Lois Murphy almost 40 years ago, the younger children usually react to another in distress with a worried, anxious look but do nothing, presumably because of fear or lack of necessary skills. Had they been in the familiar surroundings of the home, however, they might have responded more actively, as the 20-month-old son of a colleague did when a visiting friend, about to leave, burst into tears complaining that her parents were not home (they were away for 2 weeks). His immediate reaction was to look sad, but then he offered her his beloved teddy bear to take home. His parents immediately reminded him that he would miss the teddy if he gave it away, but he insisted—as if his sympathetic distress were greater than the anticipated unpleasantness of not having the teddy —which might have been indicative of the strong motivational potential of sympathetic distress.

In any event, Murphy has found that with older children sympathetic distress is usually accompanied by an overt helpful act. The laboratory studies by Feshbach and Roe and by Ervin Staub, taken together, also suggest that preschool and older children typically react to another child's distress with both sympathy and attempts to help. Finally, several other studies cited above, when considered as a group, provide evidence for a similar association between altruistic motivation and behavior in adults. Witnessing another person being shocked or failing in a task typically results in both an affective reaction, as measured physiologically, and an overt attempt to help.

It would appear, then, that sympathetic distress is accompanied by tendencies toward helpful action. Whether it motivates or is merely associated with the action is uncertain, although there is some evidence in one of Murphy's empirical generalizations that it may motivate: "As verbal and physical techniques develop to the point where the child can cope with a large portion of the varied situations to which he is exposed, an active response (to help) occurs and there is less likelihood of prolonged affective response." Therefore, when the child overtly helps the other, the affective portion of his sympathetic distress diminishes; when he does not help, the affect is prolonged. This applies both developmentally (more action and less affect with age) and within the same child at a given age. Latané and Darley have found something similar with adults: subjects who help a person who seems to be having an epileptic fit show less emotion afterwards than those who do not help. These findings are all consistent with the notion that sympathetic distress predisposes the person to act; acting reduces the sympathetic distress, whereas inaction does not.

Assuming that sympathetic distress does create a predisposition to help, a question arises concerning the time elapsing between the observation of distress and the act. Initially, a short latency is to be expected because of the child's egocentrism and lack of doubt about the appropriateness of the first act that occurs to him or her. When role taking and cognitive processing begin to play a role, a longer latency appears inevitable. With further increases in cognitive processing, the changes in the duration of decision time becomes problematic. A reduction in decision time and perhaps in duration of affective response may be expected owing to advances in the individual's ability to process information rapidly—with the result that in an emergency he or she can more quickly choose among available alternative acts. However, the latency may increase because of the entry of new types of information that must be processed, such as that bearing on the cost to the actor of the various alternative acts to be considered. Many factors within the situation, as well as differences in personal style, undoubtedly govern the latency of the altruistic response.

Although sympathetic distress may predispose the child to act altruistically, it does not guarantee that he or she will do so. Whether or not he or she acts depends on other things besides the strength and developmental level of the motive. Action will be more likely when the appropriate thing to do is obvious and within the person's repertoire, and less likely when there is little that can be done. The costs to the observer and the strength of competing motives aroused in him or her in the situation must also be taken into account. In such an individualistic society as ours, for example, altruistic motives can also often be overriden by more powerful egoistic motives. It may well be in such a society that altruistic motives have a reliable effect on behavior only in situations in which one encounters someone in distress and is not preoccupied with oneself.

Pending clarification in future research, I would suggest the following formulation of the relationship between altruistic motives and action: (a) distress cues from another person trigger the altruistic response system; (b) the observer experiences sympathetic distress and his or her initial tendency is to act; (c) if he or she does not act, for whatever reason (situational counterpressures, competing motives, lack of necessary skills) he or she will typically either continue to experience sympathetic distress, or cognitively restructure the situation so as to justify inaction, for example, by derogating the victim or otherwise convincing him- or herself that the victim wants or deserves what he or she gets.

In conclusion, I believe that the recent burgeoning interest in altruism by social scientists reflects the recognition that the topic is of more than passing academic interest. There is the obvious concern that people in our society often show a singular lack of consideration for others. Beyond that, however, looking at the larger world scene, it seems evident that the advantaged and the disadvantaged people are now more than ever aware of each other's existence; and the disadvantaged are increasingly demanding a greater share of the earth's resources. An important question is, how will the advantaged react? Will their latent altruistic conscience be pricked by the awareness of the distressful existence of others, or is there no such conscience to be pricked? Are those ethologists correct who say that the only hope lies in man's ceaseless struggle to curb the aggressive and territory-seeking tendencies inherited from our remote ancestors? Or does human nature also include proclivities for altruistic concern that can be drawn on in situations involving conflict? The answer may have a bearing on the prospects for human survival, and the search for it may therefore be as important an enterprise as any for the field of psychology.

# 8
# Moral Development and the Structure of Personality

Robert Hogan

*The Johns Hopkins University*

In the introduction to his *Social Psychology* (1965), Roger Brown suggests that social psychologists are not to be characterized by their theoretical preoccupations but by the problems on which they work. Social psychology is therefore defined by a set of problems (e.g., attitude change, prejudice, interpersonal attraction) rather than by a common theoretical perspective, and anyone who studies these problems is a social psychologist. It is not only the case that social psychology lacks an overarching conceptual paradigm but, according to Brown, that is the way it ought to be. Consequently, with regard to the conceptual Balkanization of social psychology, Brown attempts to make a virtue out of a necessity.

Brown's view illustrates what may well be the most important problem in the study of moral development; that is, theory and research in the area must be related to a broader conceptualization of social action if it is not to become merely a special topic in social psychology. That is, to the degree that research in moral development is not placed in a larger theoretical context, it risks becoming a trivial academic exercise—it is in danger of going the way of "prisoner's dilemma" and "risky shift." If research in moral development must be placed in a larger theoretical context, how may this be done? Perhaps the most obvious answer is that it must be integrated within a theory of personality.

Generally speaking, personality theories attempt to answer three kinds of questions. First, how or in what ways are people all alike? These are questions about the nature of human nature. Second, how or in what ways are people different? These are questions about the nature of individual differences. Third, what are the meanings of specific, anomalous, enigmatic actions, such as neurotic symptoms and dreams? In the tradition of depth psychology to which I subscribe, the answer to the first question is given in terms of motivational theory (all people share a common set of motives) and ontogenesis (the parameters of human development are universal and formally identical). Individual differences can be explained in terms of the strength of genetically determined instincts and in terms of social experience during development. Specific actions and neurotic symptoms are explained differently by each theory.

The remainder of this paper is organized in six sections. The first presents some necessary motivational assumptions on which the subsequent discussion depends. The second outlines some developmental assumptions that provide the framework for integrating moral development within personality theory. The third section describes the development of one's public personality, called here "role structure." The fourth section analyzes the development of one's private personality, called here "character structure." In the fifth section a detailed model for conceptualizing the development of character structure is discussed. The final section speculates on some developmental anomalies that result in behavioral pathology.

## MOTIVATIONAL ASSUMPTIONS

The human being's evolutionary history as a group-living and culture-bearing animal suggests the following somewhat oversimplified model for describing the motivational dynamics of social conduct. Let me assume first that most people have a strong need for social interaction—for recognition, approval, affiliation, and attention. Second, I shall assume that most people have a strong need for structure, order, and predictability in their lives, a need that generates the rule-following tendencies necessary for the maintenance of culture. The first assumption seems reasonable in view of the research concerning the effects of maternal deprivation (Harlow, 1958; Spitz, 1945) and attachment theory (Ainsworth, 1969; Bowlby, 1958). The second assumption is implicit in the writings of Piaget. These assumptions suggest that humans are simultaneously attention-seeking and rule-following animals, that they seem to require social interaction within a rule-governed framework, and that they are as interested in the workings of rule systems *per se* as they are in their fellows. The point of this discussion, however, is to suggest that a person's innate instinctual endowment insures that he or she will be a group-living, rule-following, norm-respecting animal, that at an instinctual level he or she needs his or her culture.

## DEVELOPMENTAL ASSUMPTIONS

People are also all alike in that there seem to be some universal patterns of human social development; the patterns and themes of personality development appear to be the same for all members of the species. As a clue to what these patterns may be, the meaning of the word "personality" can be examined. Two uses of the word recur repeatedly in ordinary language and nontechnical psychological literature; these two usages are mirrored in the German words *persönlichkeit* and *personalität*. "Personality" in the first sense refers to those distinctive and unique qualities that characterize a single individual. The emphasis is on the distinguishing features of each person's social performance. "Personality" in the second sense refers to those deep, stable, and enduring needs and dispositions that define us as we "really are" in the central core of our being. This is the person as he or she actually exists in what Yeats called "the foul rag and bone shop of the human heart."

When a distinction such as that just noted occurs with such regularity and in so many languages, it may point to something real. What I should like to suggest is that the ontogenesis of personality takes two forms that reflect the distinction made above; there are two structures in the psyche that develop more or less independently in response to different environmental demands and that taken together comprise individual personality. I call the first "role structure" and the second "character structure."

The flavor of this distinction between role and character structure is nicely captured by Ichheiser's (1970) discussion of "views in principle" and "views in fact." For Ichheiser, views in principle are those held ". . . about social facts and issues in a generalized, so to speak, philosophical way. . . . They are like a game the results of which do not carry any serious implications for ourselves. They reveal only how we think we would act, or how we think we ought to act, when confronted by certain situations or issues, but they do not reveal how we would really act [p. 42]." In contrast, views in fact seem actually to determine actions. Most people, according to Ichheiser, do not know what views they hold in fact, and if they are asked to reflect on their responses to an issue they typically report a view in principle. Views in principle are closely associated with role structure. Conversely, the totality of a person's views in fact—in Ichheiser's terms—is roughly what is meant here by character structure. The next question concerns how these two structures develop.

## ONTOGENESIS OF ROLE STRUCTURE

The assumption that people are strongly motivated toward social interaction within a rule-governed framework has two implications. First, the primary goal for each person in the interpersonal situation is to maximize the amount of positive, friendly attention he or she receives and to minimize the amount of hostile, negative rejection he or she must endure. Second, recurrent social interactions tend quickly to become ritualized. That is, the second time two people meet they tend to repeat as a matter of convenience the pattern of their first interaction. As they begin to repeat this pattern on their third meeting they may experience a sense of "Here we go again!" Specific interactions inexorably crystallize into roles—typified ways of presenting oneself in social situations that serve to facilitate interaction and ward off social disapproval. Moreover, my research at Johns Hopkins suggests that role- and rule-governed interactions begin very early in life. For example, children in the 3½–5-year age range show a remarkable ability to structure their interactions in these terms. Role play seems intrinsically enjoyable and the children become visibly upset when standard role expectations are not fulfilled.

Once roles precipitate out of standard interactions they are thereafter performed in accordance with one's perceptions or beliefs concerning specific situational requirements (e.g., what is fitting, or what one thinks others expect of one in a given situation). It should be emphasized that many of these roles are defensive in nature, designed to ward off criticism and abuse. Over time, each person also develops a small set of self-images (e.g., brave, big boy; smart little girl), model personality types that one wishes others to accept as true of oneself. Like roles, self-images are also manifested in self-presentations; however, these are longer (in a temporal sense) and more general dramatizations that, once developed, structure one's role performances. Self-images, therefore, provide the context for role performances; any single social action can be interpreted only within the context of the role a person is playing and the self-image he is attempting to foster and maintain. Thus, the kind of son, daughter, or student one becomes depends on one's self-image. Finally, over time some people articulate for themselves a broad-gauged life style, an idealized pattern of living that may organize their self-images, roles, and specific interactions. A life style becomes the context within which particular self-images are manifested. Life styles, however, are never *sui generis*; they normally reflect in subtle but distinctive ways one's cultural and religious background, social class, and modeling experience.

Roles, self-images, and life styles are usually both conscious and directly reflected in overt behavior. They are typically sensitive to the demands of a specific situation and therefore change across situations. Together they comprise role structure. Although role structure may reflect the influence of one's family, it is largely the product of peer group experience, that is, one's efforts to gain the approval and avoid the disapproval of one's age mates. These overt self-presentations (in Ichheiser's terms, "views in principle") underlie the responses obtained in most social–psychological attitude research and, I believe, generate the answers to such instruments as Kohlberg's moral judgment scale.

## ONTOGENESIS OF CHARACTER STRUCTURE

A good deal of moment by moment social conduct can be explained in terms of typified self-presentations in response to what one believes others expect of one. Nonetheless, social behavior is rarely, if ever, a simple function of the social situation. Social conduct is also determined from within by the residue of one's reactions to the demands and expectations of one's parents and family. Through the various processes of identification, introjection, imitation, and unconscious suggestion, each person "accommodates" him- or herself to the rules and guidelines that represent the conventional wisdom of his or her parents, ethnic heritage, and cultural and religious history.

Kardiner (1939) has provided one of the best discussions so far of the adaptive significance of character development. For Kardiner, each culture occupies a particular environmental and ecological niche. The environment poses certain challenges to which a culture must respond if it is to survive. Assuming that the adults of a culture have worked out a viable response to this environmental challenge, it becomes encoded in terms of the rules, values, and conventional wisdom of the group. This cultural response is passed on through the child-rearing practices of the society; if the process of transmission is successful, it insures the continued existence of the group. Erikson (1950) makes the same point, although phrased somewhat differently. He suggests that the mothers of a culture consciously develop a set of child-rearing practices that yield the character type most appropriate to the survival demands of the culture.

Character structure therefore arises from one's early interactions with parents and family. It tends to be stable, enduring, but covert and unconscious. Consequently, character structure is manifested only indirectly through overt attitude statements.

For most middle-class Americans, character structure and role structure are kept separate through a kind of segregation of consciousness. That is, much of what one does during the day is substantially unrelated to one's character structure. The reader may verify this by comparing his or her feelings and behavior when celebrating a traditional holiday with his or her family as a child with his or her feelings and behavior at an office cocktail party. The resulting discrepancy suggests the degree to which the two core aspects of his or her personality are segregated. Obviously some people are closer to one, and some are closer to the other of these psychic structures.

## THE DIMENSIONS OF CHARACTER STRUCTURE

The most important aspect of character structure is the attitudes that one develops with regard to the conventional rules and percepts of his culture. For example, character can be defined in terms of a person's orientation toward the social rules that ostensibly govern his behavior—character structure is a function of a person's largely unconscious, typified ways of selecting, using, justifying, and enforcing rules.

It has proved theoretically and empirically useful to conceptualize character structure in terms of five dimensions: moral knowledge, a dimension of moral judgment, socialization, empathy, and autonomy. These dimensions reflect certain enduring themes in philosophy and psychology; they are conceptually independent and operationally distinguishable. The next question concerns how these dimensions develop and what functions they serve as elements of character structure.

## Moral Knowledge

The first minimal requirement for social conduct is knowledge of the relevant social rules. Knowledge of a rule, however, entails no obligation to observe it; it implies only that one can state the rule, or that one acts so that his or her knowledge of the rule can be inferred.

During social development children learn three kinds of rules: (a) concrete injunctions that apply to specific situations (e.g., "Take turns," "Don't interrupt your father"); (b) values—decision rules that allow one to make moral judgments (i.e., to moralize) and to assign priorities to actions; and (c) comparison rules—cognitive strategies by which one is able to compare ongoing or intended actions with the idealized norms of conduct defined in terms of (a) and (b) above.

Moral knowledge is a necessary but insufficient precondition for rule observant behavior; however, it serves three important functions. First, it allows one to moralize, to pass moral judgments, to judge actions as praise- or blameworthy. Second, moral knowledge provides the foundations for prudential actions; that is, actions in accordance with social norms are usually in one's best interest. Third, moral knowledge affords the possibility for self-control. Knowledge of concrete injunctions and the relevant social values, combined with the ability to compare one's actions with these norms, affords one the opportunity to regulate one's actions in a socially appropriate fashion. Obviously, however, one does not regulate one's actions in accordance with the rules of a social game one does not want to play.

Moral knowledge is related to the quality and diversity of a child's social experience, and to its ability to discover the rules that regulate social conduct. This suggests that moral knowledge is probably a function of intelligence; it further suggests that people differ considerably in terms of the complexity and abstractness of their moral thought.

Evidence concerning the effects of moral knowledge on one's capacity for prudential self-control comes from the field of corrections. Given that measures of moral knowledge and intelligence are functionally equivalent (cf. Maller, 1944), and that adjudicated delinquents tend to be less bright than the normal population, it follows that delinquents have trouble comparing their actions with idealized norms of conduct.

## Moral Positivism and Moral Intuitionism

The second dimension concerns the degree to which people perceive rules as having instrumental value for regulating social affairs. The set of attitudes that characterize moral positivism are related to utilitarian ethics. The law is seen as a practical instrument of social reform, and laws are justified in terms of the degree to which they promote the common good.

The attitudes underlying moral intuitionism resemble the higher law morality of Thomas Aquinas. It is a viewpoint wherein the manifest law is regarded with detachment and even suspicion. Moral intuitionism emphasizes what the person perceives as the right thing for him or her personally to do, without great regard for established norms and conventions.

As dramatic exemplars of these two perspectives, consider Creon and Antigone in Sophocles' *Antigone*. Creon is concerned primarily with furthering the public welfare and promoting domestic harmony; as such, he reflects moral positivism. Antigone, in contrast, is concerned only with remaining faithful to her personal moral code, regardless of the effects of her actions on others.

The moral positivism–moral intuitionism continuum can be assessed reasonably well with the Survey of Ethical Attitudes (SEA; Hogan, 1970). Low scores on this reliable 35-item scale reflect moral intuitionism; high scores indicate moral positivism. The scale nicely discriminates between persons who are self-selected to occupations that preserve and defend conventional social institutions and those who seem preoccupied with promoting social change. It appears that high scorers on the SEA consider rules and codified procedures to have considerable instrumental value in the regulation of human affairs; low scorers consider rules a hindrance and an annoyance.

Research with the SEA suggests that there are obvious personological correlates of moral positivism and intuitionism; nonetheless, these perspectives are undoubtedly fostered and encouraged by adult models and by systematic instruction during development. In particular, Hogan and Dickstein (1972a) have found that moral positivists tend to doubt the natural benevolence of other people and to consider social organizations as an important check on man's less desirable natural tendencies. Conversely, moral intuitionists believe in man's natural benevolence and regard corrupt institutions as the primary source of injustice in society. Similarly, MacDonald (1971) has found that moral positivists tend to hold poor people responsible for their poverty, although intuitionists do not. Moral positivism and intuitionism therefore seem to derive in part from competing views of human nature.

## Socialization

The third dimension concerns the degree to which one has internalized the rules and values of one's society, culture, and family, i.e., the degree to which conventional prescriptions are seen as personally obligatory and binding. To the extent that one perceives these rules and values as alien and intrusive, one is unsocialized.

Durkheim (1961) suggested that the first critical stage in moral development involved acquiring an unquestioning sense of respect for the rules of one's culture. In obvious agreement, Freud attempted to account for the dynamics of socialization in terms of the Oedipus complex. G. H. Mead (1934) explained the same phenomena in terms of the evolution of role-taking ability. Although their explanations differed, these men all agreed that during socialization a rule structure was imposed on children from the outside.

More recently, however, Erikson (1950) and Waddington (1967) have argued that the disposition to comply with adult authority is a natural emergent—children are innately predisposed toward socialization, and this organic predisposition is elicited by the "proper" parent–child relationship. Moreover, there is considerable evidence to suggest that the "proper" relationship is one characterized by parental nurturance and restrictiveness.

The internalization of social rules brings about a qualitative transformation in character structure—for the first time the child becomes capable of true (i.e., rule-governed and nonegocentric) social interaction. In the absence of further developmental changes it also produces a characterological syndrome that Piaget (1965) described as "moral realism." This syndrome is exemplified by the tendency to act as if rules are sacred and immutable, valuable for their own sake.

Socialization can be assessed quite effectively by means of the socialization scale of the California Psychological Inventory (CPI; Gough, 1969), perhaps the most carefully developed and fully validated scale in the history of personality assessment. The socialization scale was originally keyed to predict the delinquency–nondelinquency criterion. Subsequent research suggests, however, that the scale is a sensitive indicator of a generalized rule-following disposition. Low scorers are rebellious, impulsive, and undependable; high scorers are mature, honest, and reliable. It is interesting to note that, in addition to serving as a global index of a disposition toward rule compliance, the scale correlates moderately but consistently with the level of a person's stated moral judgment (cf. Hogan & Dickstein, 1972b).

## Empathy

The fourth dimension involves the capacity and disposition to regulate one's actions in accordance with the expectations of others, whether or not these expectations correspond with the social rules. To the degree that one takes these expectations into account, one is considered to be empathic.

Durkheim (1961) has suggested that the second critical stage in moral development entails adopting impersonal ends for one's actions. This happens, he argues, when one becomes identified with the social groups in which one is a member and takes their goals as one's own. Consequently, according to Durkheim, to the degree that a person's social actions are guided by rational self-interest, both that person and his or her society are sick. Other, seemingly less complicated thinkers have suggested that the development of empathy is the primary transformation in moral development. This is true for the utilitarian philosophers as well as for such American sociologists as C. H. Cooley and G. H. Mead. These writers all agree with Durkheim, however, that empathy is a natural or innate capacity and that once it has emerged, it serves to regulate social conduct.

In spite of the obvious importance of an empathic disposition in the evolution of character and social conduct, its developmental antecedents are poorly understood. It is possible, however, to make some informed guesses concerning the origins of this dimension of character development. First, socialization develops in response to the demands of parental authority; empathy, however, may be a product of peer group experience and a child's attempt to accommodate him- or herself to a radically expanded set of social norms. Second, there is almost surely some association between empathy and intelligence, much as Mead (1934) has suggested. Third, empathy is probably related to role-taking practice in childhood; parents who are neither too consistently accepting nor rejecting, and who periodically ask their children to consider the other person's perspective may produce the most empathic children. Fourth, as Allport (1961) suggested, empathy is probably facilitated by adversity—experience with rejection, persecution, and discrimination may, paradoxically, promote empathic tolerance and understanding.

The development of empathy also brings about a transformation in character structure. In persons who are unsocialized, empathy serves as a compensatory incentive to prosocial behavior; that is, an increased sensitivity to social expectations can compensate for the hostility and rebelliousness that attend low socialization. Among the well socialized, empathy serves to humanize and soften the moral realism of the preceding stage. Empathy also allows the child to think in terms of "the spirit of the game," to understand the concept of "fairness" that seems to evolve into the adult notion of justice. Too much empathy, however, is as bad as too little—one can be concerned with the needs, expectations, and welfare of others at the expense of one's own legitimate plans, goals, and aspirations. Therefore, empathy can lead to indecisiveness and a kind of morbid moral oversensitivity as well as tact, sympathy, and ultimate concern.

Empathy can be assessed with the empathy scale of the CPI (Hogan, 1969; Grief & Hogan, 1973). The empathy scale was originally developed to predict rated empathy. Not surprisingly, then, high scorers on the scale tend to be tactful, sensitive to interpersonal cues, and socially acute. Low scorers appear cold, tactless, and insensitive. The scale is correlated with intelligence, rated ethical sensitivity, and the delinquency–nondelinquency criterion. More importantly, the scale significantly discriminates between delinquents and nondelinquents who are equally unsocialized as defined in terms of the socialization scale (cf. Kurtines & Hogan, 1972). Finally, the scale routinely correlates about .60 with level or maturity of a person's stated moral judgments (cf. Hogan & Dickstein, 1972b).

## Autonomy

The final dimension, autonomy, refers to the capacity to make moral decisions without being influenced by peer group pressure or the dictates of authority. Socialization and empathy leave a person committed to the status quo. The development of autonomy, however, gives a person the capacity for prosocial noncompliance with social rules; it is the source of constructive social change at the individual level.

The concept of autonomy has a decidedly nonutilitarian flavor. Kant, for example, rejects the notion that actions governed by prudential considerations or the welfare of society as a whole can be in any sense moral. Instead, for Kant moral action must arise from an autonomous will and a personal (and even somewhat irrational) sense of duty. Nietzsche mocks utilitarianism as a morality fit only for English shopkeepers. Durkheim (1961) considers autonomous rule compliance to be the final feature of the moral man. Freud's genital character understands the irrational and unconscious sources of his moral compulsions; he nonetheless remains rule observant. The difference between the pregenital character who is guided by an irrational superego and a genital character is that the latter has replaced repression with condemnation—the outward forms of social behavior remain the same. Piaget (1965), who seems to have taken many of his ideas about moral development from Durkheim, also argues that the end point of moral development is the emergence of autonomous rule compliance. Although the point is not clear in Piaget, he seems to mean more by "autonomy" than merely freedom from the constraints of adult authority. One is therefore left with the impression that Piaget's autonomous children are closely tied to the demands of the peer group. I doubt, however, that that was Piaget's intention.

The developmental precursors of autonomy have been effectively analyzed by Baumrind (1971). Her major point is that autonomous children are produced by authoritative parents. Authoritative parents label clearly certain actions as right or wrong, explain their rules, and make their praise contingent on a child's meeting specified standards of performance. In addition, such parents are strong, individualistic, independent, and demanding; as such they provide their children with clear adult models for autonomous behavior. Authoritative parents can be contrasted with authoritarian parents, on the one hand, and undemanding, overprotective, permissive parents on the other. Both authoritarian and permissive parents produce children who are less than autonomous.

The development of an autonomous sense of moral obligation produces a final transformation in the structure of moral character. A socialized person upholds social norms because he regards them as personally binding and, at a deeper level perhaps, out of respect for authority. An empathic person observes social norms because doing so affects the welfare of his or her family and

## TABLE 1
### Estimated Relationships among Five
### Dimensions of Character Structure
### and Mature Moral Judgment

| Dimensions | Correlations | | | | |
|---|---|---|---|---|---|
| | SEA | So | Em | Au | Mature moral judgment |
| Moral knowledge | .00 | .00 | .30 | .20 | .30 |
| Ethics of responsibility (SEA) | – | .26 | –.20 | .28 | –.40 |
| Socialization (So) | | – | .00 | .24 | .40 |
| Empathy (Em) | | | – | .24 | .58 |
| Autonomy (Au) | | | | – | –.04 |

social group; the possibly unconscious motive here may be fear of social disapproval. An autonomous person, however, complies with social norms because that is simply the sort of person he or she is; the primary dynamic fear of self-disapproval. Such persons understand that ultimately one must be able to live with oneself. An autonomous person may also refuse to comply with the rules on occasion, but only because he or she regards such compliance as contrary to the long-range welfare of the group. His or her noncompliance is therefore for social, not personal reasons.

In conjunction with high socialization and high empathy, autonomy produces moral maturity, a statistically rare character type. In conjunction with high socialization and low empathy, autonomy tends to produce a stern, patriarchal, Old Testament moralist—Melville's Captain Ahab; Dicken's Madame LeFarge. In conjunction with low empathy and low socialization, autonomy tends to produce strong effective, resolute, unyielding scoundrels—Shakespeare's Richard III.

Autonomy can be readily assessed with a new CPI autonomy scale (Kurtines, 1973). The scale was originally developed to predict the criterion of rated autonomy. Not surprisingly, therefore, high scorers on the scale are forceful, self-assured, and independent, particularly with regard to private and personal concerns.

Perhaps the most interesting finding so far obtained with the autonomy scale is that among undergraduates, high autonomy is associated with religious belief, whether of a liberal or a conservative variety, and with an unwillingness to use drugs. That is, students who smoke marijuana tend to be less autonomous than those who say they do not and never will. Finally, it is worth noting that autonomy seems uncorrelated with the level or maturity of a person's stated moral judgment.

Table 1 presents my best estimate of the size of the relationships between the various indices discussed above, based on all the data I currently have on hand.

## DEVELOPMENTAL ANOMALIES AND PATHOLOGY

A means for conceptualizing how and in what ways all people are alike, and how they come to differ has been discussed above. It is relevant now to attend to the issue of specific developmental anomalies and intrapsychic conflict, the explanation of which is the final task of personality theory. In the standard psychodynamic account of neurotic disorders, the primary symptom is anxiety. Anxiety results from a conflict between the demands of the instincts and the requirements of conscience. The conflict is usually unconscious, hidden from awareness by repression. Conflict-generated anxiety is the problem, and excessive but faulty repression is the cause.

There are three points with regard to this standard account of neurosis that are worth noting. First, as Sartre (1953) and others (see especially Fingarette, 1969) have pointed out, the concept of repression is extremely problematical—if the ego directs repression, then the ego must know what is being repressed; what, then, is the point of repression, as the agency from whom the undesirable impulses must be hidden is the same agency that is doing the hiding? Second, if one takes evolutionary theory seriously, then man's instinctual endowment must promote rather than disrupt group living. That is, I doubt whether instinct and conscience are sufficiently incompatible to produce conflict of the magnitude that Freud has postulated. Finally, starting with Charcot (1890) and Janet (1907) and extending through William McDougall (1926) an important tradition in psychiatric thought, largely ignored as a result of the influences of psychoanalysis (cf. Ellenberger, 1970; Hilgard, 1973), maintains that the central problem in neurosis is anxiety, but the cause of neurotic anxiety is dissociation rather than repression, lack of integration rather than unconscious defense.

I shall take this alternative perspective on neurosis seriously for a moment. In the model of personality and character development presented above, there are three points at which dissociation can become a problem. Consider first the evolution of role structure. In the absence of a small set of well-defined self-images a person's role performance (e.g., his or her interpersonal interactions) are disconnected, disorganized, and diffuse. The person flits from role to role and from interaction to interaction, giving the impression of being changeable, unpredictable, and superficial—that is, the image of the modern hysteric. Moreover, in the absence of a well-articulated life style, there is no organization between the larger segments of the person's life. He or she will drift from job to job and hobby to hobby in a seemingly random fashion. Dissociation of this type is perhaps best treated by fixed role therapy or reality therapy where the client is encouraged to specify self-images and a life style for him- or herself and then to live up to them. This is so because role structure tends to be conscious and available to introspection.

Similarly, dissociation can be a problem within the domain of character structure. In the ideal case, the rules and values that one adopts in response to the demands of family and culture are integrated under a more encompassing ideology. This may be a religion, a family tradition, or a political perspective. Where such a comprehensive ideology is missing, or when the person has been indoctrinated with competing values, he or she may be subject to unconscious dissociation and conflict as he or she attempts to comply with the requirements of inconsistent values. The ambivalence and vacillation that result resemble an obsessive–compulsive disorder. Erikson's *Young Man Luther* (1958) is a perceptive case study of a young man with unconscious value conflict. Because values (and character structure) tend to be introspectively silent, if not unconscious, conflict of this type is perhaps best treated with forms of therapy that give explicit attention to both the unconscious and the role of ideology as an organizing force in life.

A third source of dissociation results in what Erikson has termed "identity conflict." Under ideal circumstances one's character structure is compatible with one's role structure; that is, the kind of person one's parents expected one to be will be relatively consistent with the kind of person one is in the presence of one's peer group. However, many if not most of us bear little resemblance in our everyday lives to the persons our parents thought they were raising, or to the persons we actually became under the pressure of their expectations and guidance. For example, I daresay that the prevailing self-image of most readers of this paper is that of an academic–scholar–intellectual. In most cases it is unrelated to the Calvinist, Catholic, or Jewish character structure that they acquired while very young and that is still with them when their intellectual and emotional defenses are down. As Goffman (1958) observes "to the degree that the individual maintains a show before others that he himself does not believe, he can come to experience a special kind of alienation from self and a special kind of wariness of others [p. 232]." To have a sense of identity, one's sense of right and wrong must correspond with one's sense of what is socially appropriate. If one's social roles are too discrepant from one's character structure, dissociation results.

Perhaps Freud's most important insight is that in the final analysis neurosis is a moral problem, that conscience not instinct is the final foe of reason. In a sense Freud seems to have been right; when character structure is not integrated within itself, under an ideology, or with regard to one's role structure, it is a major source of unconscious conflict in life. Freud seems to have been wrong, however, in the sense that character structure (or conscience) is not pathogenic *per se*, that is, because it is unconscious; instead, conscience is harmful only when it is not integrated.

The primary burden of this chapter can be summarized in terms of six points. First, humans can be regarded as both attention-seeking and rule-following animals, as needing social interaction, on the one hand, and structure and order, on the other. Second, personality can be seen as the product of two independent psychic agencies: role structure and character structure. Third, role structure—one's public personality—develops in response to the demands of one's peer group and depends primarily on those conscious and idealized images that one would like others to accept as true of oneself. Fourth, character structure—one's private personality—develops in response to the demands of one's parents and family and depends primarily on the unconscious accommodation that one has made to their expectations. Fifth, character structure can be conceptualized in terms of five dimensions: moral knowledge, a dimension of moral judgment, socialization, empathy, and autonomy. Finally, and in contrast with psychoanalysis, character structure is seen as a psychic agency that facilitates social judgment and cultural cohesion. Character structure is the source of neurotic disturbance only when it becomes dissociated from role structure.

## REFERENCES

Ainsworth, M. D. S. Object relations, dependency, and attachment: A theoretical review of the infant-mother relationship. *Child Development*, 1969, **40**, 969–1025.

Allport, G. W. *Pattern and growth in personality*. New York: Holt, 1961.

Baumrind, D. Current patterns of parental authority. *Developmental Psychology*, 1971, **4** (1), Pt. 2. 1–103.

Bowlby, J. The nature of a child's tie to his mother. *International Journal of Psychoanalysis*, 1958, **39**, 350–373.

Brown, R. *Social psychology*. New York: Free Press, 1965.

Charcot, J. M. *Oeuvres complètes*. Paris: Progres Médical, 1890.

Durkheim, E. *Moral education*. New York: Free Press, 1961.

Ellenberger, H. *The discovery of the unconscious*. New York: Basic Books, 1970.

Erikson, E. H. *Childhood and society*. New York: Norton, 1950.

Erikson, E. H. *Young man Luther*. New York: Norton, 1958.

Fingarette, H. *Self-deception*. London: Kegan, Paul, 1969.

Goffman, E. *The presentation of self in everyday life*. Garden City, N.Y.: Doubleday, 1958.

Gough, H. G. *Manual for the California Psychological Inventory*. (Rev. ed.). Palo Alto, Calif.: Consulting Psychologists Press, 1969.

Grief, E. B., & Hogan, R. The theory and measurement of empathy. *Journal of Counseling Psychology*, 1973 **20**, 280–284.

Harlow, H. F. The nature of love. *American Psychologist*, 1958, **13**, 678–685.

Hilgard, E. R. Dissociation revisited. In M. Henle, J. Jaynes, & J. Sullivan (Eds.), *Historical conceptions of psychology*. New York: Springer Publ., 1973, 205–219.

Hogan, R. Development of an empathy scale. *Journal of Consulting & Clinical Psychology*, 1969, **33**, 307–316.

Hogan, R. A dimension of moral judgment. *Journal of Consulting & Clinical Psychology*, 1970, **35**, 205–212.

Hogan, R., & Dickstein, E. Moral judgment and perceptions of injustice. *Journal of Personality & Social Psychology*, 1972, **23**, 409–413.   (a)

Hogan, R., & Dickstein, E. A measure of moral values. *Journal of Consulting & Clinical Psychology*, 1972, **39**, 210–214.   (b)

Ichheiser, G. *Appearances and reality*. San Francisco: Jossey-Bass, 1970.

Janet, P. *The major symptoms of hysteria*. London: Macmillan, 1907.

Kardiner, A. *The individual and his society*. New York: Columbia University Press, 1939.

Kurtines, W. A measure of autonomy. Unpublished doctoral dissertation, The Johns Hopkins University, 1973.

Kurtines, W., & Hogan, R. Sources of conformity in unsocialized college students. *Journal of Abnormal Psychology,* 1972, **80**, 49–51.

MacDonald, A. P., Jr. Correlates of the ethics of personal conscience and the ethics of social responsibility. *Journal of Consulting & Clinical Psychology,* 1971, **37**, 443.

Maller, J. B. Personality tests. In J. McV. Hunt (Ed.), *Personality and the behavior disorders.* New York: Ronald Press, 1944.

McDougall, W. *Outline of abnormal psychology.* New York: Scribners, 1926.

Mead, G. H. *Mind, self, and society.* Chicago: University of Chicago Press, 1934.

Piaget, J. *The moral judgment of the child.* New York: Free Press, 1965.

Sartre, J. P. *Being and nothingness.* New York: Philosophical Library, 1953.

Spitz, R. A. Hospitalism: An enquiry into the genesis of psychiatric conditions in early childhood. *Psychoanalytic Study of the Child,* 1945, **1**, 53–74.

Waddington, C. H. *The ethical animal.* Chicago: University of Chicago Press, 1967.

# 9
# Recent Research on Moral Development: A Commentary

Shirley L. Jessor
*University of Colorado*

The chapters by Turiel, Bryan, Staub, and Hoffman provide a reasonably good sampling of the state of research and thinking about moral development at the present time. Three of the chapters deal with altruism, those of Bryan, Staub, and Hoffman; the fourth, by Turiel, deals with moral judgment. Although there are a number of common threads joining the four chapters, each represents a distinctive and separable approach to moral development. It seems best, therefore, to comment on each in its own right and then to note their commonalities at the end.

Bryan's chapter represents a continuation of the concern he and his colleagues have shown about the situational determinants of aiding behavior. This essentially empirical chapter focuses on a dimension of the independent variable of modeling—inconsistency between preaching and practice—that is termed "hypocrisy." Hypocrisy is defined as simulation, that is, as deception as to real character and feeling, especially in regard to morals and religion. Interest in the phenomenon arose partially out of an awareness of the prevalence of hypocrisy in our society, the contempt adolescents feel for adult hypocrisy, and the reaction, if not revulsion, people feel about Watergate.

The general definition of hypocrisy is translated into experimental situations in which there is a discrepancy between the preaching and practice of models who wish children to engage in charitable behavior. It is hypothesized that children will be *less* charitable, even deviant, when exposed to an inconsistent model than when exposed to a model who practices what he or she preaches, a "saint." In a series of studies of children aged 8–11, it turns out that the hypocrisy of the model does not inhibit donating behavior, nor does it facilitate cheating behavior. The children, apparently, are neither influenced in their behavior by the hypocrisy of the model nor offended by it. Their overt behavior appears to be influenced solely by the overt behavior of the model, and their verbal behavior is influenced by the exhortations of the model. Children exposed to preaching but nonpracticing models therefore learn to be "hypocrites," themselves.

Although the major hypotheses about the effects of hypocrisy are not confirmed, the introduction of reinforcement by the model, as an additional independent variable, does appear to make some difference. Children who are first exposed to hypocritical models reduce their donating behavior in reaction to this model's praise for donating behavior. Hypocrisy does appear, therefore, to have an aversive effect under such special conditions, that is, inconsistency may attenuate the socializer's ability to influence the child later on through reinforcement.

The studies that have been reported by Bryan are of interest in several ways. They deal with the role of inconsistency in socialization; they examine the relative importance of verbalization versus overt behavior on the part of a model; and they focus on the specific effects of hypocrisy on a child. The work has been pursued with ingenuity and inventiveness within the experimental paradigm, and Bryan and his colleagues have demonstrated a willingness to engage in extensive replication.

The general lack of effect, however, of model inconsistency, or hypocrisy, on behavior is not easy for Bryan to explain. It may be a function of inadequate theorizing, an inadequate test of the theory, or both. In response to the negative findings, Bryan suggests various methodological improvements. These include varying the personal characteristics of the model, using live instead of taped models, and varying the instructions. Live models who assume some salience and meaning to the subject and who have several experiences with the subjects may better approach the richness of the parent–child interaction. The exhortations to donate need improvement; as described, the preaching of the models have a simplistic and potentially irritating quality. The experiments would certainly be improved by these modifications, but I wonder whether this is the direction most likely to gain positive results.

Beyond these kinds of improvement, there are at least three important aspects of the present work that bear comment: the absence of a theoretical framework; the lack of attention to individual differences; and the persistent refusal to explore alternative methods of assessment.

The absence of a general framework or a theory of moral development, of altruism, of hypocrisy, or of social transmission is noteworthy, not only in Bryan's work, but in the field as a whole. Beyond the Kohlbergian stage notions, there is little in the moral development field that provides a logical basis for coordinating concepts and linking them to actual behavior. In Bryan's paper, for example, hypocrisy is viewed as an immoral behavior that presumably creates discomfort in the person who experiences it; but why this should reduce prosocial behavior is not made fully clear as a logical consequence of a constellation of variables. What needs to be explicated is a conceptualization of the socialization into altruism, including hypotheses about the effect of an inconsistent socializer on a child's behavior. It is certainly reasonable to assume that donating behavior is least likely to be learned or elicited through exposure to hypocrisy; but it may well be that hypocrisy is more likely to limit altruistic behavior, once learned, only in important situations, or when engaged in by important people valued by the subject, or in the eyes of the world. Hypocrisy may have its effects only after many instances, so that the socializer is viewed as unworthy and duplicitous and not worth modeling. The perceptions and attitudes mediating between exposure to a hypocrite and the behavior of the child therefore should be specified and incorporated into the theory. The effects of hypocrisy as compared to other kinds of inconsistency that may occur in the course of socialization should also be elaborated—for example, praise one day and punishment the next day for the same behavior from the same person or opposite reactions or positions about the child's behavior by two different socializers.

Second, the role of individual differences in personality, cognitive ability, moral level, sex, social status, and socialization experience of the subjects is, unfortunately, not a concern that has entered into any of the work, nor does it seem to be a future direction for which preparation is presently being made. Attributes that may make for greater or lesser sensitivity to hypocrisy need to be examined—such as the subject's definition of moral behavior, the value he or she places on being independent, and his or her general cognitive ability. For example, level of moral judgment may be related to donating behavior irrespective of the model's consistency. Level of independence in the child may be related to greater willingness to criticize a hypocrite. Cognitive ability might be related to the recognition of duplicity. Relevant personality variables, such as these or those specified by the theory called for above, need to be incorporated into hypotheses about what kind of child is more likely to be influenced by hypocrisy.

The third major point needing emphasis in regard to this work relates to the exploration of alternative methods of assessment. It would seem more fruitful at this stage, after 1500 subjects, to enlarge the method beyond the univocal concern with the experiment. The imaginative use of observation, interview, and questionnaire may lead to answers unexplored in the experiment, such as the subjects' perception of and attitudes toward hypocritical behavior in adults. Although brief posttest interviews have been attempted, the construction of a more comprehensive interview to assess children's attitudes toward hypocrisy, although complicated, may be productive. The use of a questionnaire to define children on prior relevant personality variables for subsequent correlation with behavior under hypocrisy conditions, or for control purposes, is a further potentially productive avenue that may develop from enlarging the models used.

If the aim of the series of studies is to go beyond merely demonstrating that duplicity appears to have no effects, then the responsibility to provide a theoretical framework, to look at individual differences, and to extend the method beyond its present constraints remains.

The phenomenon of hypocrisy and its effects on developing individuals is certainly worth studying, but it needs to be studied, it seems to me, in the matrix of a broader framework. In that way, it may throw further light on the complexities of socialization in general. It may then also lead to understanding, specifically, of the tolerance or intolerance of duplicity among individuals in societies that sometimes support, but often disdain, duplicity. There must be many ways to make visible to mortals the ''evil that walks invisible.'' One hopes that Bryan and his co-workers will explore some new ones.

Staub's chapter is also concerned with prosocial behavior, but the task is approached somewhat differently from Bryan. In this chapter, the aim is to look first at a complex of socialization dimensions that are presumed to influence the development of prosocial behavior in the child and then to develop experimental tests of some of these hypotheses.

The socialization dimensions considered important are affection in the home, modeling by the parents of prosocial behavior, control by the parents in a prosocial direction, and the use of such influence techniques as induction and reasoning. The research support for invoking such variables, and the conditions that enhance the relationship between parental induction and child prosocial behavior, for example, increased role-taking ability and empathy, are discussed. Induction is expected to have the most effect when used frequently and when interacting with parental control and responsibility assignment, so that these experiences lead to the internalization of a norm of ''doing things for others.'' Children learn prosocial behavior, according to Staub, indirectly, in collaboration with adults who are accomplishing important goals or in the process of teaching others.

The various hypotheses have been tested in several experiments that are part of a coordinated, ongoing series. Method of instructions, positive induction, and actual participation in responsible action are varied or combined in several ways. These conditions, for the most part, are found to influence prosocial behavior, such as donating to the needy or writing letters to hospitalized children, by girls and only the intention to do good by boys. In general, prosocial behavior is higher for girls.

Staub's work represents a contribution to our understanding of the socialization correlates of aiding behavior. He has focused on a set of important variables, such as induction, teaching, and opportunity to practice responsible behavior, and has viewed their role interactively in the production of prosocial behavior in children. The theorizing about relevant socialization conditions in the home appears to be cogent and persuasive. There have been a number of socialization studies, including those by Hoffman and others, that have supported such a position. In our own research on the socialization of problem behavior, my husband and I have found that limited parental control in conjunction with a nonconventional political, religious, and moral ideology in the home is correlated with engaging in an array of socially defined adolescent problem behaviors, such as problem drinking, premarital sex, drug use, and delinquent-type behavior.

The translation of Staub's notions about socialization antecedents into an experimental paradigm has been done with imagination; great care has gone into designing experiments so as to approach a real life situation. However, some limitations of the approach are worth noting.

For example, in the attempt to approximate and tease out the dimensions of the real-life learning situation, induction has been used as one of the independent variables. I think this influence technique, particularly, is one that requires repeated exposure, as well as the experiencing of consequences; it is therefore not easy to simulate in a single experimental situation. Perhaps the weaker results in these experiments reflect this incomplete approximation.

Combining induction, however, with an opportunity for responsible action or with the opportunity for teaching did lead to increased prosocial behavior, donating to the needy, writing letters to hospitalized children, and making puzzles. Here again, as in Bryan's work, greater approximation of a real-life situation in all its complexity apparently produced better results.

The results in the complex situation are far more impressive, as in the simple situation, for girls than for boys. Staub offers some explanation for this with respect to how girls are socialized. Perhaps more might have been discovered to boys' prosocial behavior, however, if the tasks had been more interesting to boys, e.g., building a toy rather than making puzzles or taping a record rather than writing letters. It is not clear whether the experimental conditions simulating socialization are less salient for boys or the experimental tasks are simply less interesting.

Although Staub has given more serious attention to theory than Bryan, he, like Bryan, has neglected individual difference variables. Although the work with Harvard freshmen has related subject's behavior to level of moral reasoning and general prosocial orientation, the experiments with children reported here ignore individual differences. Other attributes and experiences that children bring to a situation, such as having a strong need for affection or having learned to be nurturant, may influence the outcome as much as do the requirements of the task and the definition of the situation. Including such variations in socialization history and personality, through prior selection, concomitant measurement, or experimental manipulation, should certainly enhance understanding of the determinants of prosocial behavior.

It should be recognized that, in the final discussion of the chapter, Staub shows awareness of some of the limitations of what has been done as well as of what needs to be done in the study of prosocial behavior. His wish to extend the parameters of the situation, for example, to understand the role of experimenter attributes, to study longer term effects, and to explore the generality of prosocial behavior, can only be applauded. His discussion of the importance of knowing how the subjects view a variety of prosocial activities as well as how their own beliefs and attitudes may contribute to prosocial behavior is salutary.

The program of research, only partially reported in the chapter, shows promise of leading to further understanding of the process by which a child develops a prosocial orientation and behaves in a prosocial manner. That promise will be closer to realization when the missing links in the theory, particularly the personality links, become a specified part of the causal chain.

Hoffman's chapter differs from the other two insofar as it focuses on the early origins of the altruistic motive in the life of human beings and is not an empirical paper but a speculative one. The course of development of altruistic motives and behavior is traced from the early empathic response of the infant. With the refinement of the emotional empathic response and its interaction with a cognitive sense of the other as separate and in distress, Hoffman argues, sympathy and helping behavior are made possible. Empathy, defined as the involuntary experiencing of another's emotional state, is presumed to arise out of early conditioning in the infant–caretaker dyad; later on, distress cues on the part of another are presumed to serve as re-evokers of one's own painful experience.

Most explanations of the relationship of empathy to altruism have highlighted the affective components and neglected the cognitive components. In the development of the child, the ability for self–other differentiation, the ability to recognize that others have a different perspective, and the sense of ego and of alter identity are considered as cognitive skills that enable the person to transform empathy into sympathy. With sympathetic distress comes the desire to relieve the distress of another, not only as if it were one's own, but because it is like one's own distress. And still later comes the recognition of the diversity of inner states in others that may lead to visible distress. Understanding of the inner states as well as awareness of distress in others is thought to evoke sympathetic concern.

Hoffman's exposition is interesting and provocative. He is to be commended for the ambitiousness of his task—to transcend cultural variation and to suggest common bases for altruism in all human experience—and for the thoughtfulness with which he approaches it. Account is taken of the affective and cognitive experiences presumed necessary for recognizing distress, putting oneself in another's place, and even doing something for another. Tracing of the interrelatedness of the affective and cognitive in the life of an individual is carefully carried through. The impact of the presentation is an optimistic one in that it implies that human beings do have a sound basis for orienting in a selfless as well as a selfish direction.

The intent of the exposition is to find a common basis for altruism in all human experience rather than to build a total theory of altruism. Although this is an important step, no explanation of altruism can stand separately from an explanation of egoism, just as a theory of abnormality must come to terms with normality and a theory of moral development must come to terms with immoral development. In that sense, there is a requirement for far more specification and linkages that can provide an explanation of the factors that oppose, as well as those that support, altruism. The same set of principles, then, in conjunction with additional principles, may enable understanding of a refusal to help someone in distress.

Related to this general concern about the scope of the theory are questions about how the approach accounts for differences among people in the strength of the altruistic motive. Surely such differences do not depend solely on having had more empathic experiences or more cognitive development. The individual history of helping experiences and of reactions to and consequences of these experiences must also play a role. It is important to know about the role of other socializers in instruction, induction, and as models and sources of helping behavior. It is also important to know how much a person has come to value being a helper and how effectively he or she has learned to play the role of a helping and caring person. Finally, the role of other motives and attitudes in developing an altruism orientation; for example, responsibility for others, religiosity, seems crucial to elaborate.

The exposition needs clarification in two other respects. First, the definition of "altruism" and the distinction between motives and action is not fully consistent throughout the paper. Second, the transitions from empathy to sympathy and sympathy to an altruistic orientation need more specification. Undescribed are the factors that make concern for another's distress and a desire to help others a more likely outcome than feeling relief that one is not oneself in distress and desiring to stay safe and comfortable. If helping someone in destress may be at cost to oneself, as it often is, then one is not empathically terminating one's own distress by terminating that of another.

In Hoffman's chapter, some of the necessary conditions for learning a prosocial orientation have been explored imaginatively. Attention to other conditions can both enrich the theory and help point out the direction for making an adequate test of the propositions—the ultimate requirement if these ideas are not to remain mere speculation.

The chapter by Turiel is in another area of moral development; it is an exploration of how children develop social-judgmental concepts. The assumption is made that thinking about manners (such as forms of address, dress codes, religious rituals) may take a different form than thinking about morals (value of life, honesty, etc.). A distinction is therefore made between the two kinds of regulatory ideas—the more universal ones dealing with morals, and the more culture-bound ones dealing with customs or conventions. This kind of separation seems important and should lead to a more refined understanding of how a person comes to terms with social reality and begins to develop his or her own guides for action.

The orientation guiding the research is a structural-developmental one. Turiel is hoping to discover stagelike properties for the development of judgments about customs and conventions akin to, although perhaps different from, the properties proposed by Kohlberg for the development of moral judgment. In considering morals and mores as occupying different domains of thinking, he is attempting to distinguish how each is conceptualized through an analysis of children's responses to an interview situation.

A Piaget-type interview is used in which the subject is presented with hypothetical stories and questions about social conventions, such as modes of dress, and is asked questions about rule compliance and the rightness and wrongness of the acts. For example, children are asked whether a boy, used to calling people by their first name, is wrong in his refusal to call teachers by their last names. In addition, the children are asked to make judgments in the realm of moral behavior, such as whether to cheat an old man of his money. Responses to both types of situations are compared for children at three different age levels and are viewed as exemplars of different levels of thinking about social acts. Three levels of social–conventional judgment are derived from the responses. Level 1 respondents are considered to be rule bound and to justify an act because of the existence of a rule; Level 2 people are considered to perceive rules as originating from people and institutions and therefore as having an arbitrary character; and Level 3 people tend to legitimate rules as part of a larger functioning social system. The three levels are assumed to be related to increased understanding of social organization on the part of the child and therefore to be developmentally ordered.

The excerpts from the interview sequences with children, adolescents, and adults provide some beginning support for the utility of the differentiation between mores and morals and for the expected changes with age. Of particular interest are the reports, from the same person, of the different bases they use for making the two kinds of judgments—those about mores and those about morals. The greatest discrepancy between judgments are in the so-called Level 1 and Level 2 youngsters. They subscribe to an absolute morality about cheating—it is bad whether or not there is a rule—but with respect to dress or politeness, compliance with the requirement is validated either by the existence of a rule (Level 1) or is considered arbitrary but part of the regulatory system imposed by people or institutions (Level 2). By Level 3, there is some convergence of a functional, situational, or relativistic point of view, and both moral acts and social conventional acts may be perceived as necessary to a well-functioning society. The results therefore suggest that the separation of two types of social judgment may very well be useful.

The chapter is an interesting one and does indeed contribute to knowledge about how social judgments are made. It stems from a theoretical point of view about stages of moral development and represents a first exploratory attempt to anchor judgments about social conventions into a structural-developmental viewpoint. The research appears to support the premise that the two kinds of judgment are not isomorphic and should be isolated and compared; it also suggests there are changes in the criteria children use for making social conventional judgments with age. The interview is used as a flexible tool for investigating children's thinking.

The utility of separating the two kinds of judgments is a logical derivation from the structural developmental point of view and attests to the value of a theory for generating testable hypotheses. The findings, however, are not incompatible with other points of view, such as social learning. In such a view, the child's transformation of reality is, at least, partially a function of the value or importance placed on each kind of judgment by the socializers. Deviation from moral-type behaviors is perceived as more serious and less a function of the existence of rules.

Some limitations of conceptualization and method require comment. The very conceptualization and definition of the levels is not fully clear. Is knowledge of social organization or is attitude toward a rule the basis of differentiating the levels? It may be valuable, for example, to use separate measures of knowledge of social organization to correlate with level. Related to this criticism is the lack of persuasiveness of the coding of the responses given by the subjects to the various levels. For example, Mark is scored Level 1 for saying "If nobody else stuck to any other rules, like I was saying about the corridor, everybody would be hitting each other." Turiel says that Mark is saying that violation of the rule leads to disorder and that the reason for the rule is its very existence. However, perhaps Mark is viewing the social necessity in general of rule following to avoid disorder in general. In that respect, he may be more like Michael (scored at Level 3 as a legitimator of moral codes) who says "If rules aren't followed, there will be chaos."

Some of these problems of interpretation can be solved by developing a coding system and obtaining interjudge agreement; some of them may suggest a redefinition of levels.

The interview itself, although useful and revelatory, has some obvious limitations. It should be both more structured and more wide ranging. The examples convey a free-ranging method of inquiry that might well bias the responses—some children are asked about the fairness of rules, some about the discrepancy between belief and action, and some about rule violation. For exploratory purposes, this is desirable, but later interviews might better include specification of the domain of questions.

There are other kinds of information that also may be assessed more thoroughly in the interview, relative to the bases of the child's judgments. For example, it may be useful to assess the cognitive view subjects have as to the probable consequences of rule breaking with, for instance, such questions as "If this rule is broken, do you think it would lead to other rules being broken, e.g., about hitting other kids, cheating old men, etc.?"

This exploratory research may profit, then, by clearer definition of the differences between levels, by a coding scheme for rating responses, by some attempt at assessing reliability of judgment, by independent assessment of the child's knowledge of social organization, and by further attention, in the interview, to the child's perception of the consequences of rule conformity and rule violation.

Finally, as with the other three chapters, no attention is given to individual differences. The forthcoming promised data on repeated measurements over time of the same person should provide the opportunity to test the developmental hypothesis. It should also provide insights about how individuals vary from one another over time in the way they change their bases for making social judgments.

These four chapters, interesting, instructive, and representative of the current emphases in work in moral development, all share common strengths as well as limitations. A major strength of each is that it is part of an ongoing body of research in which self-criticism, modification, and correction are constantly being employed, in which synthesis of many observations leads to attempts at new formulations, or in which a framework suggests new pathways for research. From each can be inferred something about the conditions of socialization or development in the moral realm—the role of socializers, the effects of models, the nature of empathy, the bases of moral judgment. Each chapter also deals with socially meaningful content and, it is hoped, heralds greater knowledge about the potential good in human beings and society.

However, there are also some important limitations in the work reported in these chapters—limitations of scope and depth necessary to a full understanding of moral development. I should like to emphasize that future work in moral development can benefit from attention to the following four major issues. The first is in the area of method or strategy. There appears to be much too great reliance on the experiment in most of the work reported in this symposium. Despite its honorable history, by now many of its limitations and artificialities should be recognized. The utility of convergent validity obtainable through multiple kinds of methods and measures should not be underestimated. Furthermore, much can be gained, in all these studies, by greater attention to the perceptions of the child as derived from an interview or questionnaire.

A second important issue lies in the area of theory. Bryan's chapter is essentially an empirical one; the others are partial conceptualizations about empathy and prosocial motives, about the socialization of prosocial behavior, or about the development of moral judgment. Attention to a larger network, a wider set of concepts that links attitude and behavior, person and society, prosocial and antisocial orientations, has not been offered in this symposium.

The lack of attention to individual differences and to personality variables in all these chapters has also been disappointing to me. There has been an unbalanced emphasis on the situation—an emphasis that unfortunately restricts knowledge of individual variation—and on ontogeny. The variations between people, variations that are not only interesting in their own right but also an important source of variance, and especially when situational factors are controlled, have largely been ignored. Our understanding of altruism, for example, may be substantially increased if researchers attend to relevant personality dimensions, for example, value on affection, beliefs about society, self-concept, moral attitudes, that differentiate people and influence their behavior.

Finally, the notion of development through time, of temporally extended change in individuals, is not part of the research design of any of the present papers, although promised by Turiel. Understanding of moral development requires, I think, a much greater commitment to a longitudinal strategy so that the course of development of an attitude, a process, or a person's life style may be traced, and thereby understood. Cross-sectional comparisons at different ages, however valuable, cannot reveal and often blur the course of psychological development.

To bring these four points together, I believe the field of moral development can gain much from greater attention to theory making about how people become moral or deviant over time. Testing of such theory can be enhanced by greater attention to individual differences between people, more differentiated methods for assessing what people are like, and greater attention to the time dimension for evaluating change or development. The importance of the work on moral development and its implications for society warrant the imagination and effort involved.

# 10

# Research and Theory in Moral
# Development: A Commentary

David J. DePalma

*Loyola University of Chicago*

The chapters by Keasey, Selman, Rest, and Hogan present provocative hypotheses, data, and models for research and theory in moral development. Because the chapters originate from different "world views" and discuss various kinds of data, I shall consider them individually before making general remarks.

The chapter by Keasey discusses his research attempts to (*a*) evaluate the nature of the relationship between cognitive development and moral reasoning and (*b*) examine the factors involved in influencing an individual's evaluation of the moral reasoning of others.

Keasey correctly points out that from a Piagetian perspective one must measure cognitive development directly with Piaget-type instruments, and not with IQ tests. However, because Piaget has postulated only two stages of moral development, Keasey suggests using Kohlberg's six-stage model. Because past studies have indicated that formal operations may be important in the development of principled moral reasoning, Keasey has investigated the relationship between these variables with 12- and 19-year-old girls.

Keasey found (see his Table 1) that although some subjects had formal operations but not principled moral reasoning, there was no instance of a person who was principled in moral reasoning who did not also evidence a "substantial amount of formal operational thought." He therefore concluded (*a*) that formal operational thought is a necessary but not sufficient condition for principled moral reasoning, (*b*) that the distribution of the subjects indicates that principled moral reasoning lags behind formal operations in development, and (c) that "a specific reorganization in cognitive structures leads, in time, to a predictable reorganization in the qualitative nature of one's moral reasoning."

In order to test the implications of these conclusions, Keasey conducted a second study examining concrete operations and Kohlberg's second stage of moral reasoning in 7- and 9-year-olds. The data supported Keasey's contention that concrete operational thinking is a necessary but not sufficient condition for Stage 2 moral reasoning, and that the relationship between cognitive development and moral reasoning fluctuates as implied by the specific-dependent model (c).

These first two studies will be examined before the second part of Keasey's paper is examined. Keasey concluded that all the principled subjects showed a "substantial amount" of formal operations. However, the transitional college woman, in fact, demonstrated only 33% formal operations—yet she was principled. The resolution of this paradoxical situation may be found in a reorganization of the data.

In the first study, Keasey classified moral reasoning in terms of the subject's predominant level (a variable percentage across individuals). However, he classified cognitive ability more specifically—that is 0, 33, 67, or 100% formal operational. A more specific classification of moral reasoning within each level (e.g., by percentage of predominant reasoning) might have facilitated comparisons within and across levels of moral reasoning. With such a classification it might have been discovered, for example, that the transitional (33% formal) college woman had a low percentage of principled responses, whereas the three integrated formal (100%) individuals had a higher percentage of principled responses. Similar information could be quantified for the other subjects, and those in the second study as well. Thus, additional specificity in the classification of moral reasoning is especially important for an understanding of the developmental relationship between cognition and moral reasoning both across and within individuals.

Keasey also reports that concrete and formal operations facilitate movement from one level of moral reasoning to the next. It seems reasonable, then, to consider a few questions related to this facilitation effect and transition.

First, did cognition play an equivalent role in moral reasoning across individuals? If the transitional college woman had a high percentage of principled responses, perhaps some "noncognitive" (social and/or personality) factors were responsible for her high level of moral reasoning. Similarly, if some 12-year-olds had exhibited a degree of principled reasoning then early attainment of formal operations might have been responsible for this precocity.

Second, what particular aspects of concrete and formal operations are responsible for transition? That an index of concrete or formal operations (e.g., conservation of volume) is correlated with a level of moral reasoning does not mean that the index is a causal factor in the relationship, nor does it explain how the cognitive operations influence moral reasoning.

Third, does cognitive reorganization actually lead, in time, to reorganization in moral reasoning? It does not appear that a cross-sectional design can adequately answer this question. Furthermore, the possibility of cohort (generational) and time-of-measurement effects, and the unknown reliability of the measures (i.e., the Kohlberg and Piaget tasks) seems to suggest a different methodology (e.g., a controlled cross-sequential design; Nesselroade & Baltes, 1974).

Finally, why were boys and girls used in the second study, but only girls in the first? Research by Holstein (1973) seemed to indicate that boys and girls develop differently with regard to moral reasoning. Therefore, one might ask whether the data obtained with both sexes in study two can be compared with those from study one; or, are the factors involved in the relationship between cognition and moral reasoning the same, and do they function similarly, for both sexes?

In order to answer these questions, future studies should: (a) devote more attention to individual differences; (b) measure "noncognitive" (social and personality) factors, as well as cognitive factors; (c) use larger subject samples, of boys and girls; and (d) use a methodology that can adequately investigate the developmental dynamics of the·relationship between cognition and moral reasoning both between and within individuals.

In the second part of Keasey's paper, he examined the interaction between opinion agreement/disagreement and stage of supportive reasoning. Subjects in these studies were pretested for stage of moral reasoning. Four weeks later they were asked to evaluate agreement and disagreement opinions that were at their same stage of reasoning and one stage above (first study), or at a stage below and one stage above (second study).

Opinion agreement/disagreement exerted a greater influence than stage of supportive reasoning in both studies; stage of reasoning had a significant effect only in the second study; and same-stage and higher stages of reasoning were preferred over lower stages. The hypothesized age differences appeared only in the second study—with the younger subjects being influenced more by agreement/disagreement than the older girls.

Although these data were significant, some changes in the analyses and design might have provided valuable information for the hypotheses. First, Keasey could have classified his sixth graders and college students by their level of moral reasoning. The data could have been analyzed with regard to this subject variable, and it might have been learned whether the subject's own level of reasoning was related to the two components of moral judgment. The analysis might have revealed, for example, that subjects from one level of moral reasoning were more influenced by one or both of the two components than were subjects from other levels of reasoning—and perhaps independently of the subject's age. Certainly, cognitive and/or noncognitive factors could also have been related to the observed age difference, and these factors should also be controlled in future studies.

Second, all the subjects in these studies were girls. The obvious question is whether similar results would have been obtained with boys. A comparison by sex should prove interesting in studies on opinion agreement/disagreement in light of past research in social and developmental psychology.

Finally, it might prove interesting to conduct a modified version of Keasey's studies. However, instead of giving the subject an opinion and the supportive reasoning, he or she could be given the opinion only and asked for the reasoning. The intent of the study would be to find out how opinion agreement/disagreement influences the subject's supportive reasoning. That is, would the subject give supportive reasoning that was higher, at the same stage, or lower than his or her own level of reasoning under these conditions? Individual differences and relevant subject variables would also be investigated. This kind of research might be another way of examining the preference–comprehension issue.

The chapter by Selman and Damon is a theoretical exposition of the early stages of development of children's justice reasoning and social perspective taking. The model is an attempt to relate Selman's work on social perspective taking to Damon's research on young children's conceptions of justice.

Social perspective-taking levels describe "the way in which a child at that level understands the relations between the perspectives of self and other." Four levels are discussed: Level 0, egocentric perspective taking; Level 1, subjective perspective taking; Level 2, self-reflective perspective taking; and Level 3, mutual perspective taking. Past studies in moral judgment and role taking indicated that these two may be related. However, Selman and Damon believe that moral judgment is more than perspective taking in a moral context. Perspective taking is seen as a "separate ability that is necessary but not sufficient for moral reasoning." A given level of justice should therefore imply a specific level of social perspective-taking ability.

Because the authors studied children from 4 to 10 years of age, Damon's modifications and extensions of Kohlberg's early stages of moral reasoning were used for the justice levels. The stages were: Stage 0, justice based on the child's desires; Stage 1, justice oriented to the demands, claims, and authority of others; and Stage 2, justice involving resolution of the rights and claims of both self and others. Each stage had an A or emergent substage and a B or consolidated substage, and the application of a new level of social perspective-taking ability was seen as the prerequisite condition for the transition from A to B.

In order to study social perspective taking and justice conceptions in these children, the authors have used dilemmas presented on cards or through film strips. Recent studies (e.g., Chandler, Greenspan, & Barenboim, 1973) have indicated that such audiovisual techniques are valuable and necessary tools for research with children. In interviewing the subjects, the authors have used the "clinical method." Probe questions on perspective taking have focused on the child's *prediction* as to what the characters *will* do and think, whereas the moral issues have emphasized the child's *prescription* as to what the characters *ought* to do.

Selman and Damon have provided important information for theory and research in moral development. Although one might have hoped for older subjects as well, their theoretical notions make sense intuitively and have direct relevance for other papers in the symposium (e.g., Hoffman's discussion of altruistic motives). However, the protocol data they use to support their model raise some theoretical and methodological questions.

Justice reasoning at Substages 0-A and 0-B is especially problematic. The problem at these stages is whether children's reasons that are "merely reassertions of his desire for the choice to occur" are actually "justice" oriented. That is, can the concept of "justice" be used in a situation in which there is no consideration of what is equitable, nor even the possibility (because of cognitive and/or noncognitive limitations) that the child may think that way? Justice by definition does not appear to develop until Substage 1-A. Furthermore, the protocols do not present a clear distinction between Substages 0-A and 0-B.

When Brian (4 years, 10 months) was asked about the distribution of cake in his family, he said that he gets the most cake because he is the fastest runner. At this point, it might have been interesting if the interviewer had asked Brian whether he should (or whether it would be right to) get the most cake. Brian might have answered such a question by saying that it would be right because he wanted it that way—a Substage 0-A response. Brian's total response would then be a combination of Substages 0-A and 0-B, and it might be difficult, if not impossible, for different raters to agree on his stage of justice reasoning.

This difficulty in rating is also present in the protocol of Alan (6 years, 3 months). Alan said that Holly would not get the kitten because she does not want to get in trouble. The authors rated this response as Substage 0-B. However, from the definition of the stages of justice reasoning (Table 2), a Substage 1-A rating seems more appropriate. The protocols used to illustrate Substages 1-A, 1-B, 2-A, and 2-B are not as questionable. Therefore, the problems with the stages of justice reasoning are localized with Substages 0-A and 0-B—that is, are they reasonable conceptualizations, can they be discriminated from one another, and can they be reliably measured?

One way around some of these theoretical and methodological problems may be to use the dilemmas to assess a specific component of the model, but not both. That is, it may be valuable to use the Holly dilemma to measure justice reasoning only, instead of measuring stages of justice conception in relation to levels of social perspective taking. This can be accomplished by simply focusing in the interviews on what the characters ought to do, not on what each character will do or think regarding the others. The Tom dilemma can be used as Selman and Damon have used it—to assess social perspective-taking ability. In this way, the subjects will have a score on the justice reasoning component and one on the social perspective-taking aspect that are independent of one another. Without such independence in scoring, it seems difficult to test the hypothesis that a stage of justice reasoning implies a level of social perspective taking. Future research should focus on this issue.

Rest's chapter represents his efforts and those of his colleagues to develop a new methodology for the measurement of levels of moral judgment that can be standardized, objectively scored, reliable, and less time consuming than Kohlberg's technique.

The product of these efforts is the Defining Issues Test (DIT). The DIT presents the subject with six moral dilemmas similar to Kohlberg's. The subject reads a dilemma and then selects and ranks from among 12 statements the four that are most important to him in his decision about the dilemma. Each issue statement characterizes one of Kohlberg's stages, that is, Stages 2, 3, 4, 5A, 5B or 6. Rest also included in these statements A (antiestablishment) and M (distractor) items. The scoring system involves weighting the subject's ranking of the important issues and summing the weights attributed to Stages 5A, 5B, and 6 across the six dilemmas. The resultant score is the percentage of weights associated with principled moral reasoning. This principled (P) score can range from 0 to 95% and represents the degree to which the individual uses principled reasoning in making his moral judgments.

The data (see his Tables 1 and 2) from the studies Rest and his associates conducted show that the average P score has quite a wide range across subjects of different ages. That is, the scores range from a low of 20 in junior high school students to a high of 70 in political science and philosophy graduate students. Other studies have demonstrated that: (a) the test–retest reliability of the P score is .81 with a ninth-grade sample; (b) subjects' scores from Kohlberg's global rating method correlate .68 with their P values on the DIT; (c) a measure of subjects' comprehension of issues correlates in the .60's with the DIT; (d) the DIT correlates in the .30's and .40's with IQ-type measures; (e) the DIT correlates −.60 with the law and order scale and .63 with libertarianism; (f) an ethics class changed more on the DIT over time than a logic class, and (g) subjects can fake downward but not upward on the DIT. Because these results have been obtained with a new measure of moral reasoning, it is important to consider both their theoretical and methodological implications.

From a theoretical perspective, it is important to remember that Rest believes that a moral judgment measure assesses an individual's "sophistication in thinking and not directly anything else" (Rest, 1974). The person is demonstrating his moral problem-solving ability on the DIT, not predicting his behavior. Thus, a fair test of the DIT, according to Rest, is to find out whether people actually solve moral problems in real life the way they do on the DIT, rather than attempting to relate the DIT to resistance to temptation, cheating, altruism, or other moral behaviors.

Rest (1974) has also stated that moral judgment may play a central role only in the lives of people who live by a "reflective, autonomously accepted set of values." It therefore seems that stage of moral reasoning may predict behavior only in a small sample of the population (probably principled individuals). For most people, who are at lower reasoning stages, other factors may be emphasized (e.g., opinion agreement/disagreement, or role-taking ability), thereby producing greater inter- and intraindividual variability in these people than in the autonomous individuals. The significance of this speculative discussion is that if the understanding of moral development and the full range of moral behaviors is to be increased not only must level of moral reasoning be assessed, but also other cognitive, noncognitive (personality and social), and situational variables.

I shall now consider the data Rest has presented. Rest reports that group differences on the DIT appear to be developmental. However, longitudinal research seems especially warranted because it is very possible that the differences Rest obtained with the student and adult samples actually reflect cohort (generational) effects to some degree. Another reason for a sequential (see Nesselroade & Baltes, 1974) research strategy is that we need more information on developmental variation, both between and within individuals, in moral reasoning. We must find out, for example, how the precocious principled thinker compares and contrasts with the older principled individual and other people, with respect to development, variability in moral reasoning over time, salient experiences, and other cognitive and noncognitive dimensions.

In Table 3, Rest provides data that he feels illustrate the utility of the DIT as a measure of change in moral reasoning. Rest argues that the data show the DIT to be "selectively sentitive" to the more adequate moral reasoning of the ethics class. It may have been interesting to compare pretest and posttest changes with other classes as well. Besides this problem, the supportive data uncover a "weakness" in the use of the DIT. That is, the DIT cannot indicate the factors responsible for change in the ethics class, it can only reflect that change. It certainly is of value that the DIT has the capability to reflect change in moral reasoning. However, the change may, in fact, only reflect some sort of training effect of the ethics class without concomitant changes in "underlying structures."

Recent research I conducted using the DIT and Hogan's measure of empathy provided some information on these structures. The data showed that subjects high on principled reasoning ($P$ scores $\geq$ 48) were more likely to also be high on empathy. However, subjects with lower scores ($P < 48$) were divided equally on empathy (high versus low). The ethics class, then, could have had more students who were high on empathy than the logics class, and this difference could have influenced the DIT changes. In any case, level of moral reasoning on the DIT appears to have limited usefulness, by itself, as an explanation of change (development) and should be used in conjunction with other variables in future studies.

My research indicates two more suggestions for the DIT. First, my analyses show that high- and low-principled subjects do differ on their opinions on two of the dilemmas. In the Heinz story, 70% of the low- compared to 45% of the high-principled subjects reported that Heinz should steal the medicine to save his wife. In the Newspaper dilemma, 90% of the high- versus 67% of the low-principled subjects feel that the principal should not stop the newspaper. These data may be peculiar to our sample, but the implication is that item analysis by dilemma may prove advantageous for additional discrimination within and between levels of moral reasoning.

Second, the DIT presently is biased toward male main characters. Three of the stories involve males, two are ambiguous with regard to the character's sex, and one has a female main character. All of the stories should be ambiguous, or they should be equally divided by sex to control for possible measurement artifacts.

In conclusion, the DIT has a few problems, as do most psychological measures, but the advantages of the test are many. Not the least of these is that the DIT enables researchers to use a standardized assessment of moral judgment, to objectively score their data, and then compare their results. Furthermore, use of the DIT by many investigators should not only aid in the refinement of the instrument but also significantly assist in efforts to probe the dynamics of moral development.

Hogan's chapter represents his attempt to resolve a major problem confronting researchers in moral development. The problem, he feels, is that a broad conceptual framework, in which to couch theory and research in moral development, is vitally needed. He believes that such a formulation must consider moral development together with personality theory. Hogan explicates the theoretical and methodological components of this model in the six parts of his paper.

In the first two sections, Hogan presents the motivational and developmental assumptions on which his conceptualization is based. According to his motivational assumptions, man has strong needs for social interaction and for structure, order, and predictability; thus, man is innately a "group-living, rule-following, norm-respecting animal." It should be noted that this view is not shared by all contemporary researchers and contrasts sharply with the ideas that man must be taught the need for rules, that he is intrinsically evil, and that man is a "blank slate" at birth.

The developmental assumptions focus on Hogan's observation that "personality" has two very different and common usages. These usages, he hypothesizes, suggest that the development of personality consists of two distinct elements—role structure and character structure. Views in principle and self-presentations are related to role structure, whereas views in fact and behavioral determinants are associated with character structure.

In the third and fourth sections, Hogan elaborates on the ontogenesis of role structure and character structure. Role structure develops mainly from interpersonal (peer) interactions and from an individual's roles, self-images, and life style. It is situation sensitive, conscious, and "directly reflected in overt behavior." Hogan also believes that role structure generates responses to tests similar to Kohlberg's moral judgment scale.

In contrast to role structure, the development of character structure depends on early interactions with parents and family. Character structure is covert and unconscious and also more stable than role structure. Earlier in his paper, Hogan has stated that character structure (views in fact) actually determines our actions. However, in his discussion of role structure, he says that role structure is "directly reflected in overt behavior." This apparent contradiction is resolved to some degree by Hogan's contention that for most people character structure and role structure are separated. The implication, then, is that role structure is a prepotent behavioral determinant for some people (or in some situations for an individual), and character structure determines behavior for other individuals (or in other situations). Moreover, there is probably considerable variability across individuals in the extent to which role structure is separated from character structure. Therefore, future research must be conducted on the consequences of this separation for behavior, and on the relationship of character structure and role structure to behavior within and across individuals (and situations).

In the fifth section, Hogan discusses in more detail the five dimensions of character and the assessment tools he uses to measure each. Moral knowledge simply involves knowing social rules and has been associated with intelligence. Therefore, Hogan approximates it with IQ or IQ-type tests. The second aspect of character is "the degree to which people perceive rules as having instrumental value for regulating social affairs." This moral positivism–moral intuitionism continuum is measured with Hogan's Survey of Ethical Attitudes (SEA). Socialization, "the degree to which one has internalized the rules and values of one's society, culture, and family," is assessed by the Socialization scale of the CPI. Similarly, empathy, "the capacity and disposition to regulate one's actions in accordance with the expectations of others," and autonomy, "the capacity to make moral decisions without being influenced by peer group pressure or the dictates of authority," are also measured by the appropriate CPI scales. In his Table 1, Hogan presents the relationships between these indices and mature moral judgment.

Inspection of this table reveals that autonomy correlates only $-.04$ with maturity of moral judgment. A reasonable explanation for this result may involve the measure of maturity itself. That is, this measure involves a 15-item sentence completion test on which subjects are supposed to respond quite quickly and very briefly to statements regarding highly controversial topics. Even if it is assumed that the test is reliable and can be rated reliably, there is another problem. The time and space limitations of the test, combined with the nature of the topics, seem to be very compelling "demand characteristics." That is, these factors most probably influenced some subjects with respect to the length, nature, and quality of their responses. The test may therefore actually have induced role structure responses and thus the low correlation with autonomy, a character structure dimension.

Another character structure dimension, the moral positivism–moral intuitionism continuum, is somewhat problematic. This dimension is assessed by the Survey of Ethical Attitudes, which may possess some of the same limitations and "demands" as the measure for maturity of moral judgment. Despite this possibility, it should be remembered that the SEA only discriminates between views of human nature that are quite sophisticated developmentally. That is, the measure can only be used with older adolescents and adults. Therefore, the moral positivism–moral intuitionism continuum, along with moral knowledge, does not have the developmental ramifications of the socialization, empathy, and autonomy dimensions of character structure.

The last section of Hogan's contribution deals with a very important topic in moral development—anomalies and pathology. Hogan specifies the source, nature, and treatment of the dissociation. Based on his model, the sources are three—within role structure, within character structure, and between role structure and character structure. The last source results in identity conflict, is especially prevalent (to some degree) in our society, and occurs if "one's social roles are too discrepant from one's character structure."

With his model of personality and character development for normal and abnormal individuals, Hogan has made a significant contribution to theory and research in moral development. The theoretical dimensions for the model have been operationalized and are therefore of tremendous heuristic value. Finally, research with subjects from various age groups, with different experimental paradigms, and with many moral behaviors should furnish valuable validity and realiability information for the model.

The chapters discussed in this commentary have demonstrated that many important topics are being investigated in moral development. New theory and research on cognitive operations, social perspective taking, moral reasoning, and personality and character development have facilitated the establishment of a foundation from which other researchers can work. However, such research should be undertaken only if the following general limitations of these chapters are considered.

First, most of the chapters have not focused sufficiently on individual differences. The developmental morphology of inter- and intraindividual variability, together with consideration for situational factors and different moral behaviors, is especially important in the context of these papers. Furthermore, subjects of both sexes, and representing many ages, should be included in future research in these areas.

Second, all the papers revealed some kind of methodological problem. These problems typically involved the instruments or techniques used to assess a given subject characteristic. Further refinements in the measures, ratings, and item analyses, as well as additional reliability and validity data, should strengthen these methods.

Finally, in order to acquire an understanding of the dynamic interrelationship of the components of moral development researchers should become acquainted with recent methodological advances in developmental psychology. Of special significance to these papers is the work on sequential strategies (e.g., Nesselroade & Baltes, 1974).

The incorporations of these general recommendations and the specific ones discussed above should improve the overall quality of moral development research. The challenge is for researchers to use these ideas to more effectively study man as a changing organism in a changing world.

## REFERENCES

Chandler, M. J., Greenspan, S., & Barenboim, C. Judgments of intentionality in response to videotaped and verbally presented moral dilemmas: The medium is the message. *Child Development,* 1973, **44,** 315–320.

Holstein, C. B. Moral judgment change in early adolescence and middle age: A longitudinal study. Paper presented at the meeting of the Society for Research in Child Development, Philadelphia, Pennsylvania, 1973.

Nesselroade, J. R., & Baltes, P. B. Adolescent personality development and historical change: 1970–1972. *Monographs of the Society for Research in Child Development*, 1974, **39**, (1, No. 154), 1–80.

Rest, J. R. The cognitive-developmental approach to morality: The state of the art. *Counseling & Values*, 1974, **18**(2), 64–78.

# Toward the Future

David J. DePalma
Jeanne M. Foley
*Loyola University of Chicago*

The preceding chapters represent diverse and provocative thoughts on research and theory in moral development. This diversity has arisen from somewhat different "world views," and it is our observation that the participants have had much to say to one another. Moreover, such dialogue seems crucial in improving research and to our understanding of morality.

In considering the immediate future for research in moral development, it is clear that the participants in this symposium have much work before them. The prior recommendations, including pleas for refinement of measures, attention to methodology and individual differences, and assessment of development over time in cross-sequential studies, cannot be fulfilled quickly. Although many of the recommendations were specific to this particular group of presentations, we hope that they have a broad applicability to research and theory in moral development in general.

As editors, we have had the opportunity to read and reread the papers presented at the symposium, to listen to the tapes of the discussions, and not only to contemplate what we have heard, but also to consider what might have been included. There was, of course, a number of topics that might have received attention, but one topic stands out as worthy of attention. To illustrate from the preceding chapters, it is evident that there is a dichotomy between those participants considering moral thought or some ramification (Chapters 1–4) and those considering moral behavior (Chapters 5–8). Although we must recognize that the selection of participants has been neither random nor necessarily representative of current approaches in moral development, it does appear that this dichotomy can enable one to categorize the work of a majority of the investigators in this area.

The problem, as Wright (1971) has aptly stated it, is:

> We need to know how people's theoretical moralities relate to the rest of their moral lives. There are two aspects to this problem. The first is the link between theoretical morality and the way an individual thinks of the situations in which he is actually being called upon to make moral decisions. . . . The second aspect is the relationship between an individual's theoretical morality and the way he actually behaves in morally challenging situations [pp. 172–173].

Wright's conclusion that the evidence linking moral thought and action is "slender" is, unfortunately, almost equally applicable now. It also seems reasonable to note that the concern about relationships does not merely involve the dichotomy between moral thought and action, but, as Wright suggests, it encompasses at least five major aspects of moral behavior, that is, moral insight or judgment, belief or value systems, resistance to temptation, guilt, and altruism.

In confronting this question of relationships, there are sufficient data to indicate that multifaceted variables are involved and that simply correlating a measure of moral reasoning with a measure of prosocial behavior, for example, will not be particularly helpful. Specifically, there is considerable evidence indicating that various aspects of moral actions are not necessarily associated and that even behaviors within a particular category may not be highly correlated. This latter finding is illustrated early in the work of Hartshorne and May (1928) and continues to find confirmation in later studies (e.g., Sears, Rau, & Alpert, 1966). Similarly, one may suppose that different aspects of moral thought (reasoning in the Kohlbergian tradition and moral values or beliefs) are not necessarily associated. This possibility is suggested earlier in this volume by Keasey's work on agreement/disagreement and by DePalma's discussion of differential opinion selection related to stage of reasoning on the DIT.

The problem of investigating relationships among major aspects of moral development is further compounded by the fact that a number of the most readily available assessment techniques are especially applicable to children and to particular aspects of behavior (such as donating tokens to a child down on his luck, reacting to disappearing hamsters, or cheating in school or while playing games). These behaviors are often of little interest to those concerned with moral thought at the principled level. Although ingenuity in the development of situations relevant to adults (e.g., Darley & Latané, 1968; Rosenhan, 1969; Staub, 1971) may help to overcome these limitations, ethical considerations frequently preclude the use of many types of experimental procedures.

A third problem for the pursuit of relationships among the thought and action components of moral behavior may arise from the relative absence of theory that can guide research and aid in the development of testable hypotheses. In this context, the proposal by Hogan (Chapter 8) and the formulation by Wright (1971) each suggest theoretical orientations relating character and moral behavior that imply testable hypotheses. Each proposes, but in different ways, that particular relationships between variables may be found when they are considered in the context of particular character structures and personality development within individuals instead of pursued across individuals.

The need for integrating different aspects of research and theory on moral development scarcely requires justification. However, a better understanding of the relationships between the thought and action components seems especially important when one considers the practical implications for training and the demands for programs, whether in child rearing or in education, that will foster moral development. Because the desire for such practical applications appears to be some multiplicative function of the desirability of the behavior, it may be anticipated that interest in moral training will be high. Although one may argue that any attempts to facilitate development in this area are desirable, or at least better than nothing, we should like to suggest that certain educational approaches may be premature. That is, they may suggest that more is known about methods of training, as well as their effects, than is actually the case. This concern appears to be particularly applicable to the current translations of research and theory relevant to moral judgment into value-oriented programs of education or training. The discussion of the characteristics of these programs incorporates many of the ideas that have been presented in this volume.

In one type of program, based on Kohlberg's six-stage model, the aim of moral education is to "develop the organizational structures by which one analyzes, interprets and makes decisions about social problems [Rest, 1973]." This aim can be accomplished in a number of ways, but one frequently used method involves presenting moral dilemmas to a group (e.g., students), discussing these dilemmas, and provoking the group members with +1 stage moral reasoning. The group members are not given the answers but are encouraged to search for them. The rationale here is that the presentation of such experiences can facilitate movement to higher, more adequate forms of moral reasoning, and that this growth may generalize to other types of moral behaviors. However, this approach to value education seems questionable if we consider the evidence discussed earlier.

First, Keasey's chapter states that concrete and formal operations are prerequisite to the second and principled stages, respectively, of moral reasoning. If these cognitive operations are prerequisites for stages of reasoning, it follows that value education programs cannot be meaningful experiences unless the participants have the necessary cognitive capacities. Keasey also provides evidence that opinion agreement/disagreement is more influential than stage reasoning on subjects' evaluations of moral judgments. In value programs, researchers have not controlled opinion agreement/disagreement. It is probable, then, that individuals in these programs are affected more by opinions that agree than those that disagree with their own. That is, if most of the agreement opinions expressed in the group are at same-stage reasoning, little change is likely to occur. If most of the agreement opinions are at Stage +1 reasoning, however, movement may be facilitated. Of course, if most of the voiced opinions disagree with the individual's own, it is unlikely that transition will be encouraged—unless the person is motivated for some reason to consider the disagreement opinions. Therefore, cognitive capabilities, opinion agreement/ disagreement, and motivational factors may all affect the success of value education attempts.

Another important variable in value education may be social perspective taking. As Selman and Damon argue, levels of perspective taking are necessary but not sufficient for stages of moral reasoning. It appears, then, that value educators should be aware of an individual's level of perspective taking before exposing him to Stage +1 moral reasoning. Otherwise, others' opinions may not be assimilated into the individual's existing structures or facilitate change in his structures. Most contemporary theorists (e.g., Piaget, Kohlberg) concur on the significance of role taking in moral development. It therefore seems reasonable to suggest that direct social perspective-taking (role-taking) experiences be incorporated into value education programs.

A factor that is closely related to role taking and that may be useful for value programs is empathy. The chapters by Staub, Hoffman, and Hogan, and the discussion of Rest's chapter indicate that empathy plays a prominent role in moral reasoning and development. Because empathy is only one dimension of character structure, according to Hogan, it seems sensible to measure others, especially autonomy and socialization, as well. Besides subject variables (both cognitive and noncognitive), situational and parental factors should be determined. That is, because of the probable effects of the value education situation, and of the home environment either during or before value training, one should also assess factors related to the setting (e.g., see chapters by Turiel and Bryan), and other factors, such as parental discipline and parental character structure dimensions.

Earlier we stated that value education is aimed at moving individuals to "more adequate" stages of moral reasoning, and specifically, to principled stages of reasoning. The principled stages, according to some theorists, are better modes of thinking about moral problems than "lower" stages. However, how do we determine this adequacy? Is a principled person "more adequate" than a conventional thinker because he or she is principled or for other reasons? Recent reports have contained criticisms of the former hypothesis as involving scientific, philosophical, cultural, and sex biases (e.g., Holstein, 1973; Kurtines & Grief, 1974; Simpson, 1974). The latter interpretation—other reasons—implies that a principled person may be "better" because he or she is most likely to also be formal operational, highly empathic, and autonomous. The possibility exists, however, within this framework, and from the evidence in this volume, that a conventional person may be formal operational, highly empathic, and autonomous as well. Furthermore, as has been discussed earlier, one risk of value training is that it may merely produce individuals who can parrot the higher levels of reasoning without changing their underlying structures. Thus, principled stages may be more adequate than other stages to the extent that the principled classification reflects actual differences between individuals on "nonreasoning" dimensions.

If value training is successful in changing underlying structures, one may wonder whether change should be attempted and, if so, how it should be measured. With regard to ethical considerations one might argue that the information on moral development is incomplete and that value programs are therefore premature. Moreover, simply because researchers have some idea of the effects of deprivation of stimulation (e.g., inadequate socialization experiences) on moral development does not necessarily indicate that they can predict the effects of intervention through stimulation. Concerning measurement, Rest has shown that a direct method comparing pretest and posttest scores on stage reasoning can be used. Another approach may assess behavioral change—but herein lies a problem. What kind of behavior should be considered desirable from a person who has completed a value education program? Some proponents of value programs (e.g., Kohlberg) have avoided this problem by saying that it is not their intent nor is it constitutional to teach specific values. Instead, they aim to foster better problem-solving strategies. A further difficulty is that researchers do not know how moral judgment relates to behavior. Moral reasoning may be a salient dimension only for comparable behaviors (e.g., voting, deciding social issues), or it may also relate to the typically studied moral behaviors (e.g., cheating, altruism). It could be hypothesized that the other variables we have discussed are related to behavior either concomitantly with or apart from moral reasoning. Moreover, moral reasoning and "nonreasoning" variables may play differential roles across various individuals, ages, situations, and behaviors.

At this point in the discussion, one might ask whether we are advocating the elimination of training in moral reasoning or of value education program. Although we have outlined specific problem areas in value programs, we believe that moral reasoning should be considered in these programs. Such training should probably be continued because of the potential benefits for theory and research in moral development. However, we have proposed reasons for also including dimensions other than moral reasoning.

By examining value-oriented education, it has been our intention to demonstrate that the chapters in this volume, although representative of different perspectives, can be valuably linked together. We have only focused on the specific application of these ideas, but it should be apparent that the discussion has direct implications for basic developmental theory and research (e.g., Nesselroade & Baltes, 1974). Thus, the area appears to be "wide open," and it is our hope that this volume will encourage more multifaceted theory, research, and applied efforts in moral development.

## REFERENCES

Darley, J. M., & Latané, B. Bystander intervention in emergencies: Diffusion of responsibility. *Journal of Personality and Social Psychology,* 1968, **8,** 377–383.

Holstein, C. B. Moral judgment change in early adolescence and middle age: A longitudinal study. Paper presented at the meeting of the Society for Research in Child Development, Philadelphia, Pennsylvania, 1973.

Hartshorne, H., & May, M. A. *Studies in deceit.* New York: Macmillan, 1928.

Kurtines, W., & Grief, E. B. The development of moral thought: Review and evaluation of Kohlberg's approach. *Psychological Bulletin,* 1974, **81,** 453–470.

Nesselroade, J. R., & Baltes, P. B. Adolescent personality development and historical change: 1970–1972. *Monographs of the Society for Research in Child Development,* 1974, **39,** (1, No. 154), 1–80.

Rest, J. Developmental psychology as a guide to value education: A review of "Kohlbergian" programs. Mimeographed paper, University of Minnesota, 1973.

Rosenhan, D. Some origins of concern for others, in P. Mussen, J. Langer, & M. Covington (Eds.), *Trends and issues in developmental psychology.* New York: Holt, Rinehart & Winston, 1969.

Sears, R. R., Rau, L., & Alpert, R. *Identification and child rearing.* London: Tavistock, 1966.

Simpson, E. L. Moral development research. A case study of scientific cultural bias. *Human Development,* 1974, **17,** 81–106.

Staub, E. Helping a person in distress: The influence of implicit and explicit "rules" of conduct on children and adults. *Journal of Personality and Social Psychology,* 1971, **17,** 137–145.

Wright, D. *The psychology of moral behaviour.* Middlesex: Penguin Books, Inc., 1971.

# Author Index

# Subject Index

## J

Justice, 3, 14, 57, *see also* Moral development, Morality, Moral judgment
Justice reasoning, *see* Moral judgment, Social perspective taking

## M

Moral behavior, 5, 95–110, 194, *see also* Altruism, Moral development, Moral judgment, Social conduct
aspects of, 194
individual differences in, 5
and modeling, 95–110
Moral development, 2, 4, 5, 40, 60, 75, 115, 153, 169–179, 181–191, 193–198, *see also* Moral judgment
assessment of, 194, 197
definition of, 60
and child-rearing practices, 115
and methodological issues, 169–179, 181–191, 193–198
and parental nurturance, 115
theory of, 4, 153
cognitive–developmental, 2, 40, 75
and personality, 5, 153, 188
transitional factors in, 40
Moral education, 195–197
aim of, 195
assessment of, 197
and developmental theory and methodology, 197
issues in, 195–197
method of, 195
variables related to, 196
Morality, 8, 14, 39, 60, *see also* Moral development, Moral judgment
autonomous, 14, 60
definition of, 8, 14
development of, 14, 39
heteronomous, 14
Moral judgment, 2, 3, 7, 8, 13–15, 39–55, 60, 61, 75–91, 181–184, 193–197, *see also* Defining Issues Test, Moral development, Social perspective taking, Specific-dependent model
and behavior, 193–197
and cognitive development, 2, 39, 40, 42–47, 54, 55, 181, 182
time lag in, 46–49, 182

Moral judgment (*contd.*)
development of, 2, 42, 50, 184
and disequilibrium, 41
evaluation of, 50–55
individual differences in, 5, 49, 182
objective measure of, 2, 75–91
and opinion agreement/disagreement, 3, 51–55, 183, 184
and personality, 89, 90
and role taking, 50
sex differences in, 183, 184
and sexuality, 14, 15
and social (noncognitive) factors, 3, 41, 49, 50, 182
stages of, 2, 3, 7, 8, 13, 14, 40, 42, 60, 61
preference hierarchy for, 53–55
supportive reasoning of, 51–55, 183
transition in, 8
Moral knowledge, 158, *see also* Character structure
definition of, 158
functions of, 158
and intelligence, 158
and social experience, 158
Moral perspective taking, *see* Moral development, definition of
Moral positivism–moral intuitionism, 158, 159, *see also* Character structure
assessment of, 159
definition of, 159
personological correlates of, 159
Moral reasoning, *see* Moral judgment

## O

Orthogenetic principle, 36

## P

Personality, 155, 164–166, 188, *see also* Character structure, Role structure
and anxiety, 164
and dissociation, 164–166
definition of, 155
developmental anomalies and pathology in, 164–166
and developmental assumptions, 155, 188
Prosocial behavior, *see* Altruism

## R

Responsibility assignment, 118, *see also* Altruism